THE ABORTION
DECISION

David Granfield

THE ABORTION DECISION

Doubleday & Company, Inc.
Garden City, New York

LIBRARY OF CONGRESS CATALOG NUMBER 69-12185

COPYRIGHT © 1969 BY DAVID GRANFIELD

ALL RIGHTS RESERVED

PRINTED IN THE UNITED STATES OF AMERICA

To My Father and Mother
for the
Gift of Life

CONTENTS

Introduction   9

1. The Scientific Background   15
2. The Historical Context   43
3. The Sociomedical Crisis   83
4. The Moral Choice   123
5. The Public Interest   147
6. The Legal Implementation   175
7. The Viable Alternative   203

Notes   225

INTRODUCTION

My interest in the abortion problem has developed almost fortuitously. Although I taught criminal law and family law regularly, I would spend on abortion only a small fraction of one class hour—more or less standard practice in American law schools. Not until 1963, at a Summer Workshop in Criminal Law at New York University, did I enter the growing controversy over liberalization by taking issue with the redoubtable English jurist, Sir Glanville Williams, whose writings on abortion have been a leading factor for reform. On the strength of that encounter, Professor Gerhard Mueller of N.Y.U. and director of the Workshop, asked me to address the American Society of Criminology at its annual meeting in November 1966. My remarks were published in early 1967, the year that marked the first legislative changes.

Abortion was being given unprecedented coverage in all the communications media, but most of it, I felt, overlooked areas of concern essential if the reappraisal of the traditional abortion laws was to be sound. My brother, Patrick, a professor of theology, responded to my complaints about the lack of a fully balanced analysis of the problem with the suggestion, "You've been

working on abortion and you see what is needed. You write it."
Reluctantly at first, but with an increasing sense of urgency and
obligation, I began to analyze the elements of the abortion decision. During this time, my brother's advice, encouragement and
assistance were most helpful. I was also able to draw upon my
training as a lawyer, philosopher, and theologian in studying this
multifaceted problem, in trying to arrive at a legal judgment most
consonant with the human dignity and equality of all men, cir-
cumscribed though they may be by misery and hardship.

In reappraising traditional abortion laws, we are reassessing
our views and our evaluation of man. Although the abortion
decision is for me an in-depth study of decision-making, it is also
a rethinking of what man is, what society is, and what the relationship between the two must be for the maximization of human
potential. I would like to be able to say that I have done all that.
But I am too conscious of the book's limitations. Analysis is inevitably selective. What one hopes will be exhaustive becomes
summary and suggestive. Scholarly researchers sometimes speak
of getting control of the sources, as if they expected to grasp
truth by the throat. Rather, one ventures into recondite arenas
where even experts find themselves in sharp conflict with their
colleagues. Getting close to the sources too often means getting
close to the issues that divide men's minds and consciences.

Lawmaking, however, can never be purely academic. It is not
a leisurely and tentative exploration for hidden truth, but an
exercise in practical judgment involving matters as intractable as
they are contingent. When facts multiply, the possibility of error
increases. Law, if it can be called a science at all, is the science
of probable argument. Unlike the intellectual, the legislator must
make a decision one way or another, the judge must make a decision one way or another. Broad principles of thought and conduct are operative in law, but law operates in terms of specifics.
Are the present abortion laws to be kept on the books or are they
to be changed? If they are to be changed, what in detail will the
new laws cover?

In making "the abortion decision," I consider both basic principles and factual specifics. In Chapter One, I ascertain the relevant facts of life—the scientific findings and their philosophical implications. I look first at the empirical evidence provided by the life sciences of molecular biology, genetics, and embryology, to discover what exactly is that life process that abortion so radically interrupts; then, I consider man's reasoning about the conclusions of science in order to grasp its more general and transempirical implications. In Chapter Two, I try to situate the problem by examining the history of abortion and its rationalizations, both civil and ecclesiastical. This survey enables us to profit from the past as well as to assess the historical influences currently at work. In Chapter Three, I look squarely at the sociomedical crisis which has given rise to the abortion controversy. The incidence of fetal and maternal deaths, the public demand for liberal abortion, and the proposed grounds justifying that demand, all add up to a widespread concern which makes a reappraisal of the traditional laws a necessity. In chapters Four, Five, and Six, I evaluate abortion—the direct killing of this unborn human organism—in three different but related arenas of decision: the conscience, the community, and the court. Is liberal abortion morally right or wrong? Is it politically beneficial or detrimental? Is it legally wise or imprudent? After dealing with the moral concern, the public interest, and the legal implementation, I consider in the last chapter, the seventh, the alternate remedy to liberal abortion, really a complexus of remedies which together form the viable alternative.

In trying to formulate the right abortion decision, I write with an awareness that the problem must be worked out in a pluralistic society where the primary appeal is to human intelligence rather than to religion or other authority. I write then, not as a polemicist but as a deeply concerned participant in a dialogue over the tragic problem of abortion and its effect on human dignity.

THE ABORTION
DECISION

Chapter One

THE SCIENTIFIC BACKGROUND

I

Abortion poses many problems. Merely to reformulate the abortion laws will not solve them. Moral justification and concern for the good of the community are touchstones of all decision-making. Yet the indispensable foundation for the resolution of the abortion problem is an understanding of the relevant facts of life. What exactly is this process of human generation that is so violently interrupted by abortion? To answer this first of all questions, we need help from the life sciences—from biology, genetics, and embryology.

Unfortunately, a time lag separates scientific discoveries from their social applications. Here the legal process is conspicuously old-fashioned. Legislators, judges, and ordinary citizens often rely on a half-forgotten and drastically outdated scientific education. Little in their specialized training or their subsequent careers gives them interdisciplinary insights. Nevertheless, sound law must always adjust to an expanding scientific universe.

Abortion is a crucial happening—a matter of life and death, a biological and medical fact as well as a moral and legal issue. But biology has changed radically in the last few years. No longer is it simply descriptive biology, it is molecular biology, in which chemistry, physics, and biology join in examining the basic living structure of all organisms. In this new biological arena, abortion faces its moment of truth.

The life sciences have been in existence for a long time. Thousands of years before Christ, various peoples—the Chinese, the Egyptians, the Babylonians—were aware of the physical fact of inheritance and tried to control the transmission of desirable characteristics in corn and horses, and even in humans. The Greeks, above all Aristotle, tried to generalize, but were crippled by faulty methodologies and a lack of factual data and the instruments to obtain these facts. Much of the biological thinking of the Middle Ages was second-hand Aristotle—a kind of armchair scientism. Surprisingly, some of these theories have persisted to the present.

The advent of the microscope in the seventeenth century helped replace fancy with facts. In 1665, an Englishman, Hooke, discovered the cell. In the same century, two Dutchman made similar discoveries, de Graaf of the mammalian ovum (1672) and Leeuwenhoeck of the sperm (1677). Sound though these observations were, they gave rise, in other thinkers, to fantastic theories. A bitter controversy was waged between the homunculists and the ovists. Both were convinced that a diminutive human being was present in the sex cell of the man or the woman respectively. Thus, Swammerdam (1637–80) believed that through the microscope he could see an embryo in the head of a sperm. He concluded that all the female did was help its development. His was the first formulation of the preformation theory. On the other hand, Bonnet (1720–93) held that the woman's body contained the prototypes of all her descendants. His encasement theory postulated little men within little men within little men ad infinitum. The struggle lasted about a century, until Spallanzani (1729–99) was able to demonstrate the more reasonable theory that the child resulted from both ovum and sperm. Wolfe (1733–94), a contemporary of Spallanzani, replaced the earlier preformation theory with that of epigenesis: Human development results from the creation of new structures through progressive growth and differentiation. In 1839, two Germans, Schleiden and Schwann, developed the cell theory: the cell is the structural and functional unit of all organisms. Another German, Virchow, observed, about the time that Mendel was finishing his own experiments, that all cells were derived from preexisting cells by a process of division.

Two hundred years after Hooke discovered the cell, Mendel published, in 1865, his "Laws of Inheritance." His experiments with the sweet pea were the first real experiments with the mechanism of heredity. Mendel's "factors," later called "genes" by Johannsen, established the science of genetics. Mendel's writings made no impact on the scientific world for about fifty years. So the science of genetics really began with the twentieth century when Hugo de Vries "discovered" the earlier writings of Mendel.

Two lines of research, one on heredity and the other on the cell, were bound to intersect. The "factors" determining the transmission of characteristics would, it was argued, have to be found in the cell. Genetics, cytology, and embryology would henceforth cooperate in shedding light on the life process. Advances continued. In 1879, a German, Flemming, identified the chromosomes and the process of somatic cell division called mitosis. Then, two Americans made significant discoveries: in 1910, C. E. McClung identified the female or X chromosome; and in 1905, N. M. Stevens identified the male or Y chromosome. Although chromosomes were first identified in 1879, it was not until 1956 that the exact number of human chromosomes, forty-six, was verified.

The year 1944 marks the beginning of a new era for biology. O. T. Avery and his associates proved that the basic substance of life was deoxyribonucleic acid—DNA for short. The blueprint for growth and reproduction was finally revealed. Since 1944, with the help of electronic computers, tremendous strides have been taken in molecular biology, even to the point of breaking the genetic code, the secret of intra-organic communication.

The life continuum from conception to birth finally has its rational justification as a biological fact.

II

Advanced research affords us sound biological facts, the empirical substratum upon which to base our personal and political decision-making. Our fact-finding can be conveniently divided according to two aspects of the human being. As Hamilton says, "The actual organism produced by the normal interaction between heredity and environment is called a *phenotype,* an organism judged by its genetic constitution alone is a *genotype.*" [1] Thus we can study the process of generation phenotypically, looking to appearances, to that system of qualities and characteristics which makes up the organism—a graphic and effective approach but not a complete one. Or we can study the process of generation genotypically, that is, in terms of the gene structure of the organism. This approach is more abstract but intellectually more cogent, for it gives us a grasp of the underlying principles of embryological development.

Our procedure here will be to examine first the phenotype, then the genotype, to go from embryology to cytology, from the child to the cell. We must examine the life process in some depth to enable us to understand what it is that abortion interrupts, what kind of living thing is destroyed, before we can judge whether this interruption or destruction of life is good or bad, is to be permitted or forbidden.

The Phenotype

An investigation of the earliest days of human life, the days immediately following fertilization, is extremely difficult. The microscopic size of the new organism, its physical inaccessibility, and the limits imposed on human experimentation make the obtaining of a specimen before implantation, and even sometime later, a medical rarity. Over the years only a few such specimens have become available. As Arey summed it up in 1965, "A few cleavage stages, an abnormal morula and two unattached blastocysts are the known representatives of the first week of development." [2] Fortunately, the early developmental similarities among higher mammals have partially compensated for the lack of firsthand evidence.

In the beginning, there is the fertilized ovum, the zygote. Here, genotype and phenotype are one. The zygote is unicellular. Compared to future cells, it is undifferentiated, unspecialized, but it is an organism with the gene structure of the fully grown and highly complex adult. Cleavage is the first function of this newly produced organism. It divides repeatedly and rapidly. Each daughter cell, although smaller, reduplicates the gene structure of the original cell. Until rather recently, cleavage was thought to be simple cellular multiplication resulting in the morula, a solid mass of about a hundred cells, called blastomeres. Only with the development of a new form, the blastula, was cell specialization thought to begin. The word cleavage was then no longer used. Research in molecular biology reveals that even in the first cell division, there is a subtle cell change—not in the nucleus of the cell but in its cytoplasm. Certain cytoplasmic factors are distributed differently with each division, so that even the simple morula, a sticky cluster of apparently similar cells, has already developed radical differences, differences sufficient to effectuate a change in the organism from a solid into a spherical cluster of blastomeres. The organism is then called a blastula or blastocyst. Only five or six days old, the blastula shows obvious organization, but this is only a more evident form of an inner orientation which has existed from the beginning. The human organism is never simply a chaotic mass of cells. It is goal-oriented in form and function every step along the way to maturity.

Cell division brings swift and radical changes to the organism, but more in complexity than in size. Not until implantation in the uterine mucosa will there be the kind of outside nourishment needed for the total increase called growth. In the meantime, little blocks are made from bigger blocks—more blocks, but not more material. This fractionating process is not simple fragmentation. A new structure is formed. Apparently it is just a sphere of cells filled with a liquid. But in some ways it is like a globe of the world. On it different regions can be mapped. Areas can be pointed out in this being not yet a week old which will develop into major parts of the new embryo: the germ layers, the noto-cord, and the neural plate. Blastula maps have been made by staining with nontoxic dyes living blastulas which as they develop bear vivid witness to the accuracy of the scientific predictions.

These regions develop even before the blastula implants itself in the uterus, though it may be out of the Fallopian tube where conception occurred and already in the uterine cavity. The intra-uterine devices (IUD's) apparently prevent the nidation of the fertilized ovum and thus are abortifacient rather than contra-ceptive.[3] Before implantation is possible the zona pellucida, a transparent, noncellular-secreted membrane surrounding the ovum, must have disintegrated, exposing the sphere of blastomere cells, now called trophoblast cells, which are able to adhere to the wall of the uterus; perhaps "invade" the uterine mucosa would be more accurate, for these cells eat into the connective tissue and within a day or so the whole organism is embedded in the uterus. Where the trophoblasts have destroyed the uterine wall surrounding it, maternal blood flows in, bathing the little organism which now nourishes itself through a process of diffu-sion. This shell of trophoblast cells will very soon develop into an auxiliary organ to be cast off when birth occurs. It will not develop into the child. In the blastula, however, there is an inner cell mass. Here are the true embryonic cells. This part of the blastula involutes or invaginates into the liquid center to form the "little stomach" characteristic of the gastrula.

The stages of gastrulation correspond roughly to the second and third weeks of embryonic life, weeks denominated by the formation of germ layers. The second week is the week of the two-layered embryo. The inner cell mass has divided into the amnion, an auxiliary membrane, and the cells which will actually form the embryo. This embryonic disk is a thick plate of cells separating the amnion and the yoke sac. It consists of two layers, one of entoderm, the other of potential, but as yet undifferentiated, ectoderm and mesoderm. The first stage of gastrulation is the formation of entoderm at the beginning of the second week. The second stage of gastrulation, at the beginning of the third week, is the differentiation into the mesodermal and ectodermal layers.

From these three layers all the parts of the body spring. From the ectoderm is derived the integumentary system (skin, nails, hair, and glands), the central and peripheral nervous system, and the sense organs. From the mesoderm is derived the skeleton and muscles, the head and circulatory system, and the genito-urinary system. From the entoderm are derived the digestive and respiratory systems and the mouth and larynx. By the end of the third week, there have developed already the beginnings of the nervous system (neural plate and neural groove), the beginnings of the spinal column (the notocord), the foregut, and the heart.

Derivation from the three germ layers is predictable but not inevitable. Experiments in transferring cells from one layer to another have shown situs to be the controlling factor in early development. Though the cells have specialized, they remain flexible and adaptable for redifferentiation according to the exigencies of their new locale. Eventually most cells do reach a point where neither multiplication nor further specialization is possible, but in the earlier embryonic stages this is not so. A principle of unity places the interest of the whole organism over those of the individual cells.

The preliminary organization of the embryo is largely spatial. The gastrula allocates the cells of the inner cell mass to their functional post, but if forced mobility is in order, the reassigned cell can be trained in new skills. The subordination of parts to the whole prevails over the vested interests of any cell despite its prior specialization. This aspect of embryonic life, though not part of the ordinary procedures of growth, does make manifest the total teleology at work, not a mechanistic fabrication of structures part by part, but a fashioning of a whole organism according to a principle of vital unity and human perfection. This all-inclusive dynamism is at work, with flexible efficiency, from the very beginning.

During the fourth week, the major parts common to all vertebrates begin construction. The chief characteristics of this period are the somites, paired segments that lie along the spinal cord and eventually form a muscle mass supplied by a spinal nerve and a vertebra. Also present are primitive kidney tubules and blood vessels arising from the aorta. An embryo of the fourth week is already highly specialized. Its neural plate, which developed from the ectoderm, has grooved, folded, and become the neural tube, an independent nervous system with a clearly ascertainable and relatively large brain area. The neural tube and the notocord, the precursor of the spine, grow so much faster during this week than does the ventral portion that the embryo has a rounded back. Growth of a somewhat different kind is also occurring on the ventral side. The gut is growing in both directions, and the ends of the tube have sealed themselves off. The heart, made of the first muscle cells to develop, has initiated the pulsating motion of the blood through the paired blood vessels. The sense organs have begun. The limbs are budding.

For the next month, from the fifth to the eighth week, the rate of growth and change is amazingly rapid. The body straightens out somewhat. The head on a slight neck looks up, its face more presentable with the development of the external sense structures for seeing, hearing, and smelling. The limbs are organized, and the fingers and toes can be counted. The heart is larger, but the growth of the gut and the liver now balance the earlier cardiac protuberance. The umbilical cord is relatively smaller and more clearly distinguished from the abdomen. The genitalia are obvious but ambiguous. The sex of the child cannot yet be determined externally. Neuromuscular growth sparks body movement, perceptible with a stethoscope, but unperceived by the mother. Arey concludes about the progress made: "Almost all of the internal organs are well laid down at two months; henceforth, until the end of gestation, the chief changes undergone are those of growth and further specialization of the tissues." [4]

For the next seven months, the unborn child is called a fetus rather than an embryo. The new name denotes a new stage of existence. The fetal period is primarily one of growth, for earlier specialization has already structured the basic parts and established their relationships. The child is not complete—it will not be complete even at birth—but its essentials are well established. For example, the sex of the child is genetically determined at conception, and is determinable by the third month. From the eighth to the twelfth week, however, a progressively more accurate estimate can be made.

Compared to an adult, the fetus looks grotesque. Yet the disproportion is purposeful; immediacy of need is operative here. Embryological development foregoes prettiness for the sake of efficiency. Patten notes some of the incongruities.[5] A most obvious peculiarity, the ridiculous position of the child—standing on its head, its limbs tucked against its body, its spine curved, its rump turned toward the sky—is both economical of space and protective of the child. The head appears oversized due to the immediate and primary importance of the brain. The hips and the legs are undersized since the need for locomotion will not arise for some time after birth. The chest is conical because the lungs have not expanded. This thoracic narrowness makes the already protuberant abdomen stick out even more—a distortion only if we fail to realize that a highly developed heart and enlarged liver are necessary in a blood economy. The fetus is hairless and red and dried-up looking because there is no hair until the fifth or sixth month and no fat until a month or so later.

A brief examination of two major organs will give us a clearer insight into the character of the life of the unborn. These two, the brain and the placenta, perhaps form an unlikely combination, but one which helps us focus on basic issues. The brain is a permanent organ and a principle of independence; the placenta is a temporary organ and the product of dependence. Both develop very early. Both are indispensable to fetal existence. Together they show this new life to be separate and distinct despite its great physical and environmental needs.

The human brain has a developmental head start over other organ systems, for body building begins with the head. Growth and differentiation in this, the cephalic end, is more precocious than elsewhere. This predominance, though later reduced, is never lost. The initial imbalance shows vividly in the relationship between the two main divisions of the head, the neural and the visceral. The neural or neurocranial includes the brain, the organs of sight, hearing, and smell and supporting structures. The visceral consists primarily of the terminations of the digestive and respiratory tracts and supporting structures. The earlier growth of the neural part at the expense of the visceral keeps the embryo from looking human, but the organs needed for the specifically human activities are being fashioned. Since the child is nourished through the placenta, there is no hurry to develop the gastric and respiratory terminations so characteristic of the human face, though as a matter of fact, the face begins to be formed about the fifth week. Before this happens, however, the primordia of the eye and ear have been established on the brain by the end of the third or the beginning of the fourth week. By the sixth week, the embryonic brain will show the five major regions to be found in the adult. Proportionately, the fetus has a bigger brain than an adult. At two months, the central nervous system of a child is 25 percent of its total body weight; at birth it is 15 percent, whereas as an adult it is only 2.0 to 2.5 percent.[6]

The mysterious placenta highlights the relationship between mother and unborn child.[7] Here is the crucial point of contact between fetal and maternal life. To examine the form and function of this organic bridge is to see the child's essential independence of the mother in the context of a temporary dependence.

Physically, the placenta, as the Latin names implies, is like a flattened cake, a spongy disk, a circular, fleshy complexus of blood vessels and membranes. From the fifth month until full term, it is about an inch in thickness, six to eight inches in diameter, and a pound or so in weight. The placenta develops during the second month of pregnancy as the trophoblast cells which brought implantation in the wall of the uterus act to further maximize the benefits of this contact with the mother.

Functionally, the placenta is a blood pool, a two-way transfer point. There is a biochemical exchange between mother and child: Blood is the medium, the umbilical cord is the channel, the placenta is the mechanism, and nutrition, respiration, excretion, and protection are the purposes. The mother's blood flows into the placenta; the uterine veins drain it off. The child's blood flows into the placenta through two arteries and returns through a large vein. While the two blood supplies are in close contact, the fetal villi through the permeable walls of the blood vessels absorb from the maternal blood all that the fetus needs and gets rid of all that it does not want. But there is no intermingling of blood. The proverbial sharing of blood between mother and child is a biological myth. Mother and child have separate blood supplies and circulation.

The child may be parasitic and dependent, but it is a functioning unit, an independent life. A child is not, in the words of Mr. Justice Holmes, "a part of its mother." [8] However visceral may be its temporary residence, however dependent it may be before birth—and for some years after birth—it is a living being, with its separate principle of growth and development, with its separate nervous system and blood circulation, with its own skeleton and musculature, its brain and heart and vital organs.

The Genotype

The life of the unborn child as it unfolds phenotypically cannot fail to fascinate. The question recurs provocatively, however: How does one cell account for this developmental *tour de force?* An examination of the salient aspects of embryological life reveals three major phenotypic features which make an answer to this question even more pressing.

First, there is the phenotype's *structural size and complexity*. The one-celled zygote develops into an organism with trillions of cells, 10^{14} cells. Its weight is about six billion times heavier than the zygote.[9] Its growth rate is such that if a child had increased in height at the rate that a fetus does, 1.5 millimeters a day, he would be twenty feet tall on his tenth birthday.[10] If his body increased in weight according to his fetal rate, he would be, as an adult, two trillion times the weight of the earth.[11] Its innumerable cells have specialized as muscle, nerve, bone, digestive, respiratory, excretory, circulatory, and sex cells. The cells have formed tissues, the tissues have developed into organs and organ systems, vital parts of the living organism.

The second feature of the phenotype is its *functional perfection*. The rapid developments in size and complexity mean that the various parts of the organism must function according to the strictest exigencies of embryological life. For example, from the time of implantation, the metabolic activities of nourishment and the removal of body wastes must be carried out unceasingly. Each organ system has its own timetable, but one synchronized with the time schedules of other systems. If a stage of development does not take place when it should, the chances of recouping are slight. If the failure is a major one, we have the frightening monsters of teratology, embryology's chamber of horrors. Yet the marvel is how well all these various parts do function in the perfecting of the child.

A third and most important phenotypic feature of embryological life, though not restricted to the unborn, is implied in the two earlier considerations. It is the *regulatory mechanism*. Here is a key principle of life. This mechanism, with its biochemical system of communication, preserves the unity of the organism despite its diverse forms and functions, its complicated growth and specialization schedules. Whatever this mechanism is, and it is not yet fully understood, its control of biochemical and morphological change is a prerequisite not only for the perfection of the organism but for its very survival.

These three major features of the unfolding phenotype—structural size and complexity, functional perfection, and regulatory mechanism—demand an explanation. How can all this develop from one cell? To answer this question we must examine the genotype in the light of the advances of modern microbiology and genetics.

The zygote, called the most undifferentiated of cells, is not, for that reason, a simple structure. The life of the individual cell is a complicated mystery whose secrets the life sciences are only beginning to understand. A brief digression to look at the construction of the cell will dispel any naïve notion that the cell is just a "genetic package." [12] Actually, the cell is tremendously complicated, comprising three major parts: the membrane, the cytoplasm, and the nucleus. The *membrane* is composed of fats and protein and is selectively permeable; that is, it expands and contracts so that certain specified molecules can get into the cell and others can be let out of the cell. It can engulf liquids by forming channels (pinocytosis) and solids by forming arms of cytoplasm (phagocytosis). It is sensitive to outside beings and inner demands. It can move and can adhere to certain types of cells which in some way it recognizes. It can even repair itself if injured.

The *nucleus* is the control center of the cell. It contains the chromosomes and genes. In the human cell, there are forty-six chromosomes, twenty-three from each parent. Each chromosome has some three thousand genes which produce the physical and mental characteristics of the organism. Each gene, in turn, is composed of chains of from two hundred to two thousand molecules. Each molecule is made up of some or all of these basic elements: hydrogen, oxygen, nitrogen, carbon, and phosphorus. In the nucleus of every cell there are billions of atoms. Lest the nucleus be atomized out of comprehension, however, let us consider its other functions. It determines the structure of the individual cells as well as the functioning of the cytoplasm and the membrane. The nucleus is surrounded by a double-layered membrane with a series of pores in its outer layer. The chromosomes are in contact in the nuclear sap and among them are the nucleoli, which apparently are storage units of nucleic acid to be used for the reproduction of DNA when the cell divides.

The *cytoplasm* comprises those organelles which are within the plasma or cell membrane but not within the nuclear membrane. The nucleus determines the structure and activities of the cytoplasmic organelles whose main function is to do the work of the cell. Here raw materials are taken in and converted into energy, and specific work is done, making a controlled contribution to the total unity which is the organism. Very briefly, these are the various cytoplasmic organelles The endoplasmic reticulum is a complicated membrane. It forms something like an inner skeleton on the surface of which chemical reactions take place, materials are moved and stored. Close by but free and unattached are the ribosomes which produce protein. The complex mitochondrion expands and contracts its double membrane, with the inner one folded into cristae to increase the available surface for its role in cell respiration. There are hundreds in each cell. Lysosomes are built like the mitochondria but have no inner folds or cristae. They function as an intercellular digestive system. The vacuoles are spaces within the cytoplasm filled with liquid. They push the cytoplasm toward the cell membrane to foster an exchange of gases. Their main function is to regulate the osmotic pressure in the cell. The centrosome is important in mitosis or cell division. The lysosomes digest the cell when it breaks down, for the death and destruction of cells is essential to proper growth and differentiation. Every day billions of cells die and are replaced, so the centrosomes and the lysosomes are constantly at work. Then there is the Golgi body, clearly identifiable but symbolizing mystery, for its function is not known.

This brief excursus suggests the tremendous complexity of the zygote though it has only one cell. It took the microscope to show us the existence of the cell, and it took the electron microscope, the ultracentrifuge, and radioactive tracers to show us the intricacies of the cell and make intelligible its functioning processes.

The formulation of the cell theory and the discovery of chromosomes and genes did not adequately explain how a highly complex and delicately diversified being could develop from one cell. How, for example, to account for the invariably identical genetic structure of each cell in the human body? The mechanics of microscopic and infinitesimally accurate replication by the trillions requires a computerlike principle of order and organization. And eventually, it would take an electronic brain to decipher some of its secrets.

The key discovery, the one that eventually put the computers to work, was the role of DNA, deoxyribonucleic acid. But it took years to arrive at this point of scientific knowledge. In 1869, about a decade before chromosomes were identified and the process of cell division, now called mitosis, was observed, an Austrian, Friedrich Miescher, discovered a new substance in animal tissue. He called it nuclin, but learned little about it. In 1928, an Englishman, Frederick Griffin, performed a startling experiment. By the use of an extract made of a virulent species of pneumococcus bacteria, he was able to transform a harmless species into a virulent one. This sparked the search for the material that caused the genetic change. In 1944, three Americans, O. T. Avery, C. MacLeod, and M. McCarty performed the same kind of experiment and found that a kind of nuclin, or nucleic acid, was responsible for the transformation. They proved conclusively that only deoxyribonucleic acid—DNA—which is found exclusively in the chromosomes, could be the sought-for genetic material, the plasma of life.

A few years later, in 1953, an American and an Englishman, James D. Watson and Francis Crick, worked out the molecular structure of DNA.[13] These giant molecules, ten times larger than any other biological molecules, contain encoded instructions for the formation of the whole organism. The double helix shape and the complementary base compounds connecting the two strands like steps on a circular staircase clarify the basic functions of the cell: its ability to produce its specific characteristics as a functioning unit of the organism; and its exact reduplication, in cell divison, of the coded instructions.

The productivity of DNA is immense, for it is DNA which enables the cell to produce the proteins of which the human body is constructed. Proteins, made from only twenty different amino acids, are long, complex chains of from two hundred to two thousand molecules differing in size and amino-acid sequence. Yet the structure of DNA is so complex that it directs the production in the human body of over one hundred thousand different kinds of proteins.

The information content of DNA is even more fantastic. It has been said that a single thread of DNA from a human cell contains information equivalent to six hundred thousand printed pages with five hundred words a page, or a library of one thousand volumes. Someone else compared the stored knowledge of the fertilized ovum to fifty times more than is contained in the Encyclopaedia Britannica, as if the whole encyclopedia were written on the head of a pin not once but fifty times. This stored knowledge is found in every one of the body's trillions of cells.

These facts, interesting in themselves, are significant in helping us understand the magnificent genetic structure of the human embryo even in its most primitive stages. The complexity of the whole human body is contained in some real way in its first cell. Its human life principle irresistibly moves the organism to physical maturity. Through microbiology, we are given new eyes to enable us to see a human being in an almost invisible speck, not preformed as the homunculists would have it, but manifesting a living and human continuity from conception until death.

III

The abundance of scientific evidence for a living continuum should obviate the need of an explicit defense of the human status of the embryo. Abortion could be recognized as the sacrifice of the life of one human being for the life of another human being. Moral principles and legal rules would then help us decide whether or not this lethal choice can ever be justified. Science, however, simply presents the fact that human life begins with fertilization and continues until death without the addition of an essential human element. This straight-forward acceptance of biological realities is an indispensable prerequisite to a sound abortion decision.

A philosophic postscript to these empirical findings is necessary, however, in order to deepen our understanding of this scientifically manifest continuum, this human organism, characterized, as Niels Bohr notes, by wholeness and purposefulness, by structural perfection and regulatory mechanisms.[14] Keeping in mind the common sense principle of philosophical economy, "Ockham's razor"—entities should not be multiplied without necessity—we shall test two transempirical focal points for challenging the human status for the zygote, the theory of mediate animation and the theory of ancestral recapitulation, and we shall appraise the kinds of philosophic and scientific arguments on which they rely. Finally, we shall try to grasp the philosophic significance of abortion as seen in full biological perspective.

A. Although it is not the fashion today in scientific circles to speak of souls, an ancient theory of ensoulment has reappeared denying human status to the unborn child, at least in the early stages of pregnancy. This theory of successive souls, as it is sometimes called, is more comprehensible to the modern mind, if for "soul" we read "vital principle" or "life force." It holds that the human organism is animated successively by vegetative life, animal life, and human life. Another name for it is the theory of mediate animation, meaning that the nascent human organism is not animated by a human life principle immediately but only sometime after fertilization. According to Aristotle and Aquinas, this process of successive ensoulment takes forty days for males and ninety days for females.[15]

The philosophic rationale for successive souls in the unborn human depends on two principles of the hylomorphic (matter-form) theory so fundamental to the Thomistic synthesis. The first is the proposition defined by the Council of Vienne (1311–12) that the rational or intellectual soul is per se and essentially the form of the body. The second and subsidiary principle is that the soul can be infused only into a body that is sufficiently disposed to receive it. Aristotle and Aquinas looking at the early stages of life through the eyes of a primitive biology—they held that the embryo was organized out of the activated menstrual blood of the mother—concluded that this unformed matter could not house a human soul until it had been prepared by less perfect principles of animation, the vegetative and animal souls.[16]

The application of philosophic principles to embryological fictions engendered a theory of successive souls unsubstantiated by current biological research. Yet if we prescind from the obvious developmental incapacity of the menstrual blood and even from the acknowledged genotypic powers of the fertilized ovum, we can ask the logical philosophic question: Cannot the rational soul be the architect of its own dwelling? The standard answer is that the soul is the formal cause of the body but not its efficient cause. Yet at the same time, Thomists assumed that the vegetative soul structures the body for the reception of the animal soul, and the animal soul structures the body for the reception of the rational soul—clearly, though formal causes, they are working architecturally. If the vegetative and animal souls can do this, so can the rational soul. And apparently it does, since after the fortieth day, on which the infusion of the rational soul allegedly occurs, there is still a great deal of developmental work to be accomplished. According to Thomistic philosophy, the rational soul has the powers of the lesser principles of life. After the infusion of the rational soul, there are not three souls, but one soul with the powers of three. Hence, Aquinas can say, "The soul is the primary principle of our nourishment, sensation, and local movement; and likewise our understanding. Therefore, this principle by which we call it intellect or intellectual soul, is the form of the body." [17]

Certainly the early Thomists were excused for not knowing that after fertilization more than formless matter is present. Too many biological myths confused their philosophic judgment. Aquinas, therefore, although he considered an abortion before the soul's infusion a grave sin, did not call it the sin of homicide. His test was: "Seed and not seed is determined by sensation and movement." [18] Present-day Thomists, with the help of the piercing eye of the electron microscope and the mechanical brain of the modern computer, should not depend on the crude signs of sensation and movement to tell them whether or not human life is present. The need of the soul to be infused in suitably disposed matter does not disqualify the zygote. The true notion of this one-celled being is not that of a microscopic plastic bag of liquid with a hard little center containing directions on how to build a man. The zygote is not just a "genetic package." It is, as we have seen, a living organism with a vital principle and a physical body. It has a complex structure which functions through organelles with an over-all orientation toward full human maturity. This unique human being differs from all the vegetables and animals the world has ever known. It has a different makeup and a different pattern of unfolding, a different origin and a different destiny. It is an exclusively human phenomenon.

B. The theory of ancestral recapitulation, like the theory of mediate animation, has also been used to deny human status to the unborn child, at least during the early stages of pregnancy. It is the "biogenetic law" of Ernst Haeckel, first suggested by Karl Ernst van Baer in 1824, which holds that the developmental events resulting from human reproduction parallel the developmental events resulting from human evolution. In other words, ontogeny recapitulates phylogeny. If "every animal climbs up its family tree," then the human organism is, at different stages, a protazoon, an amphibian, a primitive mammal, and so on until, when the cerebral cortex is sufficiently developed for self-awareness, it becomes for the first time, as during the history of evolution, a human person.

No doubt in the development of any individual there is more or less of a repetition of some of the features characteristic of biologic ancestors. A kind of general parallelism may appear, but never an exact historical recapitulation of the stages of evolution. Van Bertalanffy, relying largely on De Beer's critique of Haeckel, suggests two main objections to a mathematical application of the "biogenetic law." (1) "The egg of man, this system of innumerable developmental potencies which realize themselves in the progress of development, can in no way be compared with the hypothetical unicellular organism from which phylogeny took its starting point." [19] In fact, it must be noted that the fertilized ovum of man is not the same as any other fertilized ovum or as any other organism. It differs in the number and quality of its chromosomes and genes. (2) "We can say that ontogeny cannot in principle, run through an ancestral series, because the embyro of the higher animal form is never identical with another lower animal form. The members of the phylogenetic series are independent living forms, while the embryonal stages are mere transition stages." [20] Consequently, we cannot apply this "law" literally and say that the unborn child at such-and-such a stage is a protazoon or is a fish. This is biologically impossible. The most that can be done is to point out resemblances or rudiments (*Anlagen*) from an evolutionary past "which progressively unfold in the course of embryonic life." [21]

Each organism is individualistic. A human organism remains human from zygote to corpse, but at various stages of its development it reflects its forbears. It does not become them, but it represents the ancestral features that have survived, if only as useless vestiges.

We cannot say that a particular fetus can be aborted because it is alleged that in its ascending recapitulation of the evolutionary history of man, it has not reached a high enough stage of development to be considered human. We must never forget that the human zygote begins at this human stage. This one-celled organism has within itself the end product of the evolutionary process. To make decisions about the status of the human zygote in terms of the "biogenetic law" is blatantly to disregard the findings of modern biology. A colleague of Galileo is said to have refused "to look through Galileo's telescope for fear of finding Aristotle's physics to be wrong." Today it seems that this mentality still survives in some who refuse to look through the electron microscope for fear of finding that Aristotle's or Aquinas's or Haeckel's natural philosophy is wrong.

C. Those who deny human status to the fetus in the early stages of gestation frequently appeal to the same set of unusual or experimental biological facts, sometimes with scant attention to the genotypic and phenotypic evidence of a living continuity manifested in the ordinary pregnancy. Without attempting an exhaustive biological and philosophical analysis, let us consider these facts and make some observations about their significance.

First, experimenters at Oxford University have transplanted the nucleus from an intestinal cell of an adult frog into an egg cell whose nucleus has been removed.[22] The result in thirty percent of the experiments was that the egg developed into an identical twin of the frog whose cell nucleus was used. The results suggest the fantastic possibility of producing millions of individuals all genetically identical with the original donor, frog or human. It should be noted that the union of the nucleus and the cytoplasm of the enucleated egg are not as dissimilar chemically from a normal conception as one might think. The real mystery seems to be found in the previously unsuspected powers of the cytoplasm in influencing cell development and specialization.

Second, Dr. Binz and others at the Institute for Cancer Research in Philadelphia have been able to produce hundreds of "multimice" or genetic mouse mosaics, each mouse with four parents.[23] Dr. Binz removes the embryo from two pregnant mice two days after they have mated. The embryos consist, at the time, of eight cells. The membrane surrounding each embryo is dissolved and the embryos are put together in an incubator. In two days, they become a single cluster of cells from which develops one mouse with the characteristics of both sets of parents.

Third, two American scientists, Dr. M. C. Weiss and Dr. H. Green, have produced durable hybrids that have lasted as long as six months by using human and mouse cells.[24] Hybrids were first produced in 1960, but not until recently have any lasted longer than two weeks. Most of the human chromosomes are lost in each successful hybrid cell, but most of the mouse chromosomes remain. No mouse-man develops bodily form, but the hybrid cell does live.

Fourth, two pathological growths sometimes occur. The hydatidiform mole is a malformation of the chorion or amniotic sac which surrounds the embryo and other fetal membranes. The villi, minute projections from its surface which enable it to work its way into the uterus to protect and nourish the child, sometimes develop into grapelike clusters filled with liquid. The embryo, deprived of nourishment, dies. The womb is soon totally occupied by this abnormal growth. Since it is a fetal membrane, it has the same genetic structure as the dead embryo. It survives the embryo for some time, but though it is unique and alive, it has no principle of human unity but is like a bunch of grapes made of human cells. The second pathological growth, the teratoma, is a tumor which arises from a cluster of embryonic cells which never developed when the rest of the body was growing and differentiating. If this undeveloped portion is somehow stimulated into activity, it produces an odd and usually grotesque assortment of teeth, strands of hair, tonguelike protuberances, bits of fingernail, and other less distinguishable tissues. Here is life, growth, and specialization but little organization.

To appreciate the significance of these biological facts it is necessary to avoid certain basic mistakes. First, we should not confuse being identical with being unique. An individual may have a unique set of genes. If this genetic structure is reproduced in another living being by somatic generation, as in the frog experiments, the genetic uniqueness then becomes genetic identity. The individual phenotypes, however, are unique, ever reflecting the interaction of their genetic heritage with their specific environment. The significant and indispensable uniqueness of the fetus is this phenotypic individuality, for on this is based the predication of human rights. Second, we should not confuse unity with uniqueness or identity. In both the zygote and the newly born baby, there is a common cellular denominator—genetic identity. But the baby is not simply an amalgam of genetically identical cells. It has, due to its life principle, a unity as perfect as that of the one-celled fertilized ovum. In both, the vital principle has a unifying function over its corresponding material structure despite the growing complexity of that body. The pathological growths, the hydatidiform mole, and the teratoma illustrate what happens when the principle of unity is not present. The "multimouse" shows how the continuance of a principle of unity proportionate to the species preserves normal development despite an abnormal "second conception." Third, we should not confuse universal with uniform. Dr. M. W. Nirenberg of the National Institute of Health in Bethesda, Maryland, led a team of geneticists who reported in 1967 that identical genetic code combinations acted the same way in a mammal, an amphibian, and a bacterium, thus substantiating the thesis that the genetic code is universal, "essentially one biological language." [25] The fact that hybrids are possible helps substantiate this thesis. Evolution itself is an argument in favor of a universal genetic language. But a common language does not mean all the words are uniform. Man is not simply an animal because he has an animal body. Scientists can accept, without intrinsic contradiction, both the bodily evolution of man and the direct creation of his soul. So, too, in matters embryological, the human life principle need not, even in the earliest stages, be viewed through the eyes of a reductionism which reduces life to a purely physical and chemical system. Man may be an animal, but he is much more than an animal.

In brief, modern genetics and molecular biology have made marvelous advances in the knowledge and control of life, yet we find even in bizarre experiments and revolutionary discoveries accumulating evidence of the living continuity from conception to death, the human organism. We can distinguish genotype identity and phenotypic difference. We can value the role of uniqueness and the role of unity. We can sense our biological kinship with all living creatures, and in doing so appreciate even more deeply the supreme dignity and unrivaled excellence of the human organism from its earliest beginnings.

D. How can we best classify, scientifically and philosophically, the purposeful destruction of this human life through abortion? We get a clue from looking at life itself. Although it has a goal-oriented integrity, its structures and functions aimed at full maturity, it can fail through no fault of its own. Human life involves environmental interaction. The phenotype is the result of interaction between the genotype and its environment. But the environment can be hostile and the interaction fatal to the fetus.

Embryology and genetics, in fact all the life sciences, give evidence of an evolutionary tendency operating in the universe. They show nature on the move toward more and more highly ordered enclaves. Nevertheless, another tendency is at work in the opposite direction, toward a state of utter disorder. This notion of entropy—the tendency of things to a random state of statistical uniformity of energy and temperature—gives a new scientific and philosophic dimension to that brutal happening which is abortion.

Despite the downhill direction of the universe as a whole, the world teems with anti-entropic processes. While the universe moves inevitably to the most probable state of stable equilibrium, there are beings that push toward improbable peaks of organized achievement. All living organisms are highly improbable, and man most of all. Living organisms have this anti-entropic tendency rooted in their basic functions: in the metabolic function of obtaining free energy from the environment through nutrition and respiration, thereby effecting a local decrease in entropy despite an over-all increase; in the adaptive function of using energy disproportionate to the stimulus to preserve itself in being despite the environmental hostility of an entropic universe; and in the reproductive function of perpetuating its own anti-entropic tendency dependent only on the presence of available free energy and a more or less favorable environment. All organisms do this. Man does it most perfectly.

Life is a thrust toward individual progress and perfection. It has a spark of the creative fiat that brought order out of chaos in the beginning. Nevertheless, all living beings eventually manifest entropic evidence of their own finitude. Hans Selye's work on stress—"the rate of wear and tear on the body" [26]—chronicles the operation of biological entropy. He calls aging, the speed of self-consumption, and defines life as a process of spending our limited inheritance of adaptive energy. "Vitality," he tells us, "is like a special kind of bank account which you can use up by withdrawals but cannot increase by deposits." [27] This irreversibility, so salient a characteristic of entropy, is what makes the second law of thermodynamics what Boulding calls "a dismal theory." Yet the very precariousness of life should make us respect and treasure and safeguard it all the more highly. As the poet, Francis Thompson, wrote, "Half a kiss's dainty bliss is from the day of kiss no more."

But abortion is anticipated entropy whereby the human organism with its precious inheritance of energy and potential is purposely and freely degraded. Its intricate beauty and functional dynamism are reduced to a rubble of lifeless disorder. To understand abortion in its cosmic proportions it is necessary to see it as an entropic contribution to chaos, as a devastating attack on that improbable perfection which is human life.

IV

The scientific facts of the life process have been our concern in this chapter. Since abortion interrupts this process sometime before birth and destroys the growing organism, we have tried to find out what happens after the ovum is fertilized by the sperm, and what kind of an organism abortion destroys.

To answer these questions we have examined the human organism from two points of view. The phenotypic analysis suggests the presence of a living continuum from the time of fertilization. Undeniably, an orderly process of rapid development begins with the first cleavage and continues long after normal birth. As early as the end of the first two months, the child, though not yet viable, is clearly a human being—all its essential parts and their basic relationships are well established. The fetal period is primarily a time of growth and consolidation. As we move closer to the time of fertilization, the organism is necessarily more primitive and undeveloped. But from the very beginning, it is visibly impelled by a goal-oriented impulse—and that goal is exclusively human.

If we judge merely by appearances, it is not difficult to refuse to a three-day-old morula the title, dignity, and rights of a human being. Yet appearances are often misleading, and to depend solely on appearances would be scientifically most unsophisticated. For that reason, we examine embryonic life genotypically, aided by what has been called the "genetics explosion" or "microbiological revolution." From the scientists, we learn that the human organism from the start, though no more than a one-celled zygote, has all the information and all the physical power that it needs in its uterine environment to multiply, specialize, and reach its goal of birth. This one cell is a physical body of amazing complexity, and it knows when and how to produce the various kinds of protein for the construction of a completed and mature human adult. There is a unity of life and function here which carries within itself the power of self-actualization. All the zygote needs is a favorable environment and nine busy months to demonstrate visibly what it was from the beginning—a human person.

A consideration of the life process from the philosophical point of view reinforces the scientific conclusion about the unbroken continuity of human life from fertilization to death. The theories of mediate animation and ancestral recapitulation fall under Ockham's razor as they multiply entities—successive souls and ancestral states—without any scientific or philosophic justification.

Although the moral and political and legal evaluation of the destruction of this unborn human organism will be dealt with separately, the scientific and philosophic conclusion is clear that abortion is the killing of a human person. Moreover, abortion tends to negate the evolutionary tendency in the world by its own tendency to disorder and chaos. Life is anti-entropic. But induced abortion is anticipated entropy—all the more tragic because it is freely chosen.

Chapter Two

THE HISTORICAL CONTEXT

Our current abortion problem is not a unique historical phenomenon. The earliest legal codes reflect a community concern. All peoples have known instinctively that societal survival demands sound laws to regulate the protecting and taking of human life. Abortion focuses on this life-and-death issue in a special way, because through abortion life is destroyed at its source. Nonetheless, men have differed, as they do today, over whether or not this destruction is ever justified. How they balance the competing interests involved in an unwanted pregnancy indicates the priority of values in the community.

The laws of former civilizations shine forth from the mists of the past with a clarity that few other archaeological remains possess. We learn the structure of societies by the policies and sanctions they impose on their members. The starkly prosaic style of legislation makes it an instrument of inestimable worth in re-creating the past. Laws are blunt directives. They sweep us back into the past with the immediacy of a sharp pain. They speak a universal language labeling a familiar action with a recognizable penalty. However alien modern laws would be in the ancient, and even the not too ancient world, most of the earlier laws are comprehensible to us because they deal with problems that affect every society. Unfortunately, unwanted pregnancies and the expedient of abortion are problems almost as old as mankind. In studying the historical influences on our present thinking about abortion, we focus first on two major sources: Middle Eastern culture and Greco-Roman culture. The Middle East has influenced us most significantly through Judeo-Christian thought. And yet pagan Greece and Rome contributed largely to the formation of the Christian community, which was a Greek-speaking church before it was a Roman church. Though the Catholic Church has lost its position of pre-eminence in Europe, many of its traditional values—some, in Chesterton's phrase, only as "superstitions of the skeptic"—still form part of the fabric of our Anglo-American heritage. After a survey of the history of the Church's laws on abortion we will consider the relationship of these laws to English abortion laws. From the developments in England, we see first the derivative and then the independent development in the United States.

This brief historical study shows us that the problem of abortion with its manifold dimensions is a perennial crisis stemming from the vulnerability of the process of generation in a suffering and often selfish world. It helps us assess past trends and perhaps perceive a chronologically evolving consensus about the value of nascent human life.

The Ancient Middle East

The antiquity of the abortion laws of the Middle East indicates the chronic importance of this sociomedical problem. In the "cradle of civilization," laws protecting the unborn go back centuries before Christ. The Sumerian Code of 2000 B.C., the Hammurabic Code of 1300 B.C., the Assyrian Code of 1500 B.C., the Hittite Code of 1300 B.C., and the Persian Code of 600 B.C. all prohibit the striking of a woman so as to cause the death of her unborn child. These statutes are usually both compensatory and punitive, including what we now call torts and crimes. The legal elements required to establish this combination of guilt and liability, however, vary widely from one code to another.

For an insight into the spirit of the ancient law, it is helpful to study the letter of a reasonably typical prohibition. The Assyrian Code, although not as old as the Code of Hammurabi, is perhaps the most interesting. These laws were codified under Tiglath-Pileser I, in the twelfth century B.C., but some of the laws were in force from the fifteenth century. Despite an obvious Babylonian influence, this abortion legislation is more complicated than the earlier legislation which levied fines on the defendant in all cases other than the death of a noble's wife—a capital crime. Here are the pertinent provisions of the Assyrian Code.

21: If a seignior struck a(nother) seignior's daughter and has caused her to have a miscarriage, when they have prosecuted him (and) convicted him, he shall pay two talents thirty minas of lead; they shall flog him fifty (times) with staves (and) he shall do the work of the king for one full month.

50: [If a seignior] struck a(nother) signior's [wife] and caused her to have [a miscarriage], they shall treat [the wife of the seignior], who cause (the other) seignior's wife to [have a miscarriage], as he treated her. . . . if that woman died, they shall put the seignior to death; he shall compensate for her fetus with a life. But, when that woman's husband has no son, if someone struck her so that she had a miscarriage, they shall put the striker to death; even if her fetus is a girl, he shall compensate with a life.

51: If a seignior struck a(nother) seignior's wife who does not rear her children and caused her to have a miscarriage, this punishment (shall hold): he shall pay two talents of lead.

52: If a seignior struck a harlot and caused her to have a miscarriage, they shall inflict blow for blow upon him; he shall compensate with a life.

53: If a woman has had a miscarriage by her own act, when they have prosecuted her (and) convicted her, they shall impale her on stakes without burying her. If she died having the miscarriage, they shall impale her on stakes without burying her.[1]

The Assyrian legislation contrasts significantly with the current proposal that a woman ought to be able to abort any unwanted child. The Assyrians inflicted on the woman who self-aborts one of the most horrible of punishments—impalement. In other such codes, however, there is no specific prohibition of self-abortion, or of abortion inflicted by the husband or of an abortion voluntarily agreed upon by husband and wife. The statutes looked primarily to injuries to the mother which were caused by a third party and which resulted in the death of the child. The fetal death is not necessarily the major value protected; but neither is the crime simply one of aggravated assault on the mother. There is a recognition, although imperfect, of the sacredness of human life.

These ancient statutes suggest an underlying but operative scale of values. The status of the pregnant woman is, in all the codes, a prime determinant, sometimes an exclusive one, of the compensation or punishment. The death of the fetus, too, is usually more than a necessary condition. Thus fetal sex was important in the Assyrian Code. Fetal development was important in the Hittite Code: "If anyone cause a free woman to miscarry, if it is the tenth month, he shall give ten shekels of silver, if [it is] the fifth month, he shall give five shekels and pledge his estate as security." A latter version, however, has simply, "If anyone causes a free woman to miscarry, he shall give twenty shekels of silver." [2] In the oldest of the codes, the Sumerian, the abortion was an aggravated crime if done deliberately, but even if done accidentally it was sanctioned as it is today in tort cases.[3] Considering all the codes, the punishments covered a broad spectrum: fines, public service, flogging, death, and even the death of an innocent relative of the guilty party.

We should not read into these laws, significant though they are, a greater strictness or permissiveness than is actually there.

It can perhaps be argued that within the family unit and with the consent of the father and husband, abortion would not be punished. Self-abortion, however, is explicitly penalized. Perhaps the recognized value of large families made any problem of abortion with the consent of the father largely academic. Or perhaps the absolute dominion of the father over the members of his family forstalled any extrafamilial interference by the law. At any rate, these statutes do afford the first legal precedents for offering protection, even if only indirectly, to the unborn child.

For the Jews, the Old Testament touched briefly on the problem of accidental miscarriage but with a comparative lack of juridical sophistication. Nevertheless, it was the two very different versions of this text that polarized later Jewish and Christian teaching on abortion. The germinal passage was Exodus 21:22–25:

> If, when men come to blows, they hurt a woman who is pregnant and she suffers a miscarriage, though she does not die of it, the man responsible must pay the compensation demanded of him by the woman's master; she shall hand it over after arbitration. But should she die, you shall give life for life, eye for eye, tooth for tooth, hand for hand, foot for foot, burn for burn, wound for wound, stroke for stroke.

Apparently, this ordinance of Moses, proclaimed about the time of the Assyrian Code, was not a prescription against deliberate abortion—no problem in the Jewish community at that time. Rather, it was a clarification of the more general law: "Whoever strikes another so that he dies, must be put to death." (Exodus 21:12). If after the miscarriage the woman died, the punishment was death. If she lived, the punishment was a fine. The death of the fetus was not considered a capital crime, at least in this case of manslaughter or negligent homicide.

A mistranslation of the phrase, "though she does not die of it," or more literally, "without further harm," gave a totally unintended meaning to this Mosaic law. The Samaritan and the

Karaite, but, crucially, the Septuagint translations of the Old Testament read the word "zurah" or "surah," which means "form," for the word "ason," which means "harm" or "accident." [4] As a result, the determining factor of what kind of punishment would be imposed was whether or not the child was imperfectly or perfectly formed. This distinction was in harmony with contemporary Greek thought, which had already reasoned that human life begins when the child reaches a certain stage of fetal development. The two main versions of the Bible extant at the time of Christ were the Palestinian or Hebrew Bible and the Septuagint or Greek Bible. The latter was adopted by most of the Jews and by the early Christians. Thus, Philo, a Jewish philosopher from Alexandria, wrote in the first century that one should die who kills an unborn child if it had been "shaped and all the limbs had their proper qualities, for that which answers to this description is a human being . . . like a statue lying in a studio requiring nothing more than to be conveyed outside." [5] Thus, the view of abortion as a serious crime because of the death of the fetus established the precept which was to influence the history of abortion up to the present day.

The main body of Jewish thought, as might be expected, eventually returned to the original Hebrew text and developed a less strict interpretation of abortion. This position was in conflict with that of the Hellenic Jews of the Diaspora as well as with the findings of the natural philosophers. The Talmud, however, only mentions abortion once:

> If a woman is in hard travail [and her life cannot otherwise be saved], one cuts up the child within her womb and extracts it member by member, because her life comes before that of [the child]. But if the great part [or the head] was delivered, one may not touch it, for one may not set aside one person's life for the sake of another.[6]

The rationale of this position, beyond the Exodus text, is that the child is an "aggressor" who is "in pursuit" of its mother's

life which she has a right to defend at the expense of the child.[7]
Jewish teaching, however, did not permit abortion of defective or
illegitimate children, or children who were the result of rape,
incest, or adultery. Only a serious danger to the life or health of
the mother would permit the taking of the life of the unborn
child. Even in the Rabbinical writings subsequent to the Talmud,
there was little on abortion until recent times because abortion
was not then an accepted practice or even a problem among the
Jews. Although both Reform and Conservative Jews have relaxed
the strict position of the Orthodox, it was this latter position
which was operative from the time of Christ until the last
few centuries. In contrast to the contemporary attitudes of
Greece and Rome, this position represented a major moral evolution.

Greco-Roman Civilization

Classical Greece and Rome were the unlikely arenas in which
the Judeo-Christian insight into the immorality of abortion would
begin to develop. The two cultures did not contribute equally, but
they both seemed equally hostile to any limiting of abortion on
demand. Greece affords us no clear legal prohibitions. Lycurgus
in the ninth century and Solon in the sixth century are said to
have enacted abortion laws. The closest we come to legal formu-
lations are the political works of Plato (427–347 B.C.) and
Aristotle (384–322 B.C.). Yet both the *Republic* and the *Politics*
advocate rather than prohibit abortion.

Plato recommends abortion for eugenic reasons on the grounds
that men and women above the ideal age for child-bearing should
not procreate: ". . . we have exhorted them to be very careful
that no child, if one should be conceived, should see the light;
but if one should by any chance force its way to the light, they
must dispose of it on the understanding that such offspring is not
to be reared." [8] Aristotle justified abortion for eugenic and
demographic reasons: "As to the exposure and rearing of chil-

dren, let there be a law that no deformed child shall live, but on the ground of an excess in the number of children, if the established custom of the state forbid this (for in our state population has a limit), no child is to be exposed but when couples have children in excess, let abortion be procured before sense and life have begun; what may or may not be lawfully done in these cases depends on the question of life and sensation." [9] In his *History of Animals,* he suggests that formation and sensation do not occur before the fortieth day for males and the ninetieth day for females (7.3.583ʰ).[10] This numerical pinpointing of the beginning of rational life was to have a long life in biological and legal circles.

Despite the pro-abortion attitude of Greek thought, it had within itself the germ of a philosophical argument against abortion. Culturally, abortion was widely accepted; yet Greek medical and biological ideas were to give the rational substructure or explanation for the Old Testament prohibition which Christianity was to refine and elaborate. In Greece, among the intellectuals, there were wide differences of opinion about the legitimacy of abortion. Although the Oath of Hippocrates (460–357 B.C.) was by no means representative of the consensus among physicians or philosophers, it did establish an ideal which was in opposition to abortion and which had a persuasive and rallying effect throughout the ages. The physician pledged "not to give a deadly drug to anyone if asked for it, nor to suggest it. Similarly, I will not give to a woman an abortifacient pessary. In purity and holiness I will guard my life and my art." [11] According to Soranos of Ephesus (c. A.D. 98–138), who was the leading Greco-Roman gynecologist, the deadly drug (pharmakon) mentioned by Hippocrates refers not only to poisons in general but to an abortifacient (phthorion), as he paraphrased the oath.[12] Whatever Hippocrates meant in that specific passage, his over-all condemnation of abortion was clear and was influential. The importance of Hippocrates is not in his authority but in his influence. He symbolized the new respect for life which was to join forces with philosophy and religion in implementing a protective custody for the unborn.

Rome characteristically affords more juridical prohibitions of abortion than did Greece but against a background of greater decadence. In fact, its first abortion laws were prompted by fear of human wickedness rather than by reverence for human dignity. Laws against abortion were a long time in coming. There were none at all during the Monarchy or the Republic. In fact, there was no criminal law as we know it during this period. Even with the establishment about 450 B.C. of the Twelve Tables, which enacted a body of criminal law, abortion was not included. The basic reason for this apparent omission was the institution of the Paterfamilias, which had already existed under the Republic and was even more firmly established under the Twelve Tables.[13] All family crimes were dealt with by the head of the family, the Paterfamilias, who had the power of life and death over all the members of his family as well as the right to avenge the wrongs committed against members of his family. Public criminal law, in this area, was superfluous or worse, since it would have been an interference with the rights of the family, a derogation from the dominion of the Paterfamilias.

Finally during the reign of Augustus Caesar, the first of the Roman Emperors after the dissolution of the Republic, abortion was punished, but not as a crime against the family. The rash of poisonings that spread through Rome necessitated drastic legislation. The Law, *De Sicariis et Veneficis,* On Murders and Poisons (85 B.C.), prohibited all lethal drugs including abortifacients. It punished the seller or the supplier but not the woman. In terms of abortion, it was directed more against the manufacture and sale of these poisons than against their actual use. The life of the unborn child was not of paramount importance.

This callousness about human life is not surprising. Even more frequent than abortion was the exposure of children. Though many moralists and intellectuals condemned this inhuman practice, eminent men defended it. Seneca, the Roman philosopher, argues eugenically, "Mad dogs we knock on the head; the fierce and savage ox we slay; sickly sheep we put to the knife to keep them from infecting the flock; unnatural progeny we destroy; we drown even children who at birth are weakly and abnormal. Yet it is not anger but reason that separates the harmful from the unsound." [14] The Stoics attacked on principle the practice of exposing infants, but they did not have the same ideological reasons for attacking abortion, for they considered that the human soul was infused only at birth. Abortion, therefore, was not the killing of a human being as was the exposure of a child. In general, however, since Rome accepted slavery, gladiatorial combats, inhuman punishments of crucifixion, impalement, and the wild beasts, and condoned the exposure of babies, the killing within the womb of a being considered not yet human was not likely to offend the moral sense of the community.

Nevertheless the situation at Rome became so decadent and disruptive that harsher laws were finally passed during the reign of Septimus Serverus (A.D. 193–211). In his attempt to reform the morals of the state, he was the first to forbid abortion directly. Abortion by a married woman who thereby deprived her husband of children was punished by exile. Another decree punished by temporary exile the divorced woman who through abortion deprived her ex-husband of children.

Roman law began with the Twelve Tables and reached its culmination in the *Corpus Juris Civilis* of Justinian, which was promulgated in 533–34. This was the codification of all the laws of the Empire, not a mere collection but a consolidation and even a reformulation of previous laws. Abortion was dealt with briefly. Two aspects are important: the status of the unborn child and the laws prohibiting abortion. The Stoic position that birth was the moment of the infusion of the soul permeated the *Corpus*. Thus we read in the *Digest* words that seem simplistic compared with sophisticated Greek thought.[15] The unborn child in the eyes of the law was not a human being (*homo*), not living (*animax*), not in the human class (*in rebus humanis*), but only potentially (*in spe*) a person and still part of its mother (*mulieris portio est vel viscerum*). Abortion was prohibited, however, but not because it destroyed a human being. The reasons referred to the mother—abortion was a danger to her health; to the father—abortion infringed on his rights if done without his consent; and to society—abortion gave a bad example of the use of poisons, and cut down on the number of future citizens. For illegal abortion, there were various punishments: partial forfeiture of possessions, servitude in the mines, permanent or temporary exile, and even capital punishment if the woman died.

Although these laws against abortion in the *Corpus Juris Civilis* did not outlaw the great bulk of abortions in the Roman Empire, they did stigmatize abortion as something socially harmful and therefore criminal. Greek thought and the Christian religion would together give more profound philosophical and spiritual reasons for the prohibition. The focal point would shift from the mother, father, and the community to the fetus, whose dignity and rights as a human person would gradually be recognized.

The Leaven of Christianity

The scattered and ineffectual abortion laws of the Greco-Roman civilization did little more than point out official awareness of social problems of which abortion and infanticide were symptomatic. Little can be done, however, by legislation which runs counter to the value system of the community. The killing of the unborn and the newly born was a traditionally accepted way of solving a number of social and personal problems. A new law would not radically change an old practice. Despite the instrumentalities of power at the disposal of the state, the consent of the governed, even in a totalitarian regime, has an awesome influence. It is not surprising, therefore, that political pressures were not able to change the attitude of the public toward abortion. What is surprising is that this attitude changed at all. That it did change is clear from our current controversy over the proposed relaxation of the abortion laws. Somehow the conscience of the community developed a practical concern for the lives of the unborn. Laws reflecting this new dimension in social thought eventually followed. The power that was able to accomplish more than the emperors was a new religion, Christianity.[16]

The impact of Christianity on the question of abortion was primarily a by-product of the new sense of human dignity that it engendered. Life, through the Gospel message, was given a value that anticipated birth and transcended death. The rejection of abortion by the Christian community was doubly significant in that it did not depend on a specific prohibition of Sacred Scripture. It was not the letter of the New Law that forbade abortion but its spirit of reverence for life.

The Scriptural opposition to abortion, though not explicit, is dramatically evident. The great commandment of Christian charity toward all specifically included the young. But the compelling precedent of the unborn Christ and the unborn Baptist gave this commandment a new and uterine dimension. The Gospel story is simple, a retelling of the conversation of two pregnant woman.[17] Mary, shortly after she conceived, visited her cousin Elizabeth, who was finishing the second trimester. At the salutation of Mary, who was "with child of the Holy Spirit," the six-month-old fetus in the womb of Elizabeth "leapt for joy." Elizabeth explains this unusual fetal reaction: the embryo, the fruit of Mary's womb, was "blessed" because it was "the Lord." Henceforward, future generations would recognize the dignity of the unborn child.

Yet nowhere in the New Testament is abortion clearly forbidden. Despite the frequent and detailed moral admonitions of the Pauline epistles which were in large part directed to Gentile converts for whom abortion was much more acceptable than it was among the Jews, there is no direct reference. Fornication, adultery, and incest are repeatedly condemned. And so is murder. But the killing of the innocent child that is so frequently the fruit of illicit intercourse is not mentioned. An argument can be made that the "practice of medicine" (*pharmakeia*) listed as one of the works of the flesh in the *Epistle to the Galatians* (5:20) and the "medicine men" listed with the fornicators and homicides in the *Apocalypse* (21:18) are connected with the deadly drugs used sometimes as abortifacients.[18] If abortion is meant, the message is a subtle one.

The first explicit prohibition of abortion by the Christian community is found in the writings of the Apostolic Fathers, men of the first or early second century who were taught either by the Apostles or their disciples. At the most, there are seven works with this authoritative or official characterization. Only two of them mention abortion but they do so most emphatically, certainly reflecting the consensus of the Christian community. The two works phrase the moral precept in an identical way although in a different context. Perhaps both share a common source no longer extant; or the later work may be a commentary on the earlier one. The scholarly interconnections, however, are secondary to the fact that in two of the most significant writings of the early Church, abortion, without any justification or exception, was listed among the worst of sins.

The earliest reference is in the *Didache* or, in its full title, *The Lord's Instruction to the Gentiles through the Twelve Apostles.* This work was written in Syria about A.D. 80 and is the oldest source of ecclesiastical law. Although it was not discovered until 1883, it is the most important of the so-called "subapostolic" writings: It states:

> You shall not kill. You shall not commit adultery. You shall not corrupt boys. You shall not fornicate. You shall not steal. You shall not make magic. You shall not practice medicine. You shall not slay the child by abortion. You shall not kill what is generated. You shall not desire your neighbor's wife.[19]

The second reference to abortion is in the Epistle of Barnabas, written about A.D. 138. Completely misnamed, it was not written by Barnabas and is a theological tract rather than a letter, the work was highly regarded for centuries after it was written, especially by the theologians of Alexandria. The author treats abortion not as part of a list of serious sins, as did the *Didache,* but as a corollary to the law of fraternal charity:

> You shall love your neighbor more than your own life. You shall not slay the child by abortion. You shall not kill what is generated.[20]

Subsequent Christian writers through the fourth century consistently opposed all abortion without distinctions or exceptions. The Fathers of the Church of the East and of the West emphasized the sanctity of unborn life. Their statements give a many-faceted opposition to abortion. Athenagoras wrote to Emperor Marcus Aurelius in 177 that "all who use abortifacients are homicides and will account to God for their abortion as for the killing of men. For the fetus in the womb is not an animal, and it is God's providence that he exist." [21] Clement of Alexandria, the Father of Theologians, wrote in 215 that abortions and abortifacient drugs "destroy utterly the embryo and, with it, the love of man." [22] Minucius Felix sometime between 190 and 200, spoke of the pagans who "By drinks of drugs they extinguish in their viscera the beginning of man-to-be and, before they bear, commit parricide." [23] This term, later used by St. Cyprian, meant in Roman law the killing of a close relative—a most serious crime.[24] Tertullian in 240, wrote in defense of the Christians:

> For us, indeed, as homicide is forbidden, it is not lawful to destroy what is conceived in the womb while the blood is still being formed into a man. To prevent being born is to accelerate homicide, nor does it make a difference whether you snatch a soul which is born or destroy one being born. He who is man-to-be is man, as all fruit is now in the seed.[25]

Hippolytus in 235, labeled as homicide the deliberate expelling of "a fetus already engendered." [26] Cyprian, in 258, said that one committed "parricide" because "he had killed a son who was being born" by deliberately striking his pregnant wife.[27] All these writers, whether Greek or Latin, absolutely prohibited abortion despite the Septuagint translation of Exodus and despite the position of Aristotelian and Stoic philosophers about the delayed time of the infusion of the soul.

The fifth century was a time of more refined theologizing but not of greater biological knowledge. Four main sources, Basil, Chrysostom, Jerome, and Augustine, established the poles of the dialog or controversy over the rationale of the prohibition against abortion from conception. The Church consistently forbade the destruction of life engendered in the womb, but it did not consistently call that destruction homicide. The continuing issue, reflected in ecclesiastical penal laws, was not whether abortion was a mortal sin but whether abortion was always the sin of homicide. The fifth century witnessed the formulation of the two poles, the eastern and the western.

The Eastern Church, strangely enough, first introduced into ecclesiastical literature the notion of the formed and unformed fetus. The *Apostolic Constitution,* in 400, condemned the killing of a "formed fetus." [28] Despite the name, these apocryphal Syrian canons were not of apostolic origin. Moreover, the work was not very influential on this point in the East. The major reason was that St. Basil the Great of Cappadocia had already written *Three Canonical Letters* (374–75), one of which, No. 188, was to dispel once and for all from the moral teaching of the Greek Church the distinction between formed and unformed fetus. He asserted:

Canon 2: A woman who deliberately destroys a fetus is answerable for murder. And any fine distinction as to its being completely formed or unformed is not admissible among us. For in this case, not only the child which is about to be formed is vindicated but also she herself who plotted against herself, since women usually die from such attempts. And there is added to this crime, the destruction of the embryo, a second murder—at least that is the intent of those who dare these things. We should not, however, prolong their punishment until death, but should accept the term of ten years; and we should not determine the treatment according to time but according to the manner of repentence.[29]

Canon 8: And so women who give drugs that cause abortion are themselves also murderers as well as those who take the poisons that kill the fetus.[30]

Within ten years after the death of St. Basil in 379, St. John Chrysostom wrote, presumably at Antioch, his greatest work, *Homilies on Romans* (381–98). This commentary, more ascetical and moral than speculative, continued the Eastern opposition to abortion that was so clearly formulated by St. Basil. In the twenty-fourth homily he speaks strongly against abortion. He excoriates married men who persuade the prostitutes they have impregnated to have abortions: "You do not let a harlot remain only a harlot but make her a murderess as well." Indeed, he does not know what name to call the abortion of a child after its conception, for it is a crime "even worse than murder." [31]

The Latin Church, on the other hand, although it consistently opposed abortion, made certain distinctions based on the Septuagint and on philosophy—based, one might say, on badly translated Scripture and biologically unsound philosophy. The two great names in the Church of the West on this point are St. Jerome (†420) and St. Augustine (†430). Both of these Doctors of the Church condemned abortion whenever it occurred but acknowledged that they were not sure when life did actually begin.

St. Jerome in a letter to Eustochium writes of abortion with abortifacient drugs: "Some, when they learn they are with child, practice abortion by the use of drugs. Frequently they die themselves and are brought before the rulers of the lower world guilty of three crimes: suicide, adultery against Christ, and murder of an unborn child." [32]

Augustine's mature thought on abortion is in three works written close to the time of St. Jerome's death in 420. They are his commentary on Exodus 21:22 in *Questions on the Heptateuch* (419–20), and his handbook or *Enchiridion on Faith, Hope, and Charity* (421), his anti-Pelagian tract on *Marriage and Concupiscence* (419). We will, however, deal with the problem logically rather than chronologically. First, the basic principle: "Now, from whatever moment a human being begins to live, from that moment it is possible for him to die. And, if he is dead, no matter how death came to him, I can find no reason to deny that he has an interest in the resurrection." [33] Second, he acknowledges the difficulty of solving the problem: "The following question may be most meticulously probed and disputed among the most learned (though I do not know whether man can answer it), that is, when a human being begins to live in the womb; whether there is some form of hidden life before it is apparent in the motions of the living being." [34] Third, he gives the position he thinks most reasonable, "Who is not rather disposed to think that unformed fetuses perish, like seeds which have not fructified?" [35] Fourth, in explaining the Exodus text, he gives his basic reason: "There cannot yet be said to be a live soul in a body that lacks sensation when it is not formed in flesh and so not yet endowed with sense." [36] Fifth, nevertheless all destruction of the fetus is wrong: "Sometimes this lustful cruelty or cruel lust comes to this that they even procure poisons of sterility, and if these do not work, they extinguish and destroy the fetus in some way in the womb, preferring that their offspring die before it lives, or if it was already alive in the womb, to kill it before it was born. Such persons are sinful: The wife is like the harlot of her husband, and he is like the adulterer of his wife." [37]

Scripture, together with the works of the Fathers and other ecclesiastical writers, presented the insights and evaluations out of which Church laws would eventually develop. The process was a slow one. The earliest councils to legislate on abortion took place at the beginning of the fourth century. The first, the Council of Elvira, was held about 305 at Granada in Spain and punished very severely the destruction of "what had been conceived" by prohibiting the reception of communion even at the point of death.[38] The council referred explicitly to the absence of the husband so might well have been concerned primarily with adulterous conceptions. But it does not seem to have limited its prescriptions to that specific instance. The first council in the East to forbid abortions was the Council of Ancyra in Galatia, Asia Minor in 314. Its influence was much greater than that of the Council of Elvira, partly because it represented the Churches of Syria and Asia Minor and partly because its disciplinary decrees were ratified by the Fourth Ecumenical Council at Chalcedon in 451. Its famous Canon 21 was found in most subsequent legislation up to the Middle Ages. The canon reads:

> Women who prostitute themselves and who kill the children thus begotten, or who try to destroy them when in their wombs, are by ancient law excommunicated to the end of their lives. We, however, have softened their punishment and condemned them to various appointed degrees of penance for ten years.[39]

The decrees of these first two councils dealing with abortion were clarified in subsequent centuries. In the West, the Council of Elvira was followed in Spain by the Council of Lerida (524), which continued the prohibition of all abortions, specifically after adultery.[40] But the later Canonical Collection of the Greek canons then known in the West, translated and adapted by St. Martin of Braga in Portugal (c. 580), went even farther by extending Canon 21 of the Council of Ancyra, thereby explicitly prohibiting all abortions whether the conception was from fornification, adultery, or lawful intercourse. This *Collectio Martini Bracarensis* also punished attempts at abortion, and, for the first time in ecclesiastical law, punished cooperators in abortion.[41]

In the East, Canon 21 of the Council of Ancyra and the Canonical Letter of St. Basil eventually led to the strong position

of the Trullan Synod or *Consillium Quinisextum* (692).[42] This
was not an ecumenical council. It did not legislate for the whole
Church. Yet it turned out to be the model for ecclesiastical
legislation on abortion until the twelfth-century *Decretum* of
Gratian. The Trullan Synod was essentially an incorporation of
the canons of St. Basil. Although broader than earlier abortion
laws, it was in substantial harmony with them. The Synod is a
milestone marking approximately the halfway mark of twelve
centuries of legislative unanimity on the homicidal character of
all abortion. Obviously, there were other views on abortion at
that time in the Church, but they had not reached that stage of
social acceptance that would permit their legal implementation.
The laws bore witness to the public consensus about the rights of
the unborn child.

Until the twelfth century, the Church of the East and West
followed the legislative prohibitions of these early councils, usually that of the Trullan Synod. From the fifth century, however,
canonical collections were made in jurisdictions not directly
covered by the conciliar authority. These collections of statutory
precedents so extended the influence of the early councils that
there was almost a general law on abortion, though differing
from technical common law by its many variations in particulars.

The Photian Collection, which was made in 883 and adopted
as the official law of the Eastern Church, was based on the
Council of Ancyra, the Canonical Letter of St. Basil, and the
Trullan Synod.[43] In the twelfth century there were commentaries
by such canonists as Zonares, Aristenus, Balsamon, and the
Schismatic Patriarch of Antioch. Synopses were made by
Metaphrastes, Aristenus, Blastares, and Harmenopoulus, the
latter two in the fourteenth century, but there was no basic
change in the earlier Basilian position, no distinction between
the formed and the unformed fetus.

In the Western or Latin Church, other influences were at
work. Through the ninth century, however, the canonical collections of the Latin Church were consistent with those of the

Oriental Church. This is true of the Italian, African, Spanish, and Frankish collections. But beginning with the tenth century, a new element appeared, a breach in the absolute position first showing in a stronger prohibition than usual.

Three men helped make the transition to a new way of legislating about abortion. Regino of Prum included in his *De Disciplinis Ecclesiasticis* (915), in addition to canons from the Councils of Elvira, Ancyra, and Lerida, a famous canon of source unknown, *Si aliquis:* "If anyone to satisfy lust or to implement hatred, in order that no offspring be born of him, either does something to a man or woman or gives something to drink so that the person be not able to generate or conceive, let him be held a murderer." [44] Apparently sterilization, contraception, and abortion at any stage of fetal development were here, in accord with tradition, called murder.

In the eleventh century Burchard, the bishop of Worms, included in his manual for the clergy, *Decretum* (1012), this same canon, *Si aliquis.* So far no hint of a deviation from precedent. What will eventually prove operative is not the all-encompassing prohibition, although it will become the general law of the Church for a brief few years under Pope Gregory IX, but rather the standard for punishment. In this secondary prescription was the practical recognition of a distinction based on the stage of fetal development and the alleged time of fetal animation. Private penances were measured in terms of some vague theory of mediate animation. Thus, Regino writes of a penance of one year if the fetus is under forty days, of three years if it is over forty days and unanimated, and of ten years if it is over forty days and animated. Burchard sets as penances, one year if the fetus is unanimated, but three years if the fetus is animated.[45]

Finally, St. Ives or Ivo of Chartres tried to bring some consistency into the abortion problem, and in so doing prepared the way for Gratian. First of all, he omitted the canon *Si aliquis,* the origin of which had never been clear but which, although articulating a traditional point of view, seemed to be in conflict with current penitential practice. Secondly, in his *Decretum* and *Collectio Tripartita,* he included five canons which referred to patristic authorities to justify the distinction between the formed and the unformed fetus.[46] These statements, although dating back to the fifth century, are not to be found in the canonical collections before Ivo, even those of Regino and Burchard. These five canons are innovative. The first two are from Augustine: All interference with fetal life is wrong; and only the destruction of the formed fetus is murder. The third, falsely attributed to Augustine, stated: Animation occurs only when the fetus has sufficiently developed. The fourth is from St. Jerome, and is like the second: Only the destruction of the formed fetus is murder. The fifth, from Pope Stephen V, stated: One guilty of abortion is a murderer. The *Paranomia* of Ivo of Chartres, written in 1096, was not only his most popular book, but was the canonical collection most widely read and most influential immediately before Gratian.[47] It did not contain all the five canons, for it eliminated the one allegedly by Augustine and the one by Stephen. But the substance was unchanged: Only the destruction of the formed fetus is abortion and therefore murder. This became the popular position on abortion and the one taken in the twelfth century.

In 1140, a Camaldolese monk in Bologna published a monumental work which earned him the name "Father of the Science of Canon Law." Gratian's *Decretum* was an attempt to bring order into the complex and often contradictory mass of legislation that the first thousand years of Christianity had produced. The full title of his work, *Concordia discordantium canonum,* indicates his purpose: to bring into harmony the conflicting canon law of the past. Perhaps Gratian was inspired by the rediscovery, in 1070, of Justinian's *Digesta,* lost sight of from the seventh to the eleventh century, and resolved to give ecclesiastical law some of the majesty of this Roman achievement. Gratian's task involved both the collection and the organization of past canonical legislation. His position on abortion was clear: "He is not a murderer who brings about abortion before the soul is in the body." [48] As proof of this statement, he quotes from the canons of Ivo of Chartres: the first, from Augustine, that the destruction of an unformed fetus is not murder; the third, allegedly from Augustine, that the fetus must have its body formed before the soul can be infused; and the fourth, from Jerome, that there is no murder until the fetus is formed. Gratian does not say, however, when the fetus is formed.

Gratian's position on abortion was maintained by the Decretists (commentators on Gratian's *Decretum*), by the *Decretal Letters* before Gregory IX (compilations of statutes omitted by Gratian and also of papal letters appearing after Gratian), and by the *Glossa Ordinaria* (the work of the Decretists which, however, came after the *Gregorian Decretals*). Some additions were made. Rufinus, in his commentary on Gratian's abortion canons in his *Summa Decretorum* (1157–59), pointed out that the killing of an unformed fetus was only quasi-homicide and should have a three-year penance rather than the more severe penalties for murder.[49] In the first of the *Quinque Compilationes Antiquae* (1188–92), Bernard of Pavia included the Exodus text from the Vulgate with no reference to formation as well as the *Si aliquis* canon omitted by Gratian but which classified all abortion as murder.[50] Although Bernard makes the distinction between the formed and the unformed fetus, between homicide and quasi-homicide, he does keep the traditional approach alive and in the current of canonical thought.

The *Decretals* of Pope Gregory IX (1234) have a special place in the history of ecclesiastical laws against abortion. It was the last authentic collection of law for the universal Church until the Code of Canon Law in 1917. It was the first legislation applicable to the whole Church that incorporated the theory of delayed animation. The compiler, Raymond of Pennafort, included two statements on abortion: a letter of Pope Innocent III to the Carthusians (1211), stating that if a cleric negligently causes an abortion, he is to refrain from exercizing his ministry only if the child has been animated; [51] and the canon *Si aliquis* of Regino of Prum (915), stating that sterilization, contraception, and abortion are acts of homicide. These two Gregorian canons posed an apparent contradiction, but the commentaries on the *Decretals* soon resolved the difficulty in accordance with the principles enunciated in Gratian's *Decretum*. Foremost among the commentators was Raymond of Pennafort, who drew up the compilation. He was followed by Bernard de Bottone and Cardinal Hostiensis in the thirteenth century, Joannes Andreae in the fourteenth, and Panormitanus in the fifteenth century. Their common rationale was that all abortion is murder: If the fetus is formed it is true murder; if the fetus is unformed it is quasi-murder. All abortion is sinful, but the penalties differ with the degree of fetal formation. The early Decretalists did not decide the crucial issue: When does animation take place? The ecclesiastical laws were silent on this point, though some clarification was needed if the laws were to function at all. Later Decretalists like Joannes Andreae and Panormitanus as well as others applied some variation of the old Aristotelian distinction between the animation of males and the animation of females, usually a forty-to-eighty-day norm.

After the Gregorian *Decretals* but before the Council of Trent, many particular councils passed laws that made no mention of the formation-animation distinction but did include all parties to the crime in the penalty of excommunication, not only those whom the Anglo-American common law would call principals, but also the accessories before the fact—those who advised, assisted, encouraged, or provided the abortifacient drugs or other means. This was done, for example, at the Synod of Riez (1285), and its provisions were followed by the two Councils of Avignon (1326 and 1337) and the Council of Lavaur (1368). Surprisingly, despite the Church's concern, the Council of Trent (1545–63) did not legislate directly about abortion. Since it did establish irregularities and vindictive penalties for voluntary homicide and since the abortion of an animated fetus was commonly considered to be homicide, however, there was at least indirect coverage.

About a quarter of a century after the Council of Trent, two papal constitutions established the "Sixtine-Gregorian law," which was to regulate abortion for the next 280 years. In 1588, Pope Sixtus V, in his constitution *Effraenatam,* reinstated the canon *Si aliquis* with its prohibition of sterilization, contraception, and abortion. He punished the actual destruction of a formed or unformed fetus by an automatic [*latae sententiae*] excommunication reserved to the Holy See, by irregularity (a perpetual impediment to the reception or exercise of holy orders), by deprivation of or incapacity for all clerical privileges and every office, dignity, or benefice, by deposition and degradation of clerics, and by the punishments of civil and ecclesiastical law for voluntary homicide.[52] Three years later, in 1591, Pope Gregory XIV by his constitution *Sedes Apostolica* made two drastic revisions which brought the legislation back into line with the *Decretals* of 1234: First, he limited these punishments exclusively to the destruction of the animated fetus; second, he gave the power of absolution from the excommunication to the local ordinary.[53] The punishment for the killing of the unanimated fetus remained what it was before 1588—absolution from the sin and an appropriate penance. For there was no question but that all abortion was sinful whatever the stage of fetal development. Thus, although attempted abortion was not punished by the Sixtine-Gregorian law, the absolution for the sin of so attempting could be reserved to the local ordinary as a special punishment for a gravely evil intention.

Pius IX, in 1869, radically changed the abortion law of the universal Church. By his Constitution *Apostolicae Sedis,* he eliminated the distinction between formed and unformed fetus as far as the penalty of excommunication was involved.[54] Henceforward, every direct killing of human life after fertilization would be punished in the same way. Since Pius IX was reorganizing only one area of canon law, the criminal censures, the Sixtine-

Gregorian law continued to be operative in determining irregularities, and with it the forty-to-eighty-day animation determinant. This inconsistency was eliminated when the new *Code of Canon Law* was promulgated in 1917. The provisions on abortion are brief. Canon 2350, paragraph 1 reads: "Those who procure abortion, not excepting the mother, incur, if the effect follows, an automatic excommunication reserved to the ordinary; and if they be clerics, they are moreover to be deposed." Canon 985, paragraph 4 designates as irregular by delict and thereby prohibited from receiving or exercising sacred orders, "Those who have committed voluntary homicide or procured an abortion, the effect following, as well as their cooperators. A third provision of the *Code* deals with abortion in the broad sense that includes, perhaps primarily, spontaneous miscarriages. Canon 747 states: "Care must be taken that all aborted fetuses, whatever time they are delivered, if certainly alive, should be baptized absolutely, if doubtfully alive, should be baptized conditionally." Canon 746 even allows a child to be baptized in its mother's womb if there is no hope that it will be born in a normal manner. These last two canons indicate the Church's recognition that the unborn child is a person at every stage of its development.

Without venturing into the legal complexities of the Church's present abortion law, we can clarify somewhat the main elements of this tightly formulated statute.[55] By "procure" is meant to intend deliberately to cause an abortion and to use means efficacious in themselves. By "abortion" is meant the ejection of an immature fetus. This definition is taken from Sixtus V, and has been the traditional canonical definition since that time. By "fetus" is meant the human organism after fertilization and before birth. By "immature" is meant nonviable. If a viable child is killed, even in the womb, the crime is homicide, not abortion. By "ejection" is meant the whole process by which the fetus is expelled from the womb. By "the effect following" is meant that a completed and not merely an attempted abortion is requisite. By "those who procure" is meant the mother, the co-agents who intend with the mother to do the act and physically participate in it, and the necessary cooperators, those without whom the abortion would not have taken place. It does not include those who merely facilitate the abortion or who fail to prevent the abortion when they should have. Since this is a penal statute and therefore interpreted strictly, there is a great deal of juridical development on each of these elements. Evidence of complexity, however, is not our goal, nor is canonical expertise. Our focal point is the broader concept—the extent of the protection given by ecclesiastical law to fetal life.

Papal statements on abortion have been frequent and consistent. Three important ones will point on the basic elements of the magisterial position as well as the fundamental historical continuity. The first text is from *Casti connubii,* an encyclical letter of Pius XI in 1930. It dealt with matters of marriage and divorce, sterilization, contraception, and abortion. On the latter, Pius XI wrote:

> As to the "medical and therapeutic indications" to which, using their own words, We have made reference, Venerable Brethren, however much we may pity the mother whose health and even life is gravely imperiled in the performance of the duty alloted to by nature, nevertheless what could ever be a sufficient reason for excusing in any way the direct murder of the innocent? This is precisely what we are dealing with here. Whether inflicted upon the mother or upon the child it is against the precept of God and the law of nature: "Thou shalt not kill." The life of each is equally sacred, and no one has the power, not even the public authority, to destroy it.[56]

Pius XII wrote much more frequently on abortion than did his predecessors or successors. Two texts, however, will indicate the structure of his thought on the subject.

> Now the child, even the unborn child, is a human being in the same degree and by the same title as its mother. Moreover, every human being, even the child in its mother's womb, re-

ceives its right to life directly from God, not from its parents, nor from any human society or authority, no science, no "indication," whether medical, eugenic, social, economic, or moral, that can show or give a valid juridical title for a deliberate and direct disposing of an innocent human life—which is to say, a disposition that aims at its destruction either as an end in itself or as the means of attaining another end that is perhaps in no way illicit in itself.[57]

Innocent human life, in whatever condition it may be, from the first moment of its existence is to be preserved from any direct voluntary attack. This is a fundamental right of human persons, of general value in the Christian concept of life; valid both for the still hidden life in the womb and for the new born baby; and opposed to direct abortion as it is to the direct killing of the child, before, during, and after birth. No matter what the distinction between those different moments in the development of the life already born or still to be born, for profane and ecclesiastical law and for certain civil and penal consequences—according to the moral law, in all these cases it is a matter of grave and illicit attempt on inviolable human life.

This principle holds good both for the life of the child as well as for the life of the mother. Never and in no case has the Church taught that the life of the child must be preferred to that of the mother. It is erroneous to put the question with this alternative: either the life of the child or that of the mother. No, neither the life of the mother nor that of the child can be subjected to an act of direct suppression. In the one case as in the other, there can be but one obligation: to make every effort to save the lives of both, of the mother and of the child.[58]

Subsequent Popes have remained in accord with this position but have spoken only briefly about abortion. John XXIII, in 1961, wrote in the encyclical letter *Mater et Magistra:* "Human life is sacred: from its very inception, the creative action of God is directly operative. By violating His laws, the Divine Majesty is offended, the individuals themselves and humanity degraded, and likewise the community itself of which they are members is en-

feebled." [59] Paul VI, in speaking to an obstetrical and gynecological society in 1964, reaffirmed the Church's position against
abortion by quoting the statements of Pius XII.[60] More recently,
in 1968 he used strong words in the encyclical *Humane Vitae:*
"In conformity with these landmarks in the human and Christian
vision of marriage, we must once again declare that the direct
interruption of the generative process already begun, and, above
all, directly willed and procured abortion, even if for therapeutic
reasons, are to be absolutely excluded as licit means of regulating
birth." [61] However, the most significant contribution of Paul VI
can be found in the Decrees of Vatican II, for it is his approval
that gives them their full magisterial authority.

This most authoritative recent statement on abortion comes
from the 1965 Vatican II pastoral constitution on *The Church in
the Modern World* (*Gaudium et Spes*). The constitution recognized "the advances in biology, psychology, and the social sciences" [62] as well as the fact that "for the family, discord results
from demographic, economic, and social pressures, or from
difficulties which arise between succeeding generations, or from
new social relationships between men and women." [63] It noted,
too, that "the human race is giving ever-increasing thought to
forecasting and regulating its own population growth," [64] and
that "the human race has passed from a rather static concept of
reality to a more dynamic evolutionary one." [65] Nevertheless,
the Council establishes as a fundamental principle reverence for
the human person: "Everyone must consider his neighbor without
exception as another self, taking into account first of all his life
and the means necessary to living it with dignity." [66] This reverence for human life is all important. "Everyone should be per-
suaded that human life and the task of transmitting it are not
realities bound up with this world alone. Hence they cannot be
measured or perceived only in terms of it, but always have a
bearing on the eternal destiny of men." [67]

On the question of abortion, the Council is decisive and absolute. Two passages deal with abortion specifically.

Furthermore whatever is opposed to life itself, such as any type of murder, genocide, abortion, euthanasia, or willful self-destruction . . . all these things and others of their like are infamies indeed. They poison human society, but they do more harm to those who practice them than those who suffer from the injury. Moreover they are a supreme dishonor to the Creator.[68] For God, the Lord of life, has conferred on men the surpassing mystery of safeguarding life—a ministry which must be fulfilled in a manner which is worthy of man. Therefore, from the moment of its conception life must be guarded with the greatest care, while abortion and infanticide are unspeakable crimes.[69]

These texts from Vatican II, the largest Church Council that Christendom has ever known, demonstrate in great depth the position of the Roman Catholic Church on abortion. Its stand, in complete harmony with that of the early Church, is an absolute prohibition, a necessary conclusion from the two great commandments: To love God above all and to love our neighbor as ourselves. The mind of the Council is that the unborn child is, from the time of its conception, a neighbor who must be loved and protected.

To summarize, throughout its history, the Catholic Church has resolutely opposed the practice of abortion. From the first recorded condemnation in ecclesiastical writings, in the *Didache* of the year 80 to the most authoritative recent pronouncement in the Vatican II pastoral constitution *The Church in the Modern World* of 1965, we find no authoritative deviation from the doctrine that abortion, at any stage of fetal development, is a serious sin against God, the Creator of all human life.

Ecclesiastical laws have systematically implemented this doctrinal opposition. But whereas the moral prohibition classed as sinful every destruction of the unborn, the ecclesiastical law imposed its sanction or penalty in dependence on the scientific finding about the time of the infusion of the soul into the body. The severest penalty and sometimes the sole penalty was imposed only if the embryo or fetus was considered to be a human person at the time of its destruction.

The history of these ecclesiastical laws against abortion fit into three majoɪ periods. (1) For the first eleven hundred years, the laws punished fetal destruction whatever the stage of formation or animation. (2) In the twelfth century, however, an earlier fifth century distinction between the formed and the unformed fetus—only the formed fetus was considered to have a soul—became legally operative in the *Decretum* of Gratian in 1140 and appeared in the *Decretals* of Gregory IX in 1234, an authentic collection of the laws for the entire Church. The moral prohibition against killing after conception was unchanged but from the twelfth to the nineteenth century, only the killing of a formed fetus was classed as homicide. Incidentally, the three years of the pontificate of Sixtus V (1588–1590) marked a brief return to the earlier undifferentiated position. But in 1591, Gregory XIV re-established the formation-animation distinction. (3) In 1869, Pius IX eliminated this distinction from canon law and once more penalized with excommunication every abortion occurring after conception. The present Code of Canon law incorporated this position which has been continually reaffirmed by the Church.

The conclusions from this summary history are significant. The Church has always considered direct abortion to be morally wrong whatever the stage of fetal development. On the other hand, the Church, following the theory of delayed animation, has sometimes limited its penalties exclusively to those abortions which occurred after the estimated time of the soul's infusion. Clearly, these prohibitions of ecclesiastical law have depended on the conclusions of the then current biological and philosophical sciences. As science has changed on this point, so, to some extent, has ecclesiastical penal law. This change does not mean that the moral law is a function of science, but it does mean that the application of a moral law may change in confrontation with well-verified scientific evidence.

The English Experience

The connection between ecclesiastical law and the laws of England are twofold. First of all, England was a Catholic country whose laws, despite its distance from Rome and its insular location, were in general harmony with the rest of Christendom. Second, and more specifically, the canon *Sicut ex* of the Gregorian *Decretals* (1234), a canon based on the letter of Innocent III to the Carthusians which embodied the theory of delayed animation, was incorporated into English juridical thought by Henry of Brackton (1216–72), called the "Father of the Common Law." He was a contemporary of Thomas Aquinas and was familiar with the *Decretum* of Gratian and the *Decretals* of Gregory IX. These words of his are the first mention of abortion in English law: "If there is anyone who has struck a pregnant woman or have given poison to her, whereby he has caused an abortion, if the fetus be already formed or animated, and especially if animated, he commits a homicide." [70]

Sir Edward Coke, in the third part of *The Institutes of the Laws of England*, which was published some years after his death in 1634, indicates changes in the law of abortion since the time of Brackton, changes which he either initiated or simply reported. Most probably, they reflect the struggle of lawyers and judges to develop clear and workable legal standards while recognizing that the ecclesiastical courts would deal with the moral aspects. Coke wrote: "If a woman be quick with childe, and by a potion or otherwise killeth it in her womb; or if a man beat her, whereby the child dieth in her body, and she is delivered of a dead childe, this is a great misprision and no murder; but if the childe be born alive, and dieth of the poison, battery, or other cause, this is murder." [71] As Coke chronicles it, the criminal law punished abortion only if the child had quickened—a pragmatic solution to the formation-animation problem. Secondly, the criminal law punished abortion as murder, a capital crime, only if the child was born alive. If the child was stillborn, the abortion was a serious misdemeanor, but not punishable by death. Blackstone in his *Commentaries* (1765) repeated Coke's statements, thereby influencing both England and America.

Brackton, Coke, and Blackstone reflected the case law on abortion. The first statute, however, was the Miscarriage of Women Act (1803), which punished abortion by means of drugs and also punished the use of drugs with the intent to cause an abortion, although neither the mother nor the child died. The notion of quickening which Coke brought into the law was eliminated except for determining the degree of punishment.[73] Twenty-five years later, in 1828, an amendment was made to this statute to punish abortion accomplished through instruments. The harsh penalties of the earlier law, however, were mitigated.[74] In 1837, the element of quickening was totally eliminated. There was no reference to quickening or even to actual pregnancies.[75]

The last of this series of statutes was passed in 1861, and it remained in force for over a hundred years, until 1968.[76] It made it a felony for any woman to use any means to affect her own miscarriage, if she were actually pregnant, and for others to use any means with the intent to procure an abortion whether she was actually pregnant or not. It was a misdemeanor to furnish any means for effecting abortion with knowledge that it was intended to be used for such purpose by any woman whether pregnant or not. Thirty years later, *Queen* v. *Whitchurch,* held that the woman could not be convicted under the first part of the statute unless she were actually pregnant, but that actual pregnancy need not be proved in establishing a conspiracy with others to effect her own abortion.[77]

English statutory law did not provide for any justifiable abortions until the Infant Life (Preservation) Act of 1929, which classed the destruction of fetal life a felony "unless it is proved that the act which caused the death of the child was not done in good faith for the purpose of preserving the life of the mother." [78] For the first time, the life of the child was considered to be legislatively expendable. This statute was not entirely innovative, for the common law would allow duress of circumstances as a defense to a charge of abortion when the mother's life was seriously endangered. This statute changed things by codifying this traditional defense as a clear exception to the absolute prohibition. The burden of proof, however, was still on the one who performed the abortion.

Within ten years this exception was broadened far beyond the letter of the original statute. The case of *Rex* v. *Bourne* (1938) brought about this change in a dramatic situation. A young girl of fourteen, violently raped by some soldiers, became pregnant. With her parents' consent, the pregnancy was aborted by a London surgeon who took no fee and who notified the police what he had done. He was tried by jury and acquitted under the 1861 statute. The key words of the decision are that "if the doctor is of opinion on reasonable grounds and with adequate knowledge, that the probable consequence of the continuance of the pregnancy will be to make the woman a physical or a mental wreck, the jury are quite entitled to take the view that the doctor, who, in those circumstances and in that honest belief, operates, is operating for the purpose of preserving the life of the woman." [79]

Judge MacNaghten's reasoning in the *Bourne* case amounted to this: Since the reasonable interpretation of the exception in the law could not mean simply that the mother's life is to be protected only from instant death, something short of instant death can be a justification for abortion. The problem then becomes one of distinguishing danger to life from danger to health. "Life depends upon health and it may be that health is so gravely impaired that death results." [80] Although the case gained international renown, it was not a high court decision but simply that of a trial court in the criminal division. It was not a great piece of legal writing—it had been delivered without notes, and two different versions are extant. It was not a legal justification of an extension as much as an *a priori* statement about what someone thought the law ought to be. It was judge-made law in clear conflict with the legislative mandate. No higher court ever dealt with the matter. What the *Bourne* case did was to make a policy statement which was to become a rallying cry for those in favor of liberalization. Ten years later, in 1948, an English court held in *Rex* v. *Bergmann and Feruguson,* that the "necessity" was to be judged by the doctor's subjective belief rather than by the objective facts.[81] Ten years after that, in 1958, a court held explicitly in *Regina* v. *Newton and Stunge* that the maternal exception justifying abortion included the mental health of the mother.[82] Ten years after that there was a radical liberalization of the abortion law, when the new statute went into effect in spring 1968.

Within little more than a generation after the first legislative exception to England's absolute prohibition of abortion, a law was passed which was the most liberal in the Anglo-American legal world. The heart of the bill is in the following passage:

ABORTION ACT 1967

(1) Subject to the provisions of this section, a person shall not be guilty of an offence under the law relating to abortion when a pregnancy is terminated by a registered medical practitioner if two registered medical practitioners are of the opinion formed in good faith—

(a) that the continuance of the pregnancy would involve risk to the life of the pregnant woman, or of injury to the physical or mental health of the pregnant woman or any existing children of her family, greater than if the pregnancy were terminated; or

(b) that there is a substantial risk that if the child were born it would suffer from such physical or mental abnormalities as to be seriously handicapped.

(2) In determining whether the continuance of a pregnancy would involve such risk of injury to health as is mentioned in paragraph (a) of subsection (1) of this section, account may be taken of the pregnant woman's actual or reasonably foreseeable environment.

(3) Except as provided by subsection (4) of this section, [all abortions must be carried out in approved hospitals or temporarily designated places].

(4) Subsection (3) of this section, and so much of subsection (1) as relates to the opinion of two registered medical practioners, shall not apply to the termination of a pregnancy by a registered medical practitioner in a case where he is of the opinion, formed in good faith, that the termination is immediately necessary to save the life or to prevent grave permanent injury to the physical or mental health of the pregnant woman.

Although English law before the 1967 act was fairly liberal, its permissiveness was based to a large extent on case law, a fact which made many practitioners unwilling to perform abortions without a clearer statement of their rights. The new law certainly clarified old liberties and introduced new ones. The change was in two areas; it included new grounds and new standards. The new grounds were: (1) the risk of injury to the physical or mental health of any existing children of the pregnant woman's family; and (2) the substantial risk of a severely handicapped child. The new grounds were both objective and subjective. Objectively, they were "risk," "substantial risk," and "severely handicaped." The last two, which dealt exclusively with the defective child, were not defined. The first, however, was defined, but almost out of existence: A risk justifies the termination of a pregnancy if it is "greater than if the pregnancy were not terminated." To make the decision to abort an easier one, "account may be taken of the pregnant woman's actual or reasonably foreseeable environment." Since pro-abortionists have been claiming for years that there is hardly any risk at all from an early legal abortion, no more than in having one's tonsils removed or one's tooth extracted, very little reason, apparently, is required to justify an abortion. In fact, reason is not actually required at all, for the ultimate standard is the subjective one, an opinion formed in good faith. Of course, this good faith provision is not new, but it takes on new proportions in an act which extends the grounds of justification without establishing clearly defined objective standards. The English law, now, can be distinguished from abortion on demand, in theory if not in practice, only be-

cause it still retains a built-in balancing-of-interests requirement, operating on a broad-based concept of sociomedical well-
being. In practice this distinction would be merely verbal if there
were general acceptance of the observation of the eminent de-
mographer, Kingsley Davis, who said, "When performed, as a
legal procedure, by a skilled physician, it [abortion] is safer than
childbirth." [84] According to the English principle of comparative
risk, every pregnancy could be aborted on the demand of the
pregnant woman. That English practice does not go so far is
laudable, but the doctors, not the legislators, deserve the credit.

The American Reappraisal

The history of abortion laws in the United States parallels the
British experience. The common law of England was the law for
the thirteen colonies and was the foundation for the law of the
United States. Subsequent legislation has radically changed this
common law heritage, but these changes are still in the Anglo-
American tradition. Even today, English laws have an indirect
but very real influence on American jurists and legislators.

The first law on abortion in the United States was that of the
common law as formulated by Coke and repeated by Blackstone.
Little case law survives to indicate any divergence. Generally
speaking, the law punished the deliberate killing of the child after
quickening, as murder or manslaughter if the child died after
birth or as a misdemeanor if the child was stillborn. If the
unborn child was killed before quickening—the more usual case
today—the act might have been punished as an attempt to commit a felony or, if the mother did not give her consent, as an assault and battery.

The complexities and uncertainties of the prohibitions of abortion under the common law prompted legislation in England and
in the United States. Connecticut passed, in 1821, the first abortion statute in this country.[85] It was similar to the first English
statute of 1803.[86] There were differences, however. England

punished all abortion whether before or after quickening but imposed a more severe penalty in the latter instance. Connecticut, perhaps due to Blackstone's influence, punished abortion only if quickening had occurred. In 1860, however, it eliminated the requirement of quickening.[87] Today no state considers quickening an element of the crime of abortion, though ten still consider it in determining the degree of punishment.[88]

In 1860, long before England did so, Connecticut made an exception to its absolute statutory prohibition and allowed abortion if necessary to preserve the life of the mother or her unborn child. Connecticut was not the first state to pass such a provision. New York (1828), Main (1840), Ohio (1841), and Virginia (1848) were its forerunners. It has been argued, however, that the common law justified abortion for this reason even if the abortion was not objectively necessary if the one performing it acted in good faith and on reasonable grounds. Thus, although there is no statutory exception, the Supreme Judicial Court of Massachusetts allows abortion to protect the life and health of the mother and justifies its position on common law principles.[89]

Until 1967 and the current abortion controversy, the grounds justifying abortion in the United States were very narrow. All fifty states and the District of Columbia allowed abortion to save the life of the mother. Two states, Colorado and New Mexico, also allowed abortion to prevent serious and permanent bodily injury to the mother. Three states, Alabama, Oregon, and Massachusetts, as well as the District of Columbia, allowed abortion to protect the health of the mother. Strangely, seven states allowed abortion to save the life of the child.[91] What seems to have been intended by this apparent contradiction was the protection of doctors who, in accord with accepted obstetrical practice, induced premature labor in an unsuccessful attempt to save the life of the unborn child.

The year 1967 marked the beginning of the liberal abortion laws in the United States, although a rape provision was enacted in one state the previous year. All these changes have been patterned after the Scandinavian-type proposal which the American Law Institute incorporated into its Model Penal Code in 1959. The proposed official draft came out in 1962 and has been an influential factor in subsequent legislative enactments. We will consider here some of its substantive aspects in order to see how it fits into the historical development of abortion laws.

SECTION 230.3. ABORTION.

(1) *Unjustifiable Abortion.* A person who purposely and unjustifiably terminates the pregnancy of another otherwise than by a live birth commits a felony of the third degree or, where the pregnancy has continued beyond the twenty-sixth week, a felony of the second degree.

(2) *Justifiable Abortion.* A licensed physician is justified in terminating a pregnancy if he believes there is substantial risk that continuance of the pregnancy would gravely impair the physical or mental health of the mother or that the child would be born with grave physical or mental defect, or that the pregnancy resulted from rape, incest, or other felonious intercourse. All illicit intercourse with a girl below the age of 16 shall be deemed felonious for the purposes of this subsection.

(4) *Self Abortion.* A woman whose pregnancy has continued beyond the twenty-sixth week commits a felony of the third degree if she purposely terminates her own pregnancy otherwise than by a live birth, of if she uses instruments, drugs or violence upon herself for that purpose.

(7) *Section Inapplicable to Prevention of Pregnancy.* Nothing in this Section shall be deemed applicable to the prescription, administration or distribution of drugs or other substances for avoiding pregnancy, whether by preventing implantation of a fertilized ovum or by any other method that operates before, at or immediately after fertilization.[91]

Through 1968, six states have revised their abortion laws: Mississippi in 1966; Colorado, North Carolina, and California in 1967; and Georgia and Maryland in 1968. In general, they follow the A.L.I. proposal, but there are major differences both substantive and procedural. Here is a survey of the justifying grounds enacted by the states that have liberalized their laws:

1. The life of the pregnant woman in all states.

2. The mental and physical health of the pregnant woman in all states but Mississippi. However, California, Maryland, and North Carolina speak of a substantial risk that will gravely impair the mother's health, whereas Colorado and Georgia speak of serious and permanent impairment or injury.

3. The defective child in all states but California and Mississippi. In Colorado and Maryland the defect must be grave and permanent. Georgia adds the qualification, irremediable. In North Carolina, the qualification is simply, grave.

4. Forcible rape in all states.

5. Statutory rape in all but Maryland.

6. Incest in all but Georgia, Maryland, and Mississippi.

Since our concern in this book is a reappraisal of the abortion laws, in subsequent chapters we will consider at greater length the various aspects of the abortion problem in the United States as a help in forming a sound abortion policy and in implementing this policy legally. A trend toward liberalization is obvious, but it remains for historians to decide whether the United States in the late 1960s was in transition toward an era of demographic manipulation or whether it was in a successful struggle over the reaffirmation of the inalienable rights of human dignity and equality.

Conclusion

Abortion laws reach back into the past and testify to the common response of most peoples to the fact of human generation, which is to give at least some protection to the unborn. The motives and reasons for punishing abortion have varied throughout the ages, but these very changes reflect a development in our thinking about human beings, an evolution of the human moral conscience. Two phenomena grew apace: the recognition of the human dignity of the unborn and the protection of unborn life by criminal sanctions. Whatever our ultimate evaluation of the historical facts may be, the historical continuity of the growing consensus against uncontrolled abortion is without dispute.

To call laws against abortion historically grounded is by no means the same as saying that they are outdated. Laws against slavery go back over a hundred years in this country, but far from trying to justify slavery on request, we implement more strongly the civil rights in which these laws are rooted. Most of the major substantive crimes can be traced back to ancient codes of law, yet such laws are still necessary for us today. The law does not grow old like a garment. If the reasons for the law are sound and the conditions proper, the law is as vital and as young as the community from which it springs, however far back into the past it reaches.

The history of abortion laws give perspective to our assessment of current proposals. It strikes us forcibly that the most liberal of current proposals is also the most reactionary. Abortion on demand was the original historical antecedent limited only by the capabilities of self-help and medical practice. The old laissez-faire policy of complete parental power over the life and death of the fetus almost everywhere gave way to a practical recognition of fetal rights. What is proposed today is legislative atavism, a return to the primitive practice of total dominion over the unborn and a barbaric rejection of the fruits of man's evolving conscience.

History can show the trends, the insights, and even the mistakes of the past. But history is limited. We do not want the dead hand of the past writing the laws of the present. Consequently, every generation faces fresh decision-making problems, but one enriched by the experience of the past not to coerce but to guide it. Mindful of the message of history, we must rethink the relevant facets of the abortion problem so that whatever laws we fashion will be grounded on solid facts understood and evaluated as profoundly as possible, so that when the history of our own age is written it will manifest a forward step in the maximization of human dignity.

Chapter Three

THE SOCIOMEDICAL CRISIS

Abortion, the lethal response to an unwanted pregnancy, has sparked a heated public debate. The occasion is an alleged crisis, a sociomedical crisis wherein societal needs, medically formulated, purportedly necessitate a new and greater freedom in performing abortions. Before trying to evaluate this proposed permissiveness on its merits, we should determine the actual dimensions of the problem. In doing so, we consider three factors: first, the number of deaths, both maternal and fetal, that result from abortion; second, the percentage of people who demand more liberal laws; and finally, the content of the proposed grounds for this liberalization.

Since most states already have stringent laws against abortion, we seek to assess the degree to which these laws are now working and the extent to which the existing situation points to a change. Law is only one factor—frequently only a minor one—in improving the circumstances of human life. But any reappraisal of current laws requires a weighing of the number of abortions, the character of the public demands for reform, and the stated grounds for change. Only after taking the measure of the "abortion crisis," can we proceed to the possible solutions and decide whether liberalization is an appropriate remedy or whether means other than abortion are alone permissible. Our first task, then, is to isolate the sociomedical problem with care and exactitude.

I

The Incidence of Death

The lethal quality of an abortion is twofold: It always kills the child; and it sometimes kills the mother. The first is direct and intended; the second is indirect and accidental. Both are operative factors in the abortion controversy. In fact, a frequent argument for reform, based on some thirty-year-old studies, is that there are about one million illegal abortions a year and about ten thousand resultant maternal deaths.[1] Are these statistics sound?

The Federal Bureau of Vital Statistics reports that less than forty thousand women of child-bearing age, that is, from fifteen to forty-four, die each year. It is highly unlikely that a fourth of these died from illegal abortions. More specifically, the Bureau reports that for the years 1964 and 1965, there were 247 and 235 maternal deaths respectively from abortions of all kinds; that is, from spontaneous abortions and from abortions induced legally or illegally. These figures might be challenged on the basis that some deaths are not reported. But it is most difficult today to hide a death from abortion. If the woman is brought to the hospital alive, she is usually suffering from hemorrhage or infection, both clear indications of the cause of her trouble. If the woman dies before getting to the hospital or immediately on arrival, the laws of most states require an autopsy which would quickly reveal the recent abortion. Unless the woman's body is hidden or destroyed, awkward and unlikely feats, it is virtually impossible to conceal the abortion death. Even if we use the statistical safeguard of doubling the number of registered deaths in order to be sure of including all those overlooked or concealed, there would still be less than five hundred maternal deaths a year from all abortions, spontaneous and induced, legal and illegal. Even one death from an illegal abortion is a great tragedy, but in making an abortion decision, it is necessary to grasp the true magnitude of the problem—less than five hundred, and much less than the ten thousand so mistakenly proclaimed.

The number of abortions or fetal deaths is difficult to ascertain. One must, however, distinguish between legal and illegal abortions. The incidence of the former is reasonably clear. The incidence of the latter is simply a matter of guesswork.

Legal abortions have in the past been limited by law. Although individual hospitals, cities, and states have sometimes reported the number of abortions performed, there has been no statistical clearing house, so that even in this legal area, our figures are based on an approximation. It is generally agreed that some eight thousand to ten thousand legal abortions have been performed each year. Two studies, one for the years 1957–62 and the other for the years 1963–65 have found a ratio of two legal abortions per thousand deliveries.[2] This ratio would give the figure of about eight thousand per year, since there have been about four million live births per year. Since 1967, however, the statutes of some states have been liberalized. The increase in legal abortion has been great, although even here the exact figures are difficult to obtain. Statistics from Colorado, the first state to reform its abortion laws, illustrate both the increase in the number of abortions and the statistical problem, as do California statistics.[3]

In the years immediately preceding the change, abortions had been performed, according to the Colorado State Department of Public Health, "at the rate of about one a month." Although the new statute did not require a report to the Department of Public Health, 262 abortions were actually reported during the first year. One hospital that refused to make an official report admitted performing twenty-seven abortions. These would make the total 289. Other legal abortions most probably took place. A prominent gynecologist at the University of Colorado School of Medicine believes that the total number of legal abortions was closer to four hundred. If, however, we take only the number of abortions reported officially, the number of legal abortions is twenty times what it was before liberalization. Statistical information from Colorado should be more complete in the future since a new vital statistics law which went into effect January 1, 1968 requires hospitals to report specifically all fetal deaths that are the result of abortion. There is no information available concerning the effect of liberalization on the number of illegal abortions. All we know is that, at a conservative minimum, the legal abortions have increased twentyfold.

Illegal abortions are much less susceptible of accurate assessment. Over ten years ago at an abortion conference sponsored by the Planned Parenthood Federation of America, the estimate was made that illegal abortions could range anywhere from 200,000 to 1,200,000 each year. The conclusion was reached: "There is no objective basis for the selection of a particular figure between these two estimates as an approximation of the actual frequency." [4] The editor of the study, M.S. Calderone, M.D., added a footnote: "The figures on abortion frequently used throughout the conference by various individuals were based on personal estimates by the individuals themselves. No way has yet been found of obtaining reliable statistics that would give an exact figure for the total population." Dr. Christopher Tietze, M.D., who was then Chairman of the Statistics Committee, and is now Associate Director of the Population Council, observed in 1967: "Since that time, no new data have been produced on which to base a more reliable estimate." [5] The late Dr. Alfred C. Kinsey pointed out the almost insuperable difficulty: "As long as any activity is illicit and punishable by heavy penalty, it is not going to be possible to get persons freely to tell anyone—much less anyone in official position—what has actually happened in their own lives. This has been true of a great many aspects of our whole study of human sexual behavior, and it has been equally true of abortion." [6]

The most ambitious study to date is that of the Kinsey Institute for Sex Research, *Pregnancy, Birth and Abortion.*[7] It deals mainly with 5293 white nonprison females, and concludes that by the age of forty-five, 22 percent of those who had ever been married and 20 percent of those who though single had experienced coitus underwent at least one induced abortion.[8] To apply this rate to the population at large would indicate six hundred thousand abortions a year. Certain aspects of this study prevent this conclusion.[9] The main body of the study deals exclusively with white women, although there is a very small additional sampling from 572 Negro nonprison females and 309 Negro prisoners. Ninety-six percent of the white nonprison females spent all of their lives as urban residents, with the Northeast overrepresented and the South underrepresented. Their educational level was in the upper 20 percent of the population. Their religious affiliations were: Protestant, 62 percent; Jewish, 28 percent; and Catholic, 11 percent. The ages of four-fifths of the women were between sixteen and thirty. Fifty-eight percent were unmarried. The married had a high relative percentage of separated, divorced, and widowed. In short, the study was not representative of the female population of child-bearing age.

Earlier studies are even less helpful. Kopp in 1934 concluded that there was one abortion for every 3.55 live births but based this figure on a group that was exclusively from New York City, that belonged to the Margaret Sanger Birth Control Clinic, that was 41 percent Jewish and 26.1 percent Catholic, that was 51.0 percent foreign-born or, in 21.9 percent of the cases, had a foreign born parent.[10] In 1935, Stix established, from a small group two-thirds Jewish, that 22.1 percent of all pregnancies ended in abortion, but added: "No claim is made that the experience of this group of women is typical of that of any other population. Indeed it is altogether likely that a similar study of women differently selected would yield different results." [11] In 1936, when there were 2,400,000 live births a year compared to the 3,500,-000 in 1968, Taussig arrived at 681,600 as the number of illegal abortions.[12] At the rate he used, the number of illegal abortions today would be close to a million. But as Dr. Allan Guttmacher wrote in 1958, "In the first place there are no good figures that I know of that in any way depict incidence. Taussig's book pulls out a nice round number but when you try to analyze the formulae by which the number is derived, you could have substituted other values and obtained quite a different answer." [13] In 1937, Wiehl and Berry proposed 3.1 as the rate of induced pregnancies for a sample of women from New York City.[14] In 1943, Whelpton and Kiser reported the same percentage, 3.1, for a sample of women in Indianapolis.[15] The rate of 3.1 applied to the population at large would give us about 124,000 abortions. But not one of these studies is representative. Not one of them dispels the confusion as to the exact number of illegal abortions.

The Foreign Experience

Other nations of the world also have an abortion problem. Wherever there are unwanted pregnancies, there is at least the temptation to abort. In some areas, this demand has been implemented by law. Facts from various sectors will help us view our own sociomedical abortion problem with more insight. Three areas will be considered: Scandinavia, Eastern Europe, and Japan.

1. The abortion laws of *Scandinavia* are especially relevant, because they are the pattern for recent American proposals for reform. The oldest of these laws, the Danish and the Swedish, went into effect in 1939. The Danish was revised in 1956 and the Swedish in 1946 and 1963. The Finnish law has been in effect since 1950. The most recent, the Norwegian, was the codification in 1960 which went into effect in 1964, of long-accepted medical practice.

All the familiar liberal grounds for abortion are included in the Scandinavian laws: grave danger to the life and physical or mental health of the mother; the risk of a seriously defective child; a pregnancy caused by rape or incest. There are some differences, too. The most important of these is an extension or broadening of the medical ground, a taking into consideration of what the Swedish laws label an "anticipated weakness" in the mother. The Danes and Norwegians have a similar provision. The Danish law reads: "In order to avoid this danger [to the life or health of the woman] an appreciation shall be made of all the circumstances of the case, including the conditions under which the woman will have to live, and consideration shall be given not only to the physical or mental illness, but also to any actual or potential state of physical or mental infirmity." The Norwegian law is similar: "In determining the extent of the danger, account shall be taken of whether the woman concerned is particularly disposed to organic or mental disease and likewise of living conditions and other circumstances which may make her ill or lead to a breakdown in her physical or mental health." Both the Danish and the Norwegian laws have another related provision which, though it refers to deficiency in the mother, is really a eugenic ground, for it permits an abortion if the mother is unfit to take care of the child. The law is not for the benefit of the mother but, purportedly, for the child and society. Although there have been proposals for a purely social ground, no such ground has been included. Professor Andenaes of the University of Oslo points out the biggest objection to it: "It is difficult to meet effectively the argument that if the women is living in social and economic distress this should be dealt with by appropriate measures of assistance, not by terminating the pregnancy." [16]

Of special significance here is the incidence of abortion, since one of the arguments in the United States for the adoption of Scandinavian-type legislation is the elimination of illegal abortions. As a matter of fact, in Scandinavia, there has been an increase in the number of abortions. The figures from Sweden illustrate a development which is paralleled in the other three countries.[17] In 1938, before the liberal law went into effect, there were only 443 legal abortions. Under the new law, the number of legal abortions increased greatly. The figures for 1961 through 1966 are: 2909, 3205, 3528, 4671, 6208, and 7254. The 1966 figure shows an abortion rate of 6 percent of the number of live births. If we apply this rate to the number of births a year in the United States, four million, it would amount to 240,000 legal abortions, or thirty times the present number of eight thousand legal abortions per year, a tremendous increase in fetal deaths.

The incidence of illegal abortion is somewhat more susceptible of accurate approximation in Scandinavia than in the United States. The criminal abortion rate, despite liberalization, is still too high. A 1964 Danish study indicated that although there were four thousand legal abortions, there were between twelve thousand and fifteen thousand criminal abortions each year.[18] Of great importance is a study showing what became of thirty-seven hundred women whose applications for abortion in 1958–59 were refused.[19] During that time 49 percent of the applications for abortion were refused, or the women changed their minds.[20] Of that 49 percent, 81 percent bore the child, 16 percent aborted illegally, 1 percent aborted legally at a later date, and information concerning 2 percent was unknown.[21]

A 1968 Swedish study arrived at similar conclusions. All reported pregnancies in Stockholm from 1950 to 1965 were examined. Since the purpose of the abortion law was to reduce illegal abortions, success in this area was checked. The conclusion was: "Apparently the abortion law in its present form has not sufficed to subdue criminal abortions." [22] Whereas the delivery rate and the rate of legal abortions seem inversely proportional, the rate of spontaneous and criminal abortions was more or less constant. The study confirms the Danish results in a very significant way:

> It seems reasonable to assume that most women who applied for legal abortions in vain, as well as most women who during these years found it useless even to apply, did not regard criminal interruption of pregnancy as an acceptable solution. By interviewing women, other workers have found that, when refused legal termination of pregnancy only a small proportion

of the applicants appear to undergo illegal abortions. Lindberg found 12 percent among his patients, Sjovall only 3 percent, and Hook 11 percent. Ekblad reported that 18 percent of 479 women who had a legal abortion would have sought one illegally if their applications for termination had been refused. Aren was given the same answer by 7 percent of 100 newly delivered women who had undergone legal abortions.[23]

2. The abortion laws of *Eastern Europe* are generally much more permissive than those of Scandinavia. The Soviet Union was the first to liberalize its laws, in 1920. Sixteen years later, in 1936, it restricted abortion stringently. But in 1955, it once more relaxed its prohibitions. Neither the full reason for the changes or reliable statistics are available. In the following year, 1956, Bulgaria, Poland, Hungary, and Rumania passed liberal laws. Czechoslovakia did so in 1957 and Yugoslavia in 1960.

In all of these socialist states there has been a great increase in the number of legal abortions, but there has not been any drastic decrease in the number of "other abortions." [24] This category indicates the number of those who were hospitalized after a spontaneous miscarriage or an illegal abortion. This figure does not list the number of illegal abortions, but it does help indicate whether the number is increasing or decreasing. There has been a slight decrease in this category, but its significance is questioned. Not only have antibiotics cut down the number of complications from illegal abortions, but early legal abortions have cut down on the number of pregnancies which would have eventually aborted spontaneously under stricter laws. If one statistically compensates for these facts, one finds that the number of "other abortions" has remained about the same. In other words, there has been no decrease in illegal abortions, and there may well have been an increase—all this despite liberalization. So the total number of abortions has increased greatly.

Two Soviet satellites, Hungary and Rumania, reveal important aspects of permissive abortion. From a common beginning, they have moved into two radically different positions.

Hungary allows abortion on request. A three-man medical board passes on the petition. It can dissuade but it cannot refuse. If the ground for abortion is other than illness, the social insurance system does not cover the first three days of hospitalization. The applicant must pay 360 florins, or about sixteen dollars. This charge is a relatively minor inconvenience and no deterrence. In 1964, only 5 percent of the women gave illness as a ground; the rest had abortions for personal reasons. Hungary now is in a period of crisis. It has the lowest birth rate in Europe, 13.1 per thousand, and the highest abortion rate, 17.8 per thousand. The abortion rate in 1955, the year before liberalization, was 3.5, and by 1965 it had risen to 17.8. This rate applied to the United States population would mean 3,453,200 legal abortions a year. Their rate is 140 abortions per 100 deliveries. The illegal abortion rate has remained fairly constant before and after liberalization. But the total number of abortions has risen tremendously. In 1950, there were 1700 legal abortions, 34,300 other abortions, but 195,600 live births. In 1965, there were 180,300 legal abortions, 33,700 other abortions, but only 133,000 live births. This high incidence of abortion in Hungary has resulted in a population imbalance, with a greater percentage of older people than is economically healthy. The 1980s should be critical because of an insufficient younger work force.

Although the rate of material deaths is lower under liberalization than it was earlier—due perhaps to the fact that all abortions must be performed before the 12th week and in hospitals or maternity homes—there is a high rate of medical complications. Andras Klinger of the Hungarian Central Office of Statistics stated: "Induced abortion, however, cannot be viewed as a proper and suitable means of birth control. . . . Its deleterious effects on health is sufficient reason to change the present-day situation." [25] Here are some of the medical facts. Abortions increase the incidence of premature births. The rate for premature births when there has been no induced abortion is 10 percent, when one abortion it is 14 percent, when two abortions it is 16 percent, after three or more it is 21 percent.[26] The rate of other complications is high. Of every thousand women who underwent legal abortions, 1.3 experienced perforation of the uterus, 8.5 feverish conditions, 16.5 after-hemorrhage, and 14.9 repeated hospital treatment within four weeks after abortion.[27]

The Hungarian government is trying to cut down on the number of abortions by various means, for example, by extending maternity leave from twelve to twenty weeks, by permitting unpaid leave without loss of social security rights until the child's third birthday, and by increased family allowances. But Hungary has not yet resorted to the drastic measures taken in Rumania.

After ten years of liberalization, Rumania also faced serious depopulation.[28] So in October 1966, it repealed its totally permissive abortion law and made abortion a crime for both the doctor and the woman unless the operation is justified by exceptional circumstances. The population figures explain the panic. In the thirty-five years from 1932 to 1966, the population rose from 14.5 million to 19.1 million. Despite this increase, the birth rate fell from 35.1 per thousand to 14.3, and the increase of births over deaths fell from 14 per thousand to 6.1. Since the end of World War II, contraceptives have been forbidden, but abortions were so numerous that the birth rate continued to fall. For example, in 1961, the rate for legal abortions was 12.0, which in U.S. population figures would be 2,124,000 legal abortions. This figure, obviously, does not include the number of illegal abortions which continued to be performed despite liberalization. Although the liberal law required no grounds for abortion, only 1 percent of the women gave medical reasons; 99 percent gave personal reasons. In 1961, women applying for an abortion averaged 3.9 legal abortions apiece. The 1966 law was a drastic and desperate reversal of policy in order to prevent a national calamity—extinction.

3. *Japan*'s economic crisis after World War II prompted its progressively liberalized Eugenic Abortion Laws of 1948, 1949,

1951, and 1952.[29] In less than a hundred years, Japan had reverted to its traditional nonprohibition of abortion. Influenced by Christianity and European civilization, Japan in 1880 passed its first law against abortion. An even stronger law was passed in 1907. In the thirties and forties, the Japanese expansion into China and its participation in World War II put a premium on large families. The Japanese defeat in 1945 changed all that. What was an asset became a liability. Japan was once more confined to four islands. The shortage of jobs, housing, and food highlighted the population increase. Today, Japan has the equivalent of abortion on demand, for although the grounds for abortion is impairment of the health of the mother, the doctor is the sole judge and rarely refuses to abort. No review of his decision is made.

The overpopulation problem has been solved. Japan has cut its birth rate in half. It is now just under the birth rate in the United States. In 1947, the birth rate was 34 per thousand: it is now 17 or 18 per thousand. In 1955, there were about 1,200,000 abortions, but ten years later, in 1965, it had dropped to about 843,000. This figure, however, is subject to question, for many of the abortions that are performed are not registered officially. The reasons vary: Sometimes the women want to preserve their privacy; sometimes the doctors want to avoid income taxes; sometimes the women want to avoid mortuary fees for the fetus; sometimes the doctors are not officially authorized to perform abortions. About eleven thousand doctors, only one-tenth of the profession, are so authorized. It has even been suggested that half of the abortions that are performed are not officially registered. This total, coupled with the still-persistent though apparently small number of fully illegal abortions, make the number of fetal deaths a very large one.

As in other nations with permissive abortion, there is some dissatisfaction with wholesale abortion in Japan. There is the fear of eventual depopulation, anxiety about the diminishing younger work force and fear of the military manpower of its neighbors. Businessmen, however, are the ones apparently most concerned about dwindling markets in a consumer economy. Business corporations are lessening their support of family planning programs. Abortion in Japan has done what it was intended to do, but in solving the overpopulation problem, it may well have brought even more serious problems. The abortion decision in Japan is not yet final.

II

The statistical incidence of fetal and maternal deaths, even if highly exaggerated, does not of itself engender a crisis of decision. Civilizations have a shocking tendency to overlook such deaths or to take them very much for granted. The public response to the facts of morbidity and mortality, however, is significant. Without overprizing public opinion polls, we find them suggestive both of the conscience of the community and of its goals. These surveys make available a thoughtful if impressionistic sampling of the desires, demands, claims, and interests of the community at a given time. The abortion controversy has resulted in a number of such tabulations which reveal an important dimension of this sociomedical crisis.

Four surveys suggest the general trends. They were conducted by the National Opinion Research Center, December 1965; *Newsweek*, March 1967; *Good Housekeeping*, October 1967; and The Gallup Organization, June 1968. The polls are similar, with the exception of the *Newsweek* one, which dealt entirely with Catholics. The results of the other three polls are roughly equivalent. Certain generalizations can be made. (1) There seems to be an increase in the number of respondents favoring abortion for every ground. (2) A wide majority of those responding favored abortion if the mother's health was endangered. (3) Little more than a bare majority favored abortion if the pregnancy resulted from rape or incest or if the child would be defective. (4) A wide majority opposed abortion if the grounds were that the mother was financially incapable, or was unmarried, or simply did not want to have another child.

It must be noted that these polls indicate opinions, not votes. They are not a formal participation in the decision-making process. But they are relevant. They do not state that abortion is good in itself or that abortion would be consented to by the respondent. They do, however, manifest an option for liberty, the demand for a free choice in the matter for everyone. However, before capitulating to what appear to be overwhelming odds, we should look behind the results to test the credibility of such opinion sampling. *Time* has categorized the pollsters as "a fallible priesthood" and the polls as "confusing and exaggerated." A brief consideration of some pertinent facts will enable us to treat these influential percentage points more as informed guesses than as inspired oracles.

The polls have failed in the past, spectacularly so. In 1948, when Thomas E. Dewey was the pick of every major pollster, Harry Truman could "prove the polls wrong." More recently, in the year preceding the 1968 presidential conventions, every major candidate was at one time picked as the presidential winner in a public opinion survey. In early August 1968, three major polls, Gallup, Crossley, and Harris came out simultaneously with dramatically divergent findings. Gallup picked Nixon over Humphrey by two points and over Rockefeller by four points. Crossley, however, picked Rockefeller over Nixon, who in turn won over Humphrey by three points. Harris put Rockefeller six points ahead of Humphrey, who in turn was five points over Nixon. In desperation, the three pollsters attempted a rationalization whereby all the results were "plotted sequentially, as though they were conducted by a single organization, using the same sampling techniques and using the same question-asking techniques." The conclusion was that there would be a close Nixon-Humphrey race, a finding that still showed Crossley and Harris to have been wrong and that subsequent polls putting Nixon far ahead of Humphrey seem to contradict. Since polls only attempt to indicate the thought of the moment, the most damaging failure is not in their long-run success but in their simultaneous contradictions.

The poll in its simplest form is a tabulation of the answers given by a random sampling of the community to a fixed set of questions. The sample is at best, about fifteen hundred respondents, a compromise figure insuring reasonable accuracy at reasonable expense. Gallup takes five respondents from three hundred randomly chosen localities. Harris reinterviews: Gallup does not. The accepted margin of error is two or three percentage points. The time and place are most significant, because the opinions reflected are often ephemeral. The questions are crucial. If they are too vague or too narrow or if they are leading questions or are biased questions, the poll may be completely vitiated. Consciously or unconsciously, the respondents may give false or misleading answers. To compensate for this there are "trip-up questions" and "intensity questions." In every poll, there are the "undecided" or "don't know" respondents. How this group, often a large one, is pro-rated may change the results drastically. In brief, the reliability of public opinion polls varies in terms of its various elements: who took the poll, how was it taken, what were the exact questions, the size of the sample, and why was the poll taken. To insure that the public will be able to assess more accurately the survey findings, some leading public opinion organizations, Gallup, Crossley, Mervin-field, Belden, and others have tried to introduce some self-regulation into the business so that the variables will be accessible to the public. As a matter of psychological fact, most polls make their impact on the public in terms of simple win or lose, for or against unqualified statistics.

A look at the abortion polls illustrated the confusion that results when the full structure of the survey is not revealed. For example, the Gallup poll of June 1968 which was made for the pro-abortion Population Council. The Columbus *Citizens Journal,* June 13, 1968, reported that 63 percent of the Catholics, 78 percent of the Protestants, and 94 percent of the Jews favored abortion for at least one of the four liberal grounds: health, rape, incest, defective child. But *The American Medical Association News,* June 24, 1968, misread the ground rules and stated, "A firm majority of American Catholics, 63 percent, favor legalization of abortion for the same reasons." The assent has moved from *at least one* to *all.* Even more serious a mistake than this unwarranted extension is the implication that this represents a fair statement about American Catholics. Although the total population sample may have included, as is standard practice for Gallup, some fifteen hundred respondents, there is no indication of the number of Catholics, Protestants, and Jews included. In fact, if a sample of fifteen hundred is required for accuracy, the religious breakdown would have an *a priori* unreliability, because each of the religious groups would be too small. Yet the comparative figures were reported as if they were on a par with the other figures in the survey, thereby giving the unfounded impression that a good majority of American Catholics favor some form of liberalization. The inaccuracy of this inference is seen in the March 1967 *Newsweek* poll dealing with a small, 993, but exclusively Catholic population. The questions asked are not clearly reported, but it is clear that 58 percent of the Catholics polled supported the Church's position on abortion whereas only 28 percent opposed it. Quite a contrast to the Gallup findings.

A related example of a misleading key question in an otherwise fair questionnaire is found in the National Opinion Research Center's December 1965 poll, reported in TRANS-Action, September 1966. It asked the question: "Please tell me whether or not you think it should be possible for a woman to obtain a legal abortion . . ." There were six categories listed, but the traditional ground which would justify an abortion if there is serious danger to a woman's life, was not included. The closest to the traditional ground was the first category: "If the woman's own health is seriously endangered by the pregnancy." Nothing indicates whether mental or physical health is meant or whether the seriousness is permanent or temporary or whether it is equivalent to an endangering of life itself. One who is content with the traditional law which allows abortion to prevent loss of life may well opt for this liberal health ground, since it is the only one which would provide for such a contingency. Although 71 percent of the respondents favored the health ground, it is not accurate to say that 71 percent favored liberalization.

Even without a full critique on public opinion polls, specifically abortion polls, it is evident that such surveys, though enlightening, can too easily become, if not special pleading, at least a source of mistaken reliance. Opinions change rapidly; they reflect the most sensational news item more often than a seasoned judgment; they are subject to manipulation. The tabulating of opinion is an inexact science, or perhaps we should say art; hence one must be careful not to compound its intrinsic weaknesses by naive gullibility.

III

The task of a doctor is preserve his patient's health. But what is health? The World Health Organization defines it as "a state of complete physical, mental, and social well-being." With a toothache, one goes to a dentist. With a ruptured appendix, one goes to a surgeon. With schizophrenia, one goes to a psychiatrist. But to whom does one go for that complete well-being called health? Perhaps the Divine Physician alone can guarantee such perfection.

The medical profession is not to blame for the fact that we are not in perfect physical, mental, and social health. Indeed, as physicians they are only partially involved. All men must work together if this grand ideal is to be approximated. Health in the broad sense of complete well-being is not exclusively a medical problem. The streetcleaner working for the sanitation department and the judge sitting at a sanity hearing are concerned with health. The gym instructor, the stockbroker, the spiritual adviser, the marriage counselor, the garage mechanic, the meat inspector, all these are involved with the broad concept of health. Like the rest of us, the medical doctor shares a common health goal but makes his own specific contribution within his limited area of expertise. The physician works within an important but limited area of specialization, usually formulated in terms of physical and mental disease and defect. The solution of the multidimensional health problem that is abortion is not bounded by the compass of his competence. His contribution is essential but does not pre-empt the field of decision. An examination of the suggested grounds for liberalization of abortion, the medical, psychiatric, eugenic, juridical, and socioeconomic, reveals a crisis whose breadth transcends any one profession. It is a human problem that demands the many-faceted insights of all men. Although medically formulated, the abortion decision is the responsibility of the whole society. A brief examination of the various grounds proposed as justifications for abortion will indicate both the magnitude of the problem and the division of labor that is requisite in solving it.

The Medical Ground

To justify abortion on medical grounds, the doctor must answer one of two questions. The traditional question is simply: Is this woman in danger of dying if she does not have an abortion? The liberal question is: Will the continuance of this pregnancy seriously impair the physical health of the mother? These are medical questions, sometimes difficult to determine but certainly within the competence of the medical profession. Nevertheless, the decision cannot be based only on medical evidence. If there is to be an abortion, the doctor is the one to do it. But the seriousness of the danger to the life or health of the woman is by no means the only factor to be considered before action is authorized. The doctor has done his part in giving medical evidence; now others judging the total context must make a community decision. Society must decide whether or not these medical conclusions should ever justify fetal destruction. For the most part, the answer has been a qualified yes. Usually abortion is allowed to save the woman's life, and sometimes to protect her health from serious harm. The point is, however, that even at the moment of medical crisis the ultimate decision to abort is societal, not purely medical. The physician must function within the limits set by the community.

In 1951, at the Congress of the American College of Surgeons, Dr. R. J. Heffernan of Tufts Medical School stated: "Anyone who performs a therapeutic abortion is either ignorant of modern methods of treating the complications of pregnancy or is unwilling to take the time to use them." [30] His position is not universally accepted, but it does indicate the tremendous advances that have been made in medical practice and in biochemistry. In 1954, Dr. Allan Guttmacher attributed the decline in the overall frequency of nonpsychiatric therapeutic abortions to two facts:

[F]irst, cures have been discovered for a number of conditions which previously could be cured only by a termination of pregnancy; and second, there has been a change in medical philosophy. Two decades ago the accepted attitude of the physician was that, if a pregnant woman were ill, the thing to do would be to rid her of her pregnancy. Today, it is felt that unless the pregnancy itself intensifies the illness, nothing is accomplished by abortion. [31]

Statistics from the Margaret Hague Maternity Hospital in Jersey City, New Jersey, show what can be done by "a change in medical philosophy." [32] The hospital is not a Catholic one. Its first medical director, who was there for over twenty years, was not a Catholic, and the majority of the attending staff was not Catholic. The change, however, resulted from the influence of the patients who were 75 percent Catholic. Very frequently, recommended therapeutic abortions were refused, yet the patients did much better than was predicted. The hospital's attitude changed accordingly in 1940. In the next fifteen years there were only eight therapeutic abortions in 150,000 deliveries. The maternal mortality rate was less than one out of one thousand live births. If under a different philosophy even 1 percent of the pregnancies had been aborted, fifteen hundred children, now living, would have been destroyed unnecessarily.

A great diversity of practice exists in hospitals. A questionnaire was sent to sixty-five randomly selected major U.S. hospitals. The incidence of therapeutic abortion ranged from no abortions in 24,417 deliveries to one in thirty-six deliveries.[33] The comment was made: "It seems inconceivable that medical opinion could vary so widely. Socioeconomic factors must be playing a major role in the decision to abort in certain institutions." [34] Robert Hall, M.D., President of the Association for Abortion Study, gives oblique confirmation of this observation when he says in speaking of the number of legal abortions done each year, "Of the ten thousand done within the walls of respectable hospitals, by reputable physicians, probably 90 percent are not in strict accordance with the law." [35] The law requires medical danger to the woman's life or, in some states, physical health. As we shall see in the next section, the majority of so-called "legal abortions," even under a strict statute, are for psychiatric rather than medical reasons. One thing is clear, then: The medical problem is not the major concern of pro-abortionists today. The life of the mother and even her physical health are, fortunately, well taken care of in all but infrequent instances. The focal points of current abortion concern are indications other than the medical one.

The Psychiatric Ground

The majority of legal abortions are the so-called psychiatric ones, performed because of an alleged danger to mental health of the mother. When a liberal statute is in force, the legal justification is clear and the incidence is high. For example, in Colorado during the first year, 1967–68, under the new statute, of 262 reported abortions, 144 were based on psychiatric reasons (including only two suicide risks). No reason was given for forty-five abortions. But only thirty-one were for "medical risks."

Since the great majority of statutes prohibit abortion unless it is necessary to save the life of the mother, an abortion on grounds of mental health usually requires some rationalization. Two approaches have been used to surmount this statutory impasse: one manipulates logic; the other forces facts.

The first mode of justification is found in the opinion of Judge MacNaghten in the 1938 English case of *Rex* v. *Bourne*. The judge stated in his oral instructions to the jury: ". . . if the doctor is of opinion, on reasonable grounds and with adequate knowledge, that the probable consequence of the pregnancy will be to make the woman a physical or mental wreck, the jury are quite entitled to take the view that the doctor, who in those circumstances, and in that honest belief, operates, is operating for the purpose of preserving the life of the woman." [36]

The second and more popular mode of justification is the attempt to find, in the absence of physical disease or defect, a valid suicide threat which endangers the life of the mother. The extent to which this technique is used can be seen from the tremendous increase in the percentage of therapeutic abortions based on a psychiatric diagnosis of probable suicide. Yet, as Dr. Allan Guttmacher pointed out, "Nervous and mental diseases were inconspicuous on a list [of indications for therapeutic abortion] until relatively recently." [37] His own hospital's therapeutic abortion practices are enlightening. He writes, "At Mt. Sinai, our rules are specific. The law says that one may abort to save the life of the mother, and therefore we insist that suicidal intent must be present in the psychiatric patient in order to validate the abortion." [38] In the years 1952–55 there were fifty-seven therapeutic abortions performed in Mt. Sinai Hospital. Almost half of these, 47.3 percent, were for psychiatric reasons, that is, validated by suicidal intent.[39]

These figures are not unusual. In New York City, from 1943 to 1953, the number of therapeutic abortions declined from 680 to 472, but the percentages of abortions on psychiatric grounds increased from 8.2 to 40.0. For the years 1951–53, 645 abortions, or 37.8 percent of the total number of therapeutic abortions, were performed because of alleged risk of suicide.[40] In the three years of 1960–62, 61 percent of the therapeutic abortions were done for the same psychiatric reasons.[41] A study in Buffalo, New York, over a twenty-two-year period, showed that of 504 abortions, 299 were for psychiatric reasons. The trend is seen from the fact that in 1943 only 10 percent, but in 1963 80 percent, were justified by reason of alleged suicide threat.[42]

Ostensibly, most therapeutic abortions represent the predictions of physicians about the likelihood of suicide. How accurate is this professional diagnosis? On this point there are many pertinent figures which, in practice, seem to be completely overlooked. In 1959, Dr. Milton Halpern, Chief Medical Examiner of New York City, stated that he could "hardly recall an autopsy on a death by suicide during the last twenty-five years which revealed pregnancy." [43] In a 1963 study, the coroner for the city of Birmingham, England, is reported as saying, "We have no record of any woman known to be pregnant having committed suicide." [44] In 1964, Dr. Russell S. Fisher, chief medical examiner of the State of Maryland, wrote that he could "recall only one pregnancy among the last seven hundred suicides, although some pregnancies may have been missed since we do not do an autopsy where the manner and the cause of the death are established." [45] Two Swedish studies reached the same conclusion. Lindberg examined 304 women who were refused an abortion: sixty-two threatened to commit suicide, but none did.[46] Jansson reported that in fifty-seven cases of legal abortion there were three suicides, but in 195 cases of refused abortion there were no suicides.[47]

The study of abortion in Minnesota reveals a phenomenally low incidence of suicide among pregnant women. Alex Barno,

M.D., covered sixteen years (1950–65) and 1,301,745 live births (about eighty thousand per year).[48] In that period, there were 658 maternal deaths and twenty-one criminal abortion deaths. He pointed out that auto accidents killed more pregnant women than did criminal abortions. In sixteen years there were only fourteen suicides among obstetric patients, or one per 92,982 live births. Not one of the suicides was illegitimately pregnant or had requested an abortion. Only four (one per 325,436 live births) committed suicide while pregnant; ten did so during the postpartum stage. Barno argues:

> How can pregnancy cause such a psychiatric upheaval or turmoil to alter the psychodynamics of an individual, to the extent that she will commit suicide? If she is not going to commit suicide, psychiatrists tell us that she will be very unhappy or upset. Are we all happy and content all of the time? Isn't there some unhappiness and turmoil in all of our lives? It is what is known in common parlance as everyday living. This all seems a most nebulous, nonobjective, nonscientific approach to medicine. It would seem what psychiatrists would accomplish more by using the available modalities of their specialties in the treatment or rehabilitation of the patient instead of recommending the destruction of another one.[49]

Dr. Lidz, professor of psychiatry at Yale University, summed up the all-too-frequent practice. "Let us be frank about this. When the psychiatrist says that there is a suicidal risk, in many instances he does not mean that at all, but feels that there are strong socioeconomic grounds for a therapeutic abortion. Since the only ground for abortion in many states is if it is felt that there is a threat of death, suicidal risk is thus established as the only legal way out of the situation." [50]

Even if danger to mental health were a generally accepted legal ground for abortion, there would be serious reasons against it. Here are three basic objections concerned with the standards, the decision, and the decision maker.

1. The standard is too vague. Just what precisely mental health and mental disease are has always been controverted, not only in psychiatric circles where disagreement is endemic but, at present and most crucially, in legal ones. Even if we assume knowledge of mental impairment, we have difficulty with the requisite degree of seriousness. Is it serious if it is temporary; if, in fact no irremediable harm is done? Is it serious if it is psychoneurotic rather than psychotic? Can impairment be serious if it refers only to feelings of acute distress and mental suffering? Dr. Gregory Zillboorg put the problem in perspective.

> Pregnancies that are marked by psychological tensions, severe moods, and anxieties are not really abnormal pregnancies, and common sense to the contrary, the so-called psychologically uneventful, serene, and sunny pregnancies are apt to be harbingers of severe and even malignant post-partum reactions. This does not mean that all psychologically uneventful pregnancies are forerunners of post-partum psychoses, but they frequently may be—whereas the so-called psychologically stormy pregnancies are seldom such forerunners.[51]

2. Both the diagnosis and prognosis are uncertain. Pregnancy is a physically and psychologically normal experience. Abortion is not. As Dr. Litz phrased it, "[H]aving an abortion is, by and large, an extremely deleterious experience in the continuity of the life of a woman." [52] He also states that it is practically impossible for a psychiatrist to predict when an abortion will not be more detrimental to the mental health than the carrying of the baby.[53] Even statistical information is not of much help in assessing the particular case. Dr. H. C. Taylor, a director of the Columbia-Presbyterian Medical Center, pointed out, "It is all right to take one hundred patients and say that so many are going to do well and so many are going to have unfortunate psychiatric reactions, but we must know which ones it is who are going to have such reactions, before we undertake the therapeutic abortion." [54] In other words, we must be sure of a "substantial risk"

that serious impairment will result. Most liberal provisions give no indication as to what is meant by the word "substantial."

Three factors multiply the chances that the diagnosis for a psychiatric abortion will be unsound. The patient desirous of an abortion may consciously deceive the physician about her mental state and suicidal threats. The likelihood increases in proportion to the brevity of her examination. The patient may be pressured by family, or friends, or even other doctors into asking for an abortion. The patient may well have subconsciously convinced herself that she has the requisite symptoms. Deceiving herself, she may more easly convince her physician.

3. Finally, the decision-maker is untrained. In an area as susceptive of divergent opinions and contrary predictions as that of the relationships involving pregnancy, abortion, and mental illness, even the most highly skilled psychiatrists have difficulty making consistently sound decisions. Nevertheless, the usual one to make a decision about a psychiatric abortion is the ordinary physician who has little more competence in the field of psychiatry than a lawyer, marriage counselor, or dentist. An obstetrician writing in favor of abortion has conscientiously formulated the parameters of the abortion decision that faces the ordinary physician, and in formulating them has clearly shown the impossibility of the task for the ordinary physician and, in fact, for most men. He writes:

> The real issue is this: after careful investigation of the individual's total life situation—past, present, and predictable future —are her, and to a lesser extent her family's and society's welfare and happiness best served by having her continue with the pregnancy or by having an early and therefore safe interruption of it? It is inconceivable to me to try to make such a decision without taking into account all of the manifold and interrelated considerations which may relate to the stress of a given pregnancy.[55]

The Criminal Ground

The rape victim, the incestuous woman, and in some cases the unwed mother, all qualify for an abortion under the liberal provision sometimes called the ethical or humanitarian ground—odd terms since, in most instances, there is no ethics in conceiving the child or humanitarianism in destroying it. Sometimes this ground is called the legal ground, since the essential elements of justification are matters of law rather than of medicine or psychiatry. To avoid confusion, since the other grounds for abortion can also be called legal grounds, it is helpful to specify more precisely and call it a criminal ground because of the criminal conduct that produced the pregnancy.

This criminal ground for liberal abortion is conceptually a species of the psychiatric ground—with this difference, if the fact of rape or incest is proved no further harm need be shown. The right to an abortion follows automatically on proof of the criminal act. The woman's mental or physical health, her motives, or even her guilt are irrelevant. If she wants an abortion, she is legally entitled to one. Without the criminal ground, abortions after rape or incest would be somewhat more cumbersome but not impossible. The woman may demand an abortion on the grounds that the pregnancy would make her a "mental wreck," as in the *Bourne* case, or that an abortion is necessary to save her from suicide as under traditional law, or that it is necessary to preserve her health as provided in some old and some new laws. The rape-incest provision in liberal abortion laws is not an operative necessity; its purported advantage is that it is easier, quicker, and surer.

Some but not all illegitimate pregnancies are within the scope of the criminal ground. The unwed mother, as such, is not usually provided for unless she is pregnant because of rape or incest. Legally, a man cannot rape a woman to whom he is married, nor can he validly marry a woman to whom he is closely related.

Therefore, a child who is conceived from rape or incest is illegitimate because its parents are not married. But the woman may or may not be a victim. If she has been forcibly raped, she has clearly been victimized. If, however, the woman freely consented to the illicit intercourse, but was below the legal age for consent (statutory rape) or was too closely related to the father of the child (incest), she is, despite her immoral participation in the criminal offense, permitted to abort her innocent child, the fruit of her own guilty conduct. In short, the criminal ground for abortion justifies the abortion of illegitimate children who are the result of rape or incest without regard to the moral or legal culpability of the mother or her reasons, other than the fact of the crime, for wanting the abortion.

Consider the scope of the problem. Statistics on illegitimate births, however, do not tell us the number of illegitimate conceptions which never come to term because of spontaneous or induced abortion. The changing rates are significant.[56] In a twenty-year period, from 1946 to 1966, illegitimate births have risen nationally from 125,000 to 302,400; that is, from 3.8 percent to 8.4 percent of the total number of births. The racial breakdown shows an increase of from 2.1 percent to 4.4 percent of all white births, and from 17.0 percent to 27.7 percent of all nonwhite births. The over-all increase contrasts with the uninterrupted decrease in the birth rate for the last eleven years. The estimated number of births for 1968 is 3,335,000, the fewest births since 1945.

In some urban areas, the illegitimacy rate, as might be expected, is much higher than in the nation as a whole. For example, in New York City, one out of every six births in 1967 was illegitimate.[57] Ten years ago, it was only one in every fifteen. There has been an 112.5 percent increase in illegitimate births over the last ten years, whereas the total live births declined 12.7 percent. The fastest rate of increase has been for the whites, from 1.7 to 5.3 percent. But the largest proportion was among nonwhites, an increase of from 24.0 to 38.3 percent. Puerto

Ricans, classified separately, showed an increase of from 10.7 to 21.9 percent. The actual numbers of illegitimate births for New York City in 1967 were 4454 white, 14,708, nonwhite, and 5174 Puerto Rican.

The incidence of the various kinds of illegitimate pregnancies is difficult to determine. A breakdown of the number of unwed mothers according to age gives some broad indications, especially about statutory rapes that result in pregnancies that are brought to term. These figures are for the year 1965: under age 15— 6100; ages 15 through 19—123,000; ages 20 through 24— 90,600; ages 25 through 29—36,800; ages 30 through 34— 19,600; age 35 and older—15,000, for a total of 291,000.[58] Incest is sometimes prosecuted as forcible or statutory rape, but more often is treated as a family affair or a social worker's problem. Even statutory rape eludes precise statistical evaluation. Prior to 1959, the F.B.I. Crime Reports contained figures on the frequency or statutory rape. The estimates were discontinued because of the lack of uniformity among the various law-enforcement agencies in receiving such complaints and in recording them. It was found that police, prosecutors, and grand juries freely use their discretion, especially where young people of about the same age are involved. Frequently, the only time a statutory rape charge is brought is when the girl is very young and the man much older, or when the father of an illegitimate child will not contribute to the hospital bill or to the support of the child.

Forcible rape, on the other hand, has been carefully reported. But in assessing the figures, one must be doubly cautious: first, because 18 percent of all reported forcible rapes prove to be unfounded; that is, the police, after an investigation, are not able to determine that an offense actually took place; second, because forcible rape is the most underreported of all crimes.[59] Of course, few crime statistics are completely accurate. Law-enforcement officers vary widely in their professional competence and in their reporting techniques. The most reliable statistics, however, do give some indication of the relative increase and decrease of the crime, but even here new modes of compilation recently adopted in this country have radically changed the basis for accurate comparisons.

A crude estimate of the number of rape-induced pregnancies can be made by taking the number of "forcible rapes" reported by the F.B.I. and applying to it the 2 to 4 percent rate of pregnancy from unprotected intercourse.[60] However, since the F.B.I. includes under the category "forcible rape" the following crimes: rape by force, assault to rape, and attempted rape, and "two-thirds [of all such offenses] were rapes by force and the rest were attempts or assaults to rape," the overall figure must be adjusted accordingly, for there is no danger of pregnancy in an assault to commit rape or in an attempted rape.[61]

Based on the F.B.I. Crime Reports, there were about eighteen thousand actual forcible rapes in 1967.[62] The pregnancies resulting would be, applying the rate of pregnancies from unprotected intercourse, from 360 to 720, or on an average, about 540. Even the figure of 540 rape-induced pregnancies for 1967 would be an upper limit, for what is legally rape is not simple "unprotected intercourse." Legally—and the statistics are based on the legal definition—rape requires only the slightest labial penetration and does not require any emission. If the act is interrupted before the male orgasm, the crime nevertheless has been committed and becomes a statistic.

The rate of conception from random intercourse has been experimentally verified, but an *a priori* explanation is also possible. The key factor is the woman's menstrual cycle. The ovum can be fertilized for only twenty-four hours after ovulation. The sperm can fertilize the ovum for only forty-eight hours. Thus, the possibility of fertilization exists for only about seventy-two hours, or three days, out of every twenty-eight-day cycle.[63] Statistically, then, the chance of being raped during a fertile time is about 10 percent. Of those ten women out of a hundred, some are too old, some are too young, some are pathologically sterile, some are taking contraceptive pills, some use spermicidal measures immediately after the rape, some are raped by men who have no emission, and some by men who are sterile. The percentage of pregnancies is proportionately limited.

A factor not usually considered in studies determining the rate of pregnancy from unprotected intercourse is the affect of the trauma experienced in a rape on the rate of conception. For example, in Washington, D.C., the captain of the Sex Squad of the Metropolitan Police, V. Edward Tate, recalls only three pregnancies from forcible rape in the last fifteen years. Medical research indicates that a woman about to ovulate will be thrown out of phase by a serious emotional trauma so that ovulation will not occur. Evidence supporting this conclusion comes from two very different sources. The Nazis tested this hypothesis by selecting women who were about to ovulate, sending them to the gas chambers, and, after a grimly realistic mock-killing, bringing them back to await the affects of this experience on their menstrual cycles. An extremely high percentage of these women did not ovulate in that cycle.[64] A second source is the Congo. A few years ago, many women missionaries, both Catholic and non-Catholic, were raped by bands of marauding soldiers. Surprisingly few of the women were impregnated. Those about to ovulate at the time did not do so.[65] Although it is not entirely clear whether ovulation is inhibited or implantation is prevented, it appears that the emotional shock works primarily in suppressing ovulation.

Not to be overlooked in estimating the factors that are relevant in the consideration of legislative change is that even if a statistically improbable pregnancy does result, some women, perhaps many women, will not consent to an abortion. Thus, the total number of women likely to seek an abortion seems to be very small. As a matter of medical practice, this group could easily be taken care of as they are in the District of Columbia, under a statute which allows abortion to preserve the mental health of the mother.

The Eugenic Ground

This ground differs from the three previous ones in that it shifts the emphasis from the mother to the child. In the medical, psychiatric, and criminal grounds, the child's death was not primarily intended, but was deemed necessary for the sake of the mother. When abortion is justified for fetal indications, presumably the pregnancy does not threaten the mother's physical or mental health. The death of the child is willed directly because the child is believed to be so seriously handicapped that its life is cruelly painful or worthless. In such cases, it is not a question of preserving the mother at the expense of her child. This proposal is broader than the maternal exception and demands an entirely different rationalization. This ground is not an extension of the traditional law but a radical departure from it. Although it had a Scandinavian precedent, it derived its impetus in the early 1960s from two great crises: the thalidomide scandal of 1962, which resulted in almost ten thousand defective children; and the rubella or German measles epidemic of 1963–64, which resulted in almost thirty thousand defective children. These two unfortunate episodes sensitized the American public to the agonizing reality of fetal defects. Fear of monster births has persisted despite the fact that both of these problem areas are now fairly well contained.

The source of fetal defects is twofold: genetic and environmental. Genetic defects are due to some radical failure in the basic chromosome and gene structure of the original fertilized ovum. Environmental defects are due to the interaction between the genetic structure of the organism and harmful outside influences such as viruses, drugs, radiation, and incompatible maternal antibodies. The resulting malformations can be so serious that the fetus never comes to full term, or they can be so minimal that the possessor never manifests any imperfection until long after birth, if at all. Since the causes of these defects, their seriousness and their predictability, vary widely, they are best understood if treated separately.

1. Viral Infections.

By far the vast majority of abortions for fetal defects in this country have been performed because of rubella. The first trimester is the crucial time, for that is when the various organs and parts of the body are being established. The second and third trimesters are primarily a time of growth and development. Rubella, however, differs "from such teratogens as thalidomide and radiation, which do their damage with one exposure in early pregnancy. The rubella virus probably does different things to the fetus at different times during gestation." [66] The Rendle-Short and Sallomi statistics indicate the significance of the time of exposure: If it is two to four weeks after conception, the rate of defective offspring is over 60 percent; if it is six to eight weeks, the rate is 30 percent; and if it is ten weeks, the rate is 10 percent. If the exposure to rubella occurs during the first eight weeks, there is only a 35.8 percent expectancy of a normal child. If the exposure is after the twelfth week, there is more than a 90 percent expectancy of a normal child.[67]

What kind of defects result from exposure during a crucial time? Cataract, microphthalamus, congenital heart, microcephaly, deafness, and mental retardation. Despite the possibility of irremediable defects, most of the abnormalities are correctible. A British project tested, with an eleven-year followup, 227 mothers who were exposed to rubella and found that their children had no greater incidence of mental retardation than that occurring in the general population.[68]

Fortunately, most viruses do not cause fetal defects. This is especially true of the commonest one, the cold and influenza virus. Thus, with effective control of rubella, the viral threat to unborn children is almost eliminated.

2. Drugs.

Thalidomide, a German tranquilizing drug, caused grotesque deformities among many children whose mothers took the drug during the first trimester, specifically between the fifth and the eighth week when the human limbs are developing. Before or after this time, the drug was harmless to the child. The medical profession and the general public have been warned about the dangers of thalidomide, and its specific teratogenic factor has been isolated, the phthalic acid and glutamic acid which are present in the thalidomide molecule.

Other chemicals have an embryopathic effect. Too much vitamin D can cause serious fetal damage, as can the dye, trypan blue, and the salts of certain heavy metals. Hormonal excess in the mother or hormonal deficiencies in the child are harmful. Nitrogen mustard and urethane are dangerous growth inhibitors. Recently, lysergic acid 22, LSD, has appeared to produce chromosomal change with the possibility of fetal malformation. Folic acid antagonists used in the treatment of leukemia sometimes have injured the fetus by its metabolic action.

3. Genetic Defects.

Genetically caused fetal defects are of two kinds: an inheritance of faulty genes from one or both parents, or an abnormal distribution of chromosomes. In the first category, a mutation originally produces a defective gene, either dominant or recessive, causing, for example, congenital cataract, albinism, or finger fusion. Sometimes these genes are sex-linked, that is, they are carried by the mother in the X-chromosome and affect only the male offspring, for example, by hemophilia and color blindness. In the second category, there are a number of defects due to an excess or deficiency in the number of chromosomes. The normal person has forty-six chromosomes—forty-four autosomes (nonsex chromosomes) and two gonosomes (sex chromosomes). Owing to an imperfect cell division in forming the gonosomes, the child may have a defective genetic package.

The most familiar example of this anomaly is Mongolism, with its physical and mental deficiency. The Mongoloid child has an extra chromosome, making a total of forty-seven. When the mother's forty-six chromosomes split to form the ova, chromosome No. 21 sometimes does not do so correctly. The egg, then, either gets both parts of No. 21 or neither. In the first instance, the child becomes a Mongoloid; in the second, it usually dies before birth. Only two cases have been reported of a child missing any of the forty-four nonsex chromosomes: one died at birth; the other was severely retarded. The missing chromosome was No. 21 or No. 22.

The chance of having a Mongoloid child is about one in seven hundred. The probabilities, however, vary with age. For a twenty-year-old woman, it is one in three thousand; for a forty-five-year-old woman it is one in forty. It is possible to photograph chromosomes through an electron microscope and make a karyotype of the individual cell, thereby checking on numerical chromosomal normality. Since the fetal cells are obtained from the placenta or the amniotic fluid which contains sloughed-off body cells, there is danger of terminating the pregnancy or injuring the fetus if the attempt is made during the first trimester. When a karyotype can be made, it does indicate clearly certain kinds of abnormality. It is helpful in only a few problem areas, but not where defects are caused by sex-linked recessives which do not appear on a karyotype. Certain abnormal distributions of the sex-chromosomes, however, can be picked up by a karyotype. Turner's syndrome is found in females with forty-five chromosomes, but only one X chromosome. These women are frequently mentally retarded. Males with a genetic structure of XYY or XXYY are usually aggressive and of borderline intelligence. If the male's structure is XXY, he has some female characteristics but no intelligence problems. In general, the current prediction rate in the area of genetic fetal abnormalities is very limited.

4. Radiation.

Radiation can cause malformation and death, but it does not necessarily do so. If the dosage is extreme, such as would be prescribed for cancer of the cervix, the effects on the fetus would presumably be serious. If, however, the X-ray usage is primarily diagnostic, there is little likelihood that the child will be affected even though the radiation occurred during the first trimester.

5. The Rh Factor.

Another common problem during pregnancy is the presence of an incompatibility between the blood of the mother and that of the unborn child, when one is Rh negative and the other is Rh positive. The antibodies formed by the mother's blood make their way through the placenta and reduce the formation of red blood cells in the child. The amount of antibodies can be measured and the danger to the child can be easily assessed, however. The formation of antibodies is not always serious, though it tends to increase with subsequent pregnancies. Today it is possible to prevent fetal death by a transfusion immediately after birth or, in an emergency, by an intrauterine transfusion if the child's anemia or lack of red cells has reached dangerous proportions. Thus, erythroblastosis fetalis or Rh incompatibility is no longer an indication for abortion.

The Socioeconomic Ground

A socioeconomic justification for abortion is not as radical as abortion on demand. Almost any reason will do, but there has to be a reason. It is the penultimate liberalization; the next step would be complete permissiveness. In considering the various liberal grounds for abortion, we have moved farther and farther away from the traditional one, the necessity of saving the life of the mother. The medical, psychiatric, and criminal grounds retain some connection, however attenuated, with this original justification. The eugenic ground is an abrupt departure, although it does deal directly, if only partially, with the presumed welfare of the child. The socioeconomic ground is not directly and necessarily concerned with either mother or child; we are in the realm of social advantage and the economics of the good life.

The socioeconomic ground has two aspects: the microcosmic, which looks to the individual and family, and the macrocosmic, which looks to the community and the state. The first considers the family's social competence and financial ability to provide for the health, education, and welfare of all its members. If the birth of another child will hamper this realization, that unborn child is to be sacrificed for the sake of the living. The second aspect is also one of allocating a limited amount of resources among an increasing number of persons, but it transcends the family and considers the total community. The abortion decision has moved from a concern for the mother to an affair of state. This new socioeconomic argument can be formulated in terms of traditional abortion law: If abortion is justifiable to save the life of the mother, is it not all the more justifiable to save the life of the whole society? The argument can be formulated even more broadly in terms of liberal abortion laws: If abortion is justifiable to prevent harm to the physical or mental health of the mother or, *a fortiori,* of the existing members of her family, is it not all the more justifiable to allow abortion to prevent similar harm to the whole society? These arguments are already persuasive to many people. But if this justification becomes a legally acceptable ground, will the individual woman have the right to refuse an abortion which is deemed necessary for the life or the health of the larger society? Do not the reasons given to justify liberal abortion also justify involuntary abortion?

Perhaps we can better answer this question by first considering the reason underlying current preoccupation with the socio-economic ground. It is fear. Technology is optimistically conquering the universe, but technopolitan man is scared. His feeling of psychic security seems to be in inverse proportion to his scientific progress. He is disturbed about many things. His total environment is being contaminated: air pollution, noise pollution, thermal pollution, and fallout pollution. Accidents, crimes, riots, and revolts are multiplying. Wars and atomic destruction are an ever-present threat. Even if these evils are avoided, overpopulation and wholesale starvation seem to foretell man's ultimate fate.

In 1798, before the first industrial revolution had transformed

Great Britain, Malthus pessimistically observed that the population grows by geometric progression, whereas food production increases by arithmetic progression. In modern terms that would make a population explosion as disastrous as a nuclear holocaust. Perhaps the current mentality can be phrased best in Sartre's phrase, "Hell is other people." The remark is doubly appropriate for a crowded world, since it was taken from a work entitled *No Exit*. Since the 1950s, we have entered the second industrial revolution, the cybernetic age with new techniques for exploiting the material world. But overpopulation continues to be a world problem. The population of the United States, in 1967, passed the two-hundred-million mark. Some demographic predictions are that by the year 2000 the U.S. population will be 308 million. In that same year the world population, now 3.4 billion, will have doubled.

Many exponents of family planning, instead of implementing the human capacity for overcoming obstacles, concentrate solely on limiting human reproduction by contraception and abortion to achieve zero population growth. They argue that any growth rate at all, if continued, will eventually use up the earth.[69] Some, looking at Japan, believe that voluntary contraception and abortion are sufficient. Others, looking at India, believe that stronger methods are necessary. For some, then, family planning begins with information, moves to motivation, and ends with coercion. The word coercion may not always appear, yet its equivalents are frequent, such as collective determination, societal regulation, and imposition of restraints. Professor Kingsley Davis of the University of California at Berkeley questions the demographic effectiveness of present family planning programs because of the absence of strong governmental control.[70] He believes that control over population should parallel control over dangerous drugs, explosives, public property, and natural resources. The family, he says, must be de-emphasized, "(i) by keeping present controls over illegitimate childbirth yet making the most of factors that lead people to postpone or avoid marriage, and (ii) by instituting conditions that motivate those who do marry to keep their families small." Professor Davis considers it the task of society to develop such attractive substitutes for family interests that there will be no need to turn to "hardship as a corrective." Abortion, he claims, is a necessary technique if population control is to be achieved without resort to extreme measures. Professor Davis's reasoning is as follows: Induced abortion is one of the surest means of population control, especially suited to the threshold stage; it is hair-splitting to argue whether or not some contraceptive agent [e.g., I.U.D.] is really an abortifacient; the main objection to abortion is its illegality; when done by a skillful physician it is safer than childbirth; abortion is a backstop to contraception; therefore, cease outlawing abortion, have abortions paid for by the state, and require that all illegitimate pregnancies be aborted.

What we see in such a proposal is ultimately a lethal shortcut. The problem becomes simply one of arithmetic, of addition and subtraction. Man's dark tendency to push this control of life into avenues of monstrous inhumanity does not enter the realm of consideration. The problem is formulated in terms of manipulating units rather than in terms of maximizing the values of free individuals while preserving their dignity and their equality.

All men should be concerned with both the quality and the quantity of life in the world. One radical flaw in the liberal abortion solution is that it tries to preserve the right quantity at the expense of the quality, for it sacrifices human worth for socioeconomic security.

Conclusion

To assess the present abortion problem in the United States is not an easy task. Even when the initial exaggerations have been toned down, the actual dimensions of the problem are not clear. We know that there are not as many illegal abortions as has been claimed, and we know that there are not as few as we would wish. Is there an abortion crisis? At the least, there is a serious problem. Many people find that their pregnancies are unwanted pregnancies. How often they choose abortion as the solution is difficult to determine.

Despite many abortion polls, the number of those actually favoring liberalization, like the number of those actually undergoing illegal abortions, is at least disputed. A trend in favor of liberalization does exist. At least more people than ever before are expressing a preference that previously they would not have mentioned.

The traditional grounds that justified abortion are rarely resorted to today except as they have been broadly interpreted. The new grounds, however, have moved so far beyond the maternal exception that liberal abortion has become a new tool for social engineering. Perhaps the abortion crisis is not a medical crisis at all, but a social crisis. Perhaps for this reason, the abortion decision must be worked out, not in terms of medicine, but in terms of morals, politics, and law. For the abortion crisis presents us ultimately with a crucial decision about the right to life. Medicine may be its context, but human dignity is its core.

Chapter Four

THE MORAL CHOICE

The abortion decision involves a moral choice and thus is part of a plan for happiness. Although phrased in terms of good and evil, morality aims at happiness. The primary precept of morality is: Do good and avoid evil.[1] The reason for this imperative is that the good leads to happiness, the evil leads to misery. This principle is both descriptive and deontic: It tells us what men do as well as what men ought to do. The "is" and the "ought" are combined in this wellspring of behavior, which is sometimes formulated as the *maximization* postulate: "Men act to maximize their values, conscious or unconscious."[2] Whatever a man does, whether he is driven by submerged impulses hidden within the murky depths of his psyche or by conscious and well-articulated motives directing him to eminently reasonable goals, he does so to actualize his potential, to realize his destiny, to achieve his optimal perfection. Objectively, he may choose unwisely and make himself miserable, but whatever he feels is necessary for his happiness, he seeks. Although a man necessarily chooses happiness in everything he does, he is not for that reason happy, for he fails again and again to choose the things that will make him happy. Man has no freedom in his choice of the ultimate goal, which is happiness, but he does have a limited freedom in

the choice of means. This is the arena of responsible decision—
of morality.

Paradoxically, honest men can make diametrically opposed
moral choices. Abortion anarchists and abortion absolutists can
both be seeking honorable solutions to the same desperate problem. On the other hand, even the backstairs abortionist trafficking
in human life seeks good. He too acts for happiness. The difference is revealing. The honest man seeks out good in its
existential entirety. He tries to discover what is best for himself
and for all men, individually and socially. The bad man myop-
ically seeks only his own subjective good. If he does not ration-
alize, he admits at least to himself that in gratifying a narrow
personal preference, he is sacrificing the good of other men.
Somehow he sees his own happiness as dependent on this exploitation. This refusal to consider the good of others, this denial
of equality, is characteristic of crime and sin. Good is the object,
but it is the choice of a lesser good when the situation demands
the choice of a greater good. A half-hour nap may be a good
thing, but not for one on guard duty. We cannot close our eyes
to the total situation without vitiating our choices and impeding
our happiness. If we consciously refuse to recognize the interests
involved, we act immorally; if we fail to consider all the interests
because of ignorance or error, we act unwisely. In both situations our moral choice is defective and leads to misery. To make
sure that we view the abortion decision in true perspective, we
should consider both the person and the community, the person
as a member of a community. To do so, we must try to understand the pillars of communal personalism, equality and authority.

Equality and Authority

The abortion choice must reconcile the rights of equality with
the limits of authority. Scientific and philosophic findings reveal
the fundamental dignity and equality of all men, even before

their birth. Yet abortion is a use of power by one human being over another: It establishes a drastic inequality. The moral issue is: May this power over life and death ever be permitted?

Men have consistently exercised power over one another. Much of this power is authoritative, and in harmony with the expectations of the community. The state has this moral power over its citizens, and parents have this moral power over their children. Those who exercise power lawfully are said to have authority. They can establish a policy and impose it on others under pain of a sanction. Does the existence of widespread authority belie the principle of equality between rulers and subjects, between parents and children? Not at all, as is clear from the true function of authority.[3]

That power which is authority is usually reinforced by physical power but is essentially a moral power—the right to make a decision for others. Authority is not measured by the amount of force it can wield. A frail and sickly father has authority over his minor son though the boy is bigger and stronger than he is. This lack of physical might may limit the effectiveness of the moral power but it does not take away the rightfulness of its commands. On the other hand, the weakness of the subject does not break down protective barriers and allow those in authority unrestricted use of force. In fact, accountability for the abuse of power is proportionate to the helplessness of the victim.

Service, not superiority, is the purpose of authority. A society exists for the sake of the community, to fulfil the needs of its members. Authority exists that the society may, with unified effort, work toward that goal which is the value maximization of its individual members. The authority of the government is for the sake of the people, not for the sake of the prestige and privileges of those who rule. Parental authority is not for the self-aggrandizement or security of the mother and father, but for helping the child pursue patterns of conduct which will bring him to more and more perfect maturity. Authority is not a diminution of equality but a social necessity in protecting and implementing that equality. Authority is power in the service of equality.

Abortion, as the authorized killing of an innocent equal, brings discord into the apparent harmony between authority and equality. This jarring note prompts us to examine more deeply the right to life which forms the basis of the prescription against the direct killing of the innocent. Liberal abortion undermines human society by attacking the fact of equality and by attacking the right to life. Without these two interrelated elements human society remains at a primitive level of naked power disguised somewhat by the mask of expediency. But liberal abortion also harms society by attacking the notion of authority as service. Those in authority are given some control over the lives of others, but it is a limited control—a service, not a sovereignty. God alone has full and perfect dominion over others, the power of life and death. As the Creator of all men, He implements their individual right to life by his power and commandments: "The innocent and the just person thou shalt not put to death, because I abhor the wicked" (*Ex.* 23:7). God's superior authority over all men is the ultimate guarantee of the inalienability of the right to life, even in the womb. For human authorities to try to arrogate to themselves, for reasons of expediency, this power over the life and death of the innocent is to usurp a divine prerogative and to change authority into tyranny and equality into a myth.

The right to life is basic to a personalistic view of community. It is the first condition of equality, the first limitation of authority. Contemporary thinkers have deepened our awareness of this truth so important in an abortion decision. Of special value is the witness of existentialists as they search out the meaning of life in a suffering, if not absurd, world.

An Existentialist Evaluation

Two contemporary existentialists, Albert Camus and Victor Frankl, have written deeply of human dignity, and can give us a somewhat oblique insight into the area of ultimate concern in the abortion decision. By their intellectual independence, these two thinkers strengthen the Judeo-Christian ethical preference which has been responsible for the traditional strictures against abortion. Together they make a humanistic case against violating the sanctity of human life.

A. Absurdity and Abortion.

Albert Camus (1913–60) called himself a moralist rather than a philosopher, but won the Nobel Prize in literature (1957) for predominantly psychological studies of the response of the human conscience to the hard facts of an absurd world. Inevitably linked with existentialism, he tried to disassociate himself from the movement. In two works, separated by about ten years, he assesses the validity of suicide, *The Myth of Sisyphus* (1942), and murder, *The Rebel* (1951). These complementary evaluations do not treat abortion but do examine its underlying assumptions through, one might say, an existential confrontation of life and death.

For Camus, absurdity refers to the conflict between man's inquiring mind and the silence of the universe. Man has nostalgia for unity in a fragmented world. Camus complains, "The world itself is not reasonable, that is all that can be said. But what is absurd is the confrontation of the irrational and the wild longing for clarity whose call echoes in the human heart." [4] Man's life is absurd because it is impossible to reconcile man's quest for truth and the density of the world. So he adheres to the facts of his experience without demanding a transcendental explanation of them. The absurd man relies on his courage and his reasoning.

"The first teaches him to live without appeal and to get along with what he has; the second informs him of his limits." [5]

The methodology of the absurd man is humanistic. He does not resort to eternal values in attempting to solve his greatest problem, the value of life. "Judging whether life is or is not worth living amounts to answering the fundamental question of philosophy." [6] It is enlightening for us to examine the reasoning here since the abortion problem is at the root a conflict over the value of life, all life, not just the life of the unborn child. Since the most frequent arguments against abortion are religious or at least ethically theistic, the arguments of an atheistic humanism which denies knowledge of transcendental truth can be very revealing. Without accepting Camus' denial of a reasonable explanation for the universe, we can share with him a sense of absurdity. So little does man know, so much is there yet to learn. We do have some answers, some truths, our lives are not totally absurd. Yet it is most instructive to see what can be done to shed light on the abortion controversy if we work exclusively from the premise of absurdity.

Camus' fundamental question is: Does a philosophy of absurdity dictate death? Does it lead logically to death? His affirmation of life is clear. "Even if one does not believe in God, suicide is not legitimate." [7] From the point of view of absurdity, the reasoning is as follows: Suicide would end the encounter, the tension between the appetite for unity and the irrationality of the world. Suicide would deny the premises of absurdity which allows neither flight nor deliverance, because absurdity demands a confrontation with the irreconcilables without hope of reconciliation. Only in this courageous facing of things as they are is authenticity realized, is one's destiny fulfilled.

When Camus wrote *The Rebel,* the psychology of the times had changed. The intellectual problem was no longer suicide but the idea of murder, and murder on the grand scale of the Third Reich. Philosophically, however, Camus perceived an essential identity. "In terms of the encounter between human inquiry and the silence of the universe, murder and suicide are one and the same thing, and must be accepted or rejected together." [8] He establishes a principle which seems self-evident, yet is so consistently overlooked in justifications for liberal abortion. "From the moment that life is recognized as good, it becomes good for all men." [9] To bring this point home more sharply, he compares the absurdist position with that of the nihilists, whose acceptance of suicide as legitimate brought them logically to the acceptance of murder. Nihilism is a total rejection of the value of life. The philosophy of the absurd, on the other hand, is a limited but vigorous affirmation of life. "Absurdist reasoning cannot defend the continued existence of its spokesman and simultaneously accept the sacrifice of other lives. The moment that we recognize the impossibility of absolute negation—and merely to be alive is to recognize this—the very first thing that cannot be denied is the right of others to live." [10]

By setting up this fundamental affirmation—"the right of others to live"—Camus hit at the heart of nihilism, which reduces men to expendable units of social utility. His life had been beset with terrorism and vilification so characteristic of the nihilistic regimes of communism and fascism. In passionate reaction, Camus forged a philosophic defense of all human life. He isolated that ideological disease which has so infected modern civilization—the objectification of man.

This objectification is at the root of the problem of liberal abortion. Are the unborn expendable objects? Are they things of mere social utility? Can we as true humanists accept the sacrifice of others without destroying the meaning of our own lives? Would we not through liberal abortion be denying that "the very first thing that cannot be denied is the right of others to live"?

We may see in liberal abortion the same tendency to treat persons as things, and like Camus we reject this vilification of man. But most people need more than a great stone upon a bleak landscape to symbolize their hopes for humanity. However valid Camus' affirmation of life is for us, we need a more positive presentation of the value of life in adversity if we are to act on our instinctive sense of the dehumanizing aspects of liberal abortion. Camus' apologia is more convincing than it is motivating.

The absurd man can strike an heroic pose. He takes his stand against an adverse fate, convinced that the whole universe is an adverse fate. For him, the secret of the universe is that it has no secret—no explanation. As in Chesterton's phrase, the village atheist writes about the village idiot. Camus knows that he is both the atheist and the idiot, but his pride in this pessimistic truth sustains him. He fights a losing battle for truth, but he fights it as a man. He affirms life as he decries its destruction. The meaning of life is in its affirmation, though it is lost in a cloud of unknowing that covers the world. For a man of intellect, a man of genius and sensitivity, this may be meaning enough, these may be words to live by. Most people, however, even most intellectuals, require that life manifest for them a deeper significance for it to be worthwhile. Man searches for meaning, for evidence that life has dignity even in adversity. If a man despairs of that, he will erect a nihilistic ideology which he will worship and to which he will sacrifice his fellow men, as the Carthaginians once sacrificed their children to the god Moloch.

B. The Search for Meaning

Victor Frankl, too, gives an existentialist answer to Camus' first philosophic question: Is life worth living? He does so with a conviction equal to that of Camus, but gives a richer psychological explanation. He tested his theories in the crucibles of Auschwitz, Dachau, and other concentration camps where the reasons for suicide were most pressing and the evidence of murder most horrible. He discovered how meaning and dignity can be realized even in the face of hopeless odds—the certainty of imminent torture and death. The satanic methodology of the Third Reich for destroying both souls and bodies reveals the face of evil in one of its most overwhelming guises, but even against such an adversary, Frankl found life worthwhile. Compared with Nazi atrocities, the sufferings and deprivations used to justify liberal abortion are almost inconsequential. Because of that, these justifications need a complete reappraising in the light of Frankl's findings.

Life for Frankl is an opportunity to realize values, to become better by doing and enjoying, realizing thereby creative and experiential values. Certain situations, however, confront us with no other choice but to endure. Yet values are not lost when evil enters our lives. "The right kind of suffering—facing your fate without flinching—is the highest achievement that has been granted to man." [11] These are the "attitudinal values" which spring from man's response to tragedy. Frankl frequently quotes Goethe's remark, "There is no predicament that we cannot ennoble either by doing or by suffering." [12] Herein lies the key to full human dignity, to a perfecting of the personality in all its uniqueness. No longer does man seem to exist at the whim of fate, his destiny determined by luck. Here is liberation, not from pain and suffering but from that frustration of personal fulfillment which such deprivations seemed inevitably to bring with it.

The mother who wants an abortion because of the unborn child's foreseen defects or her own mental or physical or financial limitations is making her lethal decision on a false assumption: namely, that life with these defects or limitations is a life not worth living. Yet defects and limitations are unavoidable. The process of aging with the piece-by-piece breakdown of the human body and with death as the final physical dissolution of that same body convinces us of that unavoidability. Is the decision to abort an admission of despair? Is it an acceptance of a dismal and nihilistic fate? If, nonetheless, we recognize value in every human life however wounded or diminished, we need never lose hope that we too are able to achieve our own personal destiny. Frankl's basic premise is: "The so-called life not worth living does not exist." [13] He takes an extreme case, most relevant in a consideration of abortion, the better to combat the nihilism which is so destructive of human values and even of human life. He writes:

> When I was in Paris seven years ago for the first World Congress of Psychiatry, I was asked by Père Beirnaert whether I, as a psychiatrist, believed that idiots could become saints. I answered in the affirmative. But more than that I told him that the very fact, horrible as it is, of having been born an idiot could be an occasion and a chance to prove oneself so well—by an inner attitude—that one might well be tantamount to a saint. Of course, other persons, even we psychiatrists, would hardly notice anything, since the very possibility of manifesting the self outwardly would be blocked by mental disease. Only God can know how many saints were concealed behind the miens of idiots. But then I asked Père Beirnaert whether it was not intellectualist self-conceit even to doubt this possibility. Did not doubting it mean supposing that saintliness or any other moral qualifications of man were dependent on his I.Q., so that one might for instance say: Below an I.Q. of 90 there is not a chance. And another thing: who would doubt that a child is or has a personality? Yet what else is an idiot but a man who is infantile and has thus remained a child?" [14]

The contributions of a personalistic existentialism to the abortion decision consists in a sharpening of our focus on the meaning and value of every human life and in a warning of the nihilistic implications of liberal abortion. Indispensable and controlling though these insights are, they are subject to ethical analysis and elaboration. Therefore, we next consider from the point of view of systematic theology the moral structure of the act of abortion.

Theological Determinants

Some authorization to kill the unborn child is found in most moral systems—even that of the Roman Catholic Church. The rationalizations may differ, but the fate of the unborn child is the same. Despite the insistence on the equal dignity of the fetus and despite the prohibition about the killing of the innocent, at least indirect abortion has been almost universally permitted.

The common ground has been the need to sacrifice the life of the child to save the life of the mother. Most moral systems, for example that of conservative Protestantism and Orthodox Judaism, make such an abortion an exception to the fundamental prohibition against the killing of the innocent. Roman Catholic moralists, in an attempt to preserve the prohibition against direct killing of the innocent, permit only indirect abortion. The rules justifying this indirect taking of innocent life were formulated in the principle of double effect, a well-established part of moral theology but a complex and controversial one.

A. The Traditional Formulation

Man's experience of an action having two effects, one good and one bad, is certainly older than his awareness of the possibility and problems of abortion. But the formulation of a moral principle to guide man's conduct in this area goes back only to the thirteenth century when Aquinas fashioned it in his *Summa Theologiae* to enable him to justify killings in self defense.[15] Two hundred years later, it next appeared in Cajetan's *Commentary on the Summa*.[16] From the sixteenth century, however, theologians began to apply the principle in an *ad hoc* way to various particular areas of moral concern. By the seventeenth century, it was frequently applied to problems arising over material cooperation, sexual pleasure, passive scandal, personal danger, and wartime killings. Domingo de Santa Teresa, in 1647, was the first to conceive of the principle as a general theological one. In his treatise on sins in the *Cursus Theologicus* of the Salmanticensis, he applied the principle specifically in determining when otherwise illicit sexual pleasure can be indirectly permitted for the sake of a proportionate good, but he also asserted its universal applicability.[17] In 1850, with the *Compendium*

Theologiae Moralis of John Gury, the principle finally reached its current maturity and formulation.[18] Nevertheless, the subsequent years have had their share of bitter dispute over the theoretical and practical aspects of the principle of double effect which, even today, is being radically reassessed. To analyze this principle in its present formulation, however, will enable us to assess, with historical perspective, its theological future, especially as it governs the abortion decision.

The principle of double effect is formulated as follows: When from a licit act there immediately follow two effects, one good and the other bad, and the good outweighs the bad, it is licit to intend the good and permit the evil. This definition can be broken down into four essential elements or conditions, all four of which must be present if the act is to be licit.

First, the intention must be good and not evil. Otherwise, one is purposely doing something evil. If morality means anything, such an act must be forbidden, for this first condition is simply a subjective restatement of the primary precept of morality: Do good and avoid evil.

Second, the act must be good or indifferent. Otherwise one is actually doing something evil and therefore forbidden, whatever the results of the action may be. If the first condition were not supplemented by this second one, the Machiavellian principle that the end justifies the means would be licit.

Third, the evil effect must not be the cause of the good effect. Otherwise, one would, in St. Paul's words, "do evil that good may come of it." (*Rom.* 3:8). This condition combines the first and the second and opposes Machiavellianism on a stage farther along.

Fourth, the good effect must outweigh the bad effect. Otherwise, the disproportion would bring more evil into the world than good. It would not be the avoidance of evil that is enjoined by the primary precept of morality but a doing of good that evil might come of it.

Three abortion situations help clarify the meaning of this

principle.[19] First, a woman has an operable cancer of the cervix. If the womb is removed before metastasis, in accord with accepted medical practice, the woman will live but the child will die. The abortive action may be performed, however, since the destruction of the child is indirect and unintended, is not caused by the good effect, and has a proportionately grave reason. Next, a woman has an ectopic pregnancy with a nonviable fetus in the Fallopian tube. The tube will certainly rupture and hemorrhage long before viability, thereby gravely endangering the lives of both mother and child. In such a case, the removal of the tube to prevent the hemorrhage is considered licit since the sacrifice of the child is only indirect. Finally, a pregnant woman has a serious kidney, lung, or heart disease and will die before she can bear her child to term. Although such a case would be a medical rarity nowadays, if it did occur, no abortion of the child could be permitted, since the killing would be direct.

In all three cases, the child's life is sacrificed to save the mother. In the first case, the womb happens to be cancerous—a fact not related to the child. In the second case, the child is the cause of the harm to the mother owing to its misplaced nidation. In the third case, the child's presence puts a lethal burden on the mother's already weakened constitution. But the decision to permit the sacrifice of the child in the first two cases but not in the third is not because of the degree of danger to the mother or because the child is the cause of the danger to the mother, but primarily because the causality involved is only indirect. The child cannot be killed directly for any reason—even to save the mother from imminent death. The child may be killed indirectly as the result of a licit operation for a proportionately good reason. Although the intention of the aborter is significant, the physical causality is primary. The doctor may not intend the death of the child; but even if his primary intention or motive is directed toward saving the mother, that fact does not make the killing of the child indirect if the child's death is the means whereby the mother is saved.

Clearly and emphatically, Catholic moral teaching forbids the direct killing of the unborn child. Authoritative contemporary statements are frequent. Pius XII wrote:

> Now the child, even the unborn child, is a human being in the same degree and by the same title as its mother. Moreover, every human being, even the child in its mother's womb, receives its right to life directly from God, not from its parents, nor from any human society or authority. Therefore, there is no man, no human authority, no science, no "indication," whether medical, eugenical, social, economic or moral, that can show or give a valid juridical title for a deliberate and direct disposing of an innocent human life . . . that is a disposition which looks to its destruction either as an end or a means to another end perhaps in itself not illicit.[20]

By the time that Pius XII had given the allocution to the midwives in 1951, Catholic moralists were in general agreement about the medico-moral aspects of abortion. This unanimity was the result of involved theological disputes and periodic Holy Office clarifications. The crucial period was from 1884 to 1902, during which time the Holy Office issued its major decisions on abortion, which decrees were both a response to theological controversy and an occasion of it. Gradually, however, the protection over the life of the unborn was extended to its present coverage, moving from the prohibition of craniotomy in 1884 and all direct killings in 1889, to the prohibition of the extraction of a nonviable fetus to save its mother in 1895 and 1898. The problem became more complicated with the 1902 decree prohibiting the removal of an ectopic fetus before the sixth month. What was spoken of here was the direct removal, but the question was hotly disputed whether or not an indirect removal was also illicit. Eventually, the silence of the Holy Office and the consensus of moralists indicated the liceity of the indirect abortion in this case, as in the case of a cancerous womb. It should not be thought, however, in viewing these decrees, that the Church was prohibiting for the first time such acts as craniotomy or direct abortions.

These responses, reflecting the traditional stand of the Church, were rather a strengthening of that stand, occasioned by the controversy over the interpretation and application of basic moral principles to more clearly understood medical facts.

T. Lincoln Bouscaren, the eminent dean of American canonists, was a most persuasive voice in the controversy and wrote a definitive text, *The Ethical Aspects of Ectopic Operations,* in which he presents in detail the magisterial and theological interaction.[21] The story of this controversy reflects the deepening awareness and articulateness of churchmen about the implications of the right to life.

B. The Current Challenge

The moral disputes continue. Even the abortion controversy among theologians is not completely dead. Most of the arguments trying to justify abortion are familiar, formulated perhaps in more contemporary language, but familiar nevertheless. They all attack one or another element in the basic moral principle: The direct killing of an innocent human being is prohibited. There are four main arguments to justify abortion: (1) The killing is not direct; (2) the fetus is not, at least in early pregnancy, a human person or is only doubtfully a human person; (3) the fetus in some cases is not innocent; and (4) the fetus in some cases has lost its right to another or has surrendered its right to another.

The first argument is that the killing in what is commonly called direct abortion is not really direct. The argument is one that the Jesuit moralist Lempkuhl used in justifying craniotomy before the Holy Office decree of 1884, but it owes its currency not to Lempkuhl but to Aquinas, who first suggested the principle of double effect. Historically, perhaps, Lempkuhl was accurate in following Aquinas, but the principle developed differently than someone in the thirteenth century might have suspected.

Aquinas was concerned with the right of a person to defend

himself, even to the point of taking another's life.[22] Although
he refers to an "attacker" who uses "violence," he did not limit
his principle to the formally or materially unjust aggressor. He
does not make a distinction between direct and indirect killing,
but his own criteria lend themselves to that dichotomy with the
unfortunate result that the direct-indirect formulation for some
refers to final causality in accord with Aquinas, and for others
it refers to efficient causality in accord with most modern Catholic moralists. His basic distinction is: "Moral acts receive their
species [character] according to what is intended, not from what
is beyond intention, since the latter is accidental." [23] His argument, easily applied to abortion as an act with two effects, is as
follows: "Therefore, from the act of someone defending himself
a double effect can follow: one is the preservation of his own
life, the other is the killing of the attacker. Such an act, wherein
one intends the preservation of one's life, does not have the character of the unlawful, since it is natural for everyone to preserve
himself in being as far as he can." [24]

Following the original Thomistic formulation, a therapeutic
abortion could be considered an indirect killing if done with
the direct intention of saving the life of the mother. The in-
directness would not by itself justify the abortion, but it would
certainly remove a major obstacle to that justification. For a few
contemporary moralists, this rationale, implemented by a balancing of interests, suffices. For example, one would classify an
abortion as indirect if there were a "commensurate reason" for
the causally direct killing. Such a reason is found by examining
values "in terms of the horizon of the whole reality." [25] Another
ignores the direct-indirect distinction to justify abortion as a
choice made in terms of "the community building or destroying
aspect of the situation." [26] Another referring to "conflict situations involving human life" justifies abortion by weighing values,
"even though the action itself aims at abortion 'as a means to
an end.'" [27]

Under the guidance of the Church, the Thomistic formulation

developed along lines other than intentionality and proportionate reason. The requirement of indirect efficient causality was incorporated into the principle of double effect, thereby limiting fetal destruction to very few instances. This addition reflects the magisterial evaluation of unborn life. In practice it limits indirect abortion to cases of cancerous womb and tubal pregnancy. In both situations there is, almost invariably, a factor which turns the balance of equality in favor of the mother; namely, that if the operation is not performed, both the mother and the child will die, but if it is performed, the mother will probably live. The fact that both would die is not sufficient by itself to justify a direct abortion, but it does seem sufficient to justify an indirectly permitted and unintended death. To protect that highly perishable human person, the unborn child, the principle of double effect becomes a weight which is always on the scales of decision. It is the handicap that all other arguments must overcome before the unborn child can be permitted to die. It seems less a principle and more of a conclusion—an almost irrebuttable presumption in favor of fetal life.

Sound judgment about the morality of abortion requires clear recognition of the subordinate position of the principle of double effect, for to exaggerate the function of the latter is to undermine man's primary right to life. The principle of double effect is a secondary one. The Christian community had convictions against abortion long before the principle of double effect was formulated. Yet this human construct enables us to solve problems occasioned by the fact that so much of our conduct, however well intentioned, results in both good and bad effects. The problem is crucial where life and death are involved. The principle is an attempt on the part of theologians to free us to do as much as possible, even though indirectly intended evil—in this case, the death of the unborn—results. In no way does the principle of double effect compete with the principle of the inviolability of innocent life.

In the debate over the morality of abortion, an imbalance has developed whereby the primary assumption is given less attention and held less important than the secondary implementation. The fight to justify abortion has centered in the arena of double effect, as if the discovery of a loophole here would be equivalent to divesting the child of its inalienable right to life. These narrow interpretations, however, must be tested outside the system of the double effect. Since we are dealing with human life, we must face it squarely and not endeavor to achieve liberalization as the tortured inference from a resurrected principle.

The second argument questions the human status of the unborn. Despite scientific and philosophical evidence of immediate animation, some deny or doubt this fact. We must, therefore, examine the moral implications of their position. Even when, from the twelfth to the nineteenth century, the penal laws of the Church reflected the theory of delayed animation, the moral opposition of the Church to all abortion from the time of conception was clear. The authoritative moral teaching of the Church has ever insisted on the grave sinfulness of even the earliest fetal destruction, as a radical disordering of the sacred processes of human generation. This sinfulness is present whether the embryo is a human person or not. The issue over the factual doubt is helpful primarily in deciding whether or not the sin is homicide. A principle of morality and common sense is that when there is a doubt of fact, the safer course must be chosen. This principle binds most strongly when another's life is involved. The purpose of the principle is to help us decide how to act when we lack knowledge about an important fact. Not to take the safer course implies a willingness to commit the sin or crime if the facts turn out as well they might. Sometimes the direction of the principle is misunderstood. The word "safer" implies to some that, for example in abortion, the comparison is made between the interests of the mother and those of the child, as if the moral question were: Is it safer for the family to risk killing an unborn person than to risk losing a wife and mother? This tangential reasoning misses the point of the principle, which indicates the safer course of conduct for one who wants to avoid sin or crime. In case of doubt about the existence of a person in the womb from conception, the moral choice will be to avoid the risk of killing a human being and to refrain from abortion.

The third argument is a denial of fetal innocence. Here the witness of the criminal law may help more than that of moral theology. A crime has two elements: a *mens rea,* or unlawful intention, and a *actus reus,* or unlawful conduct. Although the law does not punish *mens rea* alone, it may impose civil liability if there is an *actus reus* without *mens rea,* thereby sanctioning the actor for his unintended but unlawful conduct. An automobile fatality subjecting the driver to imprisonment if intended, may subject him only to tort damages if unintended, and even to no damages if he is excusable. The physical act was the same, but the responsibility in each case was radically different.

In view of these legal principles, what is the status of the fetus? The law does not use the technique of some moralists to justify abortion on the grounds that the fetus is an unjust aggressor. Anglo-American common law did allow abortion to save the life of the mother but not through the legal fiction of an act of self-defense. More realistically, it treated the case as one of duress of circumstances—the one exception to the rule of law which "forbids the intentional killing of an innocent person even to save the life of the slayer or the lives of several." [28] The law recognized the existence of circumstances which made it equitable to allow the child's life to be sacrificed for the life of the mother, thereby making one exception, the maternal exception, to the general rule. Many non-Catholic moralists have incorporated this practical norm into their own code of ethics. Some, including a few Catholics, however, have attempted to justify this inclusion on the grounds of self-defense.

Dr. Joseph Fletcher presents an illustrative case: an insane patient rapes and impregnates another insane patient. Can she justifiably get an abortion? Dr. Fletcher says she should be able to. He compares the child to a lunatic rapist running amuck. He finds no differences: "The embryo is no more innocent, no less an aggressor or unwelcome invader!" [29]

Let us compare the lunatic rapist and the rapist's illegitimate embryo, both of whom, Dr. Fletcher insists, can be justly killed in self-defense. Legally, a man who has been found not guilty by reason of insanity is held to have done the evil deed but without the evil intention requisite for criminal responsibility. The Model Penal Code of the A.L.I., section 4.01 formulates a test: A man is not responsible "if at the time of such conduct and as a result of mental disease or defect he lack substantial capacity either to appreciate the criminality of his conduct or to conform his conduct to the requirements of the law." [30] If a lunatic killer knew and could control his acts, he would be criminally guilty, for what he is doing is something a human being should not do. If he tries to do it to us, even though he is acting irresponsibly, we can protect ourselves, at his expense, against this objectively unjust and illegal aggression. The Model Penal Code, section 3.04 focuses on the *actus reus* and justifies the use of defensive force "when the actor believes that such force is immediately necessary for the purpose of protecting himself against the use of unlawful force by such other person on the present occasion." [31] A person then becomes an aggressor against whom one can use lawful force in self-defense, irrespective of the attacker's intent or motive, when he uses "unlawful force."

The unborn child's conduct, on the other hand, is neither immoral nor criminal. No law requires the fetus to stop growing. Even if the child knew fully what was happening, he would find it impossible to control his normal and natural embryological development. The child is doing what all children do. It is not solely the lack of an evil intention, an infantile *mens rea*, that makes the child innocent; it is primarily the lack of any evil deed, any even infantile *actus reus*. In total innocence, the child has an inviolable right to life. He forfeits this not by any principle of justice, but only by the principle of expediency.

The fourth argument focuses on an alleged conflict of rights between the mother and the child. The term used in current discussions is interests rather than rights. On the level of interests, the mother would more easily succeed because of the number and the quality of her claims and commitments. The older formulation of a conflict of rights paid lip service to the right to life in the very act of denying it. Appeal was made to the principle that where there is a conflict of rights, the stronger rights should prevail. The principle is workable where both parties have rights in the same thing, but no one can have rights in someone else's life. Such a right cannot be given up by the one or possessed by the other. In this area, mother and child are equals. Both have an equal right to life. Neither has the right of life or death over the other. To say that the stronger should prevail is, in practice, to allow direct killing on the grounds that might makes right.

Nor does the principle that the lesser of two evils should be chosen justify an abortion. The principle makes an obvious point. It states that the lesser of two physical evils should be chosen; that the lesser of two moral evils is preferable though still evil, for to rob may be less evil than to rob and kill, but it remains a serious crime; and that physical evil should be chosen rather than moral evil. Two natural deaths are a lesser evil than one murder. In the conflict of interests between mother and child, the rights of both to life must be preserved. The conflict cannot be resolved morally by the killing of the weaker party without thereby destroying all morality.

A corollary to the conflict of rights argument is that of the surrender of rights. The child is considered to have given up his life for the sake of a benefit to himself, for example, the opportunity to be baptized before its inevitably premature death, or more currently, the avoidance of the life of a rubella or thalidomide defective, or that of a ghetto dweller, or for the sake of a benefit to others, for the sake of his mother who will die or be mentally or physically unhealthy unless the child is aborted, or for his older brothers and sisters who will be economically deprived by the burden of his birth, or for society which is threatened with overpopulation. The reasoning behind this theory is flimsy: (1) The child has not given any consent at all to its destruction; (2) even if we use the fiction of interpretative intention, the child would have no more right to allow himself to be killed directly than he would have the right to commit suicide; and (3) the act of the one who kills the child, whatever the child's consent might be, would be a direct and therefore forbidden abortion.

Conclusion

The moral elements of the abortion question translate the facts of life into terms of good and bad. Morality adds to the findings of science a sense of obligation. We learn to use our freedom wisely in maximizing our values. Abortion is forbidden morally because it is an abuse of human power. It is a destruction of a human being by another human being, and as such strikes at the heart of human dignity. The usurpation of authority which is abortion is not wrong simply because it kills unborn children, but because it results in the vilification of all men. To give moral justification to abortion is to condemn all men to the level of expendable things. Morally, the fight against abortion is not primarily to protect the human dignity of the unborn, but is above all to safeguard that dignity in all mankind.

The true response to the fact of human life is reverence for life. To grasp the beauty and the dignity of human nature, however circumstanced, is to see the image and likeness of God. The depth of our insight into what it means to be human is measured, for the world to see, by the way we love one another. To those who love, the commandment, "Thou shalt not kill," is totally unnecessary. For those who kill, the commandment, "Thou shalt love thy neighbor as thyself" is indispensable.

Most men will accept, in principle, the moral prescription against destroying innocent human life, yet differ radically in their application of this shared conviction. A facile explanation of a pro-abortion mentality is an accusation of wickedness or cruelty or insensitivity. Yet among the ranks of those zealously promoting liberal abortion are men and women acutely sensitive to the sufferings of mankind, perhaps more sensitive to the sufferings of mankind than to mankind itself. So acutely aware are they of pain and anguish that they can more easily countenance a quick death than a protracted ordeal. The problem of evil has panicked them into seeking victory over suffering at any price, even at the price of killing members of the very human community they are dedicated to help. This tragic inconsistency is a betrayal of their finest ideals.

Their temptation or conviction, however, is understandable, for we live in a world with a built-in bias. Despite the highest ideals and the best intentions, otherwise acceptable actions frequently result in an unhappy combination of good and bad effects. Life, we discover, is not as simple or as straightforward as we would like it to be. But this is our life. Moralists faced with the actuality of double effects have worked out a principle of double effects to enable us to live reasonably, responsibly, and lovingly in a world of double effects. The principle helps us achieve a delicate balance: We are not totally incapacitated by a moral impasse, nor are we irresponsibly dispensed from moral choice. We are still bound by our basic insights into the reality of human dignity. We must always value the inalienable right to life. We cannot intentionally destroy this life directly or indirectly. Nevertheless, if the object of our intention and our action is good and reasonable, if the grounds for seeking it are compelling and proportionately grave, we are morally free to pursue our goal even if unfortunate and unintended effects result. The principle of double effect is by no means a casuistical trick to enable us to do indirectly what we cannot do directly. Its sole function is to enable us to do good things directly when the total situation justifies that direct action, despite the presence of bad effects as an unintended and indirect by-product of that good action. The thrust of moral theology is toward the positive and progressive maximization of human value through responsible choice. The moral choices, to be fruitful, however, must be in harmony with the basic insights into the dignity and equality of men. Morally, liberal abortion fails because it threatens the meaning and value of life, because it destroys equality among men by recourse to a despotic authority, because, in attacking the fetus, it atacks the principle of morality and the foundations of civilized life.

Chapter Five

THE PUBLIC INTEREST

I

The emotional impact of abortion sometimes impairs sound legal judgment. Even concrete facts and moral evaluations do not of themselves, however, necessarily produce good laws. For laws are not isolated units of behavioral guidance. Disparate as they may be—civil ordinances, zoning regulations, wrongful death statutes, intestacy provisions, excise taxes, criminal penalties, or constitutional amendments—laws are functional parts of a larger unity.

Laws do not fragment society, they unify it. In fact, law as a system of value judgments authoritatively implemented by sanctions is, first of all, directed to that most widely accepted value which is survival, to that minimal public order which is peace. Unless a political community survives in peace, the maximization of man's potentials which is optimal public order is impossible.

Society must examine proposed abortion laws calmly and must scrutinize their insertion into the legal fabric in terms both of the survival of the political community and the fulfillment of its destined role in maximizing human dignity. The main point of this chapter is that a sound political decision would oppose the passage of liberal abortion laws because they are against the public interest of the community, not merely because these laws are immoral but primarily because they undermine the basic principle of our democratic structure, the equal dignity of all men before the law and their legal right to equal opportunity for personal fulfillment.

Whether our ethical convictions are that "the direct killing of an unborn child is always immoral," or that "every woman has the right to abort a child she does not want," we are faced here with a political question which transcends the individual case: How do these permitted killings or the prohibition of them affect the common good? In order to answer this question, we must discover the fundamental principles at work in this crisis of decision-making. As sources of understanding and order, these principles will help delineate not only the areas of agreement and discord, but more important, the crucial political issue of the abortion decision. After considering these libertarian principles we will try to assess the compatibility of liberal abortion with our political commitment to human dignity. To do so, we consider specifically the legal status of the unborn and then, more generally, the political consensus on human equality: its positive platform in the United States and its negative embodiment in Nazi Germany.

The Libertarian Principles

Three general principles form the ideological context of the abortion decision. The first is: *Liberty is in possession; law must be justified.* Intelligence and freedom are the essential properties of human dignity. They distinguish man from the other beings of his immediate experience. A unique potential enables him to fulfill his destiny by maximizing his values through a process of reasonable and responsible decision. To achieve this fulfillment, man has recourse to law, although law restricts his precious liberty. Through law, man is able to reverse the inevitabilities of entropy and bring highly sophisticated islands of meaningful order into the universe. Without law, man's energies would dissipate into lukewarm mediocrity. There is no need here for an apologia for the rule of law in human society, but there is need to set up guidelines for allocating the priorities between the antinomies of law and liberty. In legal terms, one might say that the burden of proof is on the lawmaker. The presumption is that any restriction of liberty is bad; the lawmaker must rebut that presumption, and do so conclusively. That freedom is in possession means that compelling reasons are necessary to dislodge it from its place of preferment. If there be any doubt about the necessity for the law, we must give the benefit of that doubt to freedom. Thus the principle can be phrased: As much liberty as possible; as much law as necessary.

Abortion, then, is not forbidden by civil society unless it proves necessary to do so. The key word is "necessary." Because abortion has a significant moral dimension, an inevitable question arises concerning the role of morality in constituting the reguisite necessity. Two corollaries on this point should be noted briefly. (1) Morality *as such* should not be legislated. The positive law is not simply a deduction from the natural law or from the moral law or from some conceptual ideal. It possesses criteria of its own. Even a unitary society in total agreement about the validity of a moral precept should require more than ethical interests to justify establishing a parallel positive law. The second corollary complements the first. (2) Morality, *for appropriate reasons,* can be legislated. Mr. Justice Stewart, in *Griswold* v. *Connecticut,* made the point obliquely: "To be sure, the injunction contained in the Connecticut [birth control] statute coincides with the doctrine of certain religious faiths. But if that were enough to invalidate a law under the provisions of the First Amendment relating to religion, then most criminal laws would be invalidated." [1] In establishing necessity, morality is relevant, but it neither coerces nor disqualifies. Morality does not by itself constitute the necessity that is required for that restriction of liberty which is positive law. Liberty is still in possession unless law is justified by something more than reasons of conscience. The Wolfenden Report attempted to formulate for the criminal law that extra ingredient:

> In this field, its function, as we see it, is to preserve public order and decency, to protect the citizens from what is offensive or injurious, and to provide sufficient safeguards against exploitation and corruption of others, particularly those who are specially vulnerable because they are young, weak in body or mind, inexperienced or in a state of special physical, official, or economic dependence.[2]

This liberal position on the function of the criminal law has a traditional natural law parallel. Thirteenth-century Europe was far less libertarian and far less pluralistic than the present-day United States. The classical European statement on the relation of morals to the criminal law, however, is pragmatically modern. Thomas Aquinas formulates the basic question in a twofold way. He asks whether it pertains to human law to repress all vices or to prescribe the acts of all the virtues. In no way compromising his own moral convictions or denying the need for virtuous men in a healthy society, he adjusts his legal methodology to human beings as they actually are, to men who have both dignity and defects. His jurisprudence is existential, not mechanistic, as his general norm clearly indicates: "Law imposed on men should be in keeping with their condition, for law, should be possible both according to nature and according to the customs of the country."[3] He deals first with prohibitive laws:

> Now human law is framed for a number of human beings, the majority of whom are not perfect in virtue. Wherefore human laws do not forbid all vices from which the virtuous abstain, but only the more grievous vices from which it is possible for the majority to abstain; and chiefly those that are to the hurt of others without the prohibition of which human society could not be maintained. Thus human law prohibits murder, theft and suchlike.[4]

In answering the second question on positive commands, Aquinas focuses more sharply on the public interest as the touchstone of decision. His answer here complements the earlier statement on negative laws:

> Human law does not prescribe concerning all the acts of every virtue, but only in regard to those that are ordainable to the common good—either immediately, as when certain things are done directly for the common good, or mediately, as when a lawgiver prescribes certain things pertaining to good order whereby the citizens are directed to the upholding of the common good of justice and of peace.[5]

The libertarian reason, whether ancient or modern, for placing the heavy burden of legal justification on the shoulders of those who rule is that political power is given for the sake of the people and not for the sake of their rulers. Those in authority must act to help all men maximize their values in community. Political power is limited by the exigencies of the common good. But it is a good which is common to individuals. Although the law protects all, it has extra concern for the young, the weak, the inexperienced, the dependent—all those who are not adequately able to protect themselves from exploitation, corruption, and death. And who is younger, weaker, more inexperienced, and more dependent than an unborn child?

The second principle is: *Human equality is the first limitation on individual liberty*. The paradox of equal liberty is that it imposes equal restrictions on liberty. Men are alike not only in their freedom, but in the limitations which are protections of this freedom. The criminal law restricts my liberty so that I will not restrict the liberty of another. A crime inflicts harm on its victim in depriving him unjustly of life, liberty, or property. The victim of a crime, to a greater or lesser degree, finds his use of freedom diminished. The law, therefore, by its penal sanctions, tries to ensure the equal opportunity of each man for the free development of his potentials.

Despite our religious and moral pluralism, we in the United States, are committed, however imperfectly, to the principle of the equal dignity of all men. Only in terms of this principle is democratic absolutism, so feared by Jefferson, effectively avoided. Without the protection of minorities, democracy becomes another form of despotism, nonetheless real because the despots are in the majority and the minority yet unborn.

The third principle is: *An equal right to life is the first condition of individual liberty.* The recognition of the right to life of everyone in the community is fundamental to democracy. If the lives of the minority are not sacred and immune from violation, then no one is safe, for everyone is a member of some kind of minority. In fact, in our personal uniqueness, each one of us forms a minority of one. Our democratic ideals are impossible of full realization if the life of any minority member is in jeopardy simply because he is a member of a minority. Little comfort is given to the American Negro, whose race puts him in this precarious position. Indeed, the same unsettling realization should sooner or later dawn upon the American male who, since universal adult suffrage, finds himself politically outnumbered.

Traditionally, this right to life is forfeited by the commission of a capital crime. But even an accused is guaranteed due process and equal protection of the law. With but one exception the law has not allowed the taking of a totally innocent life. That exception is an abortion to save the life of the mother, with some few states granting an extension where there is proportionately grave danger to the mother's health. Although the law does excuse killings in self-defense even if, due to insanity, the unjust aggressor was not responsible for his otherwise criminal conduct, it does not class the maternal exception as self-defense. The ground is one of duress of circumstances without any imputation of even material culpability to the child. The law does not consider the fetus an unjust aggressor, but rather the unfortunate victim of circumstances beyond human control.[6]

These general principles of liberty, of equality, and of the right to life, structure for us the jurisprudential context of the abortion decision, but they do not make the decision for us. Their role is to help us focus with greater clarity and depth on the other issues that must be worked out before sound law can become a reality. Lawmaking is not the myopic setting up of unrelated directives with appropriate sanctions. One law, as the implementation of social policy, cannot be isolated from other laws. The unity of the body politic and the demands of the common good require consistency between individual laws and the over-all public interest. Ultimately, every law is tested in terms of the fundamental goals of society, whether found in a written constitution or in the broader political consensus. In that perspective, we face a crucial issue of the abortion decision: Is liberal abortion compatible with the political ideology of the United States?

II

To answer the question about the compatibility of liberal abortion and our political ideology leads us to consider two main areas: (1) the past trends and present state of the law governing the rights of the unborn; and (2) the fundamental political consensus regarding the dignity and equality of all men.

The Legal Status of the Unborn

How radical a departure from traditional law, liberal abortion proposals are, can be best seen from a cursory glance at the historically evolving consensus over fetal rights. In assessing the laws that manifest that consensus, we must remember that a moral right cannot always be equated with a legal right, nor a natural personality with a legal personality. Although legal personality is generally held to begin with birth, rights have been predicated of the unborn child, specifically in three different ways.[7] The Civil-law approach grants legal personality to the unborn child whenever its birth would be to its benefit, as in property law. Birth, however, is the donor of the right. The causal approach bypasses the problem of fetal status at the time of the injury and looks solely to the cause of the harm. At birth, the child has the legal personality which enables it to take advantage of this antecedently grounded right. The biological approach identifies the legal personality with the natural personality and thus easily protects the child at any time during its uterine life.

The attribution of legal personality is a statement that certain interests of the individual will be recognized and protected by the community. A legal personality is a creature of the positive law: It means what the law intends it to mean. Yet legal personality is not usually a mere fiction, even in the extreme case in which a corporation is considered to be a moral person for Fourteenth Amendment purposes.[8] This attribution is based on factual realities and implies a value judgment.

To study the legal rights of the fetus is to see the fetus through the eyes of the law. To give an unborn child a legal personality does not necessarily mean that the child has a human personality, any more than the classification of a slave in ancient Greece as a "human instrument" without legal personality deprived the slave of his human personality. Nevertheless, a consistent and growing recognition of fetal rights and an evolving legal personality for the fetus does argue forcefully that the community recognizes an underlying human personality. We cannot, however, press the argument too far, for the law is not simply a vehicle for legislating moral evaluations or scientific conclusions. It acts to fulfill community needs. The positive law, however, has clearly done one thing: It has set up a complex structure of protections and compensations for the unborn, thereby granting legal personality in pertinent areas of need. Liberal abortion, on the other hand, tears from the fetus this legal personality by depriving it of the traditional benefits which have accrued to it through positive law. In so doing, it has implicitly denied or ignored the vested legal rights of the unborn child, whose legal personality ought to have no less protection than does a modern corporation.

Frequently overlooked is the fact that Anglo-American law has always accorded legal rights to the unborn child—some from the very moment of conception. Like the rights of adults, fetal rights differ in scope, and like adult rights they have been an ever-present part of our legal system. Three areas of law grant rights to the unborn child: property law, criminal law, and tort law. The first two areas are relatively stable. The last, however, has shown an amazing evolution, a creative recognition of fetal rights.

Laws of property and decedent's estates have for ages guaranteed the right of an infant *en ventre de sa mère* to inherit without any restriction based on the stage of fetal development, though the rationale has varied with the times. In *The Earl of Bedford's case* (1586) we read: ". . . although *filius in utero matris est pars vicerum matris* . . . yet the law in many cases hath consideration of him in respect of the apparent expectation of his birth." [9] Blackstone spoke of the child in its mother's womb as being supposed in law to be born for many purposes: ". . . it is capable of having a legacy, or a surrender of a copyhold estate made it. It may have a guardian assigned to it; and it is enabled to have an estate limited to its use, and actually to take afterwards by such limitation, as if it were then actually born. And in this point the Civil law agrees with ours." [10]

The criminal law, as we have seen, protects the unborn child's right to life.[11] Originally, quickening, which occurs at the end of the fourth month, was required, but if subsequently, due to some poison or beating or other means, the child should die immediately after birth, the crime would be murder; if it were stillborn, the crime would be a serious misdemeanor. Statutes in England and in the United States eliminated the requirement of quickening. It is preserved in some states, however, as a determinant of the degree of punishment. The sole justification for abortion was the maternal exception. If that ground was not present the crime was a felony at whatever stage of fetal life. As soon as the child was born it was protected as fully as an adult by the general homicide laws. Frequently, additional laws have been passed to protect the child more easily by eliminating some of the evidentiary problems in distinguishing between abortion and infanticide and between accidental and culpable killings. These laws make it a crime to conceal the birth or the death of a child. The common law protected the unborn child, also, in an infrequent situation. If a pregnant woman was sentenced to death, she received a stay of execution until the child was born.[12] This contrasts with the Talmudic concern with the woman who despite the pregnancy would not receive a stay of execution because she was sentenced to die rather than to suffer as she would if she had to wait till the baby came to full term.[13]

Tort law, on the other hand, has manifested an inner dynamism which, contrasted with the relative stability of property law and criminal law, takes on a special significance. In 1884, the Massachusetts case of *Dietrich* v. *Inhabitants of Northampton* established a long-lived precedent by denying recovery for the wrongful death of a child injured before its birth. Judge (later Mr. Justice) Holmes quoted Coke, but refused to allow the criminal law analogy. It must be remembered, however, that the common law did not allow recovery even for the wrongful death of an adult. All such compensation was statutory. Holmes concluded with technical precision that "such child was not a 'person' within the meaning of Public statutes c. 52, § 17." [14] In 1900, Judge Boggs, dissenting in *Allaire* v. *St. Luke's Hospital,* an Illinois case, opposed the *Dietrich* holding and suggested that viability, creating a state of relative independence, should be the test for recovery.[15] It took almost fifty years for this suggestion to be adopted, but in 1949, the Minnesota Supreme Court became the first to allow recovery for the wrongful death of an unborn viable child in *Verkennes* v. *Cornelia.*[16] Today, even in Massachusetts, the *Dietrich* case is no longer followed. In Massachusetts, recovery was allowed in 1960 for the wrongful death of a viable child [17] and in 1967 for the wrongful death of a nonviable child.[18] Almost every state that has considered the question in the last two decades has allowed recovery.[19] Forty percent have allowed it only if the child was born alive, but 60 percent have allowed it even if the child was stillborn. All, however, require that the stillborn child be viable when the injuries occurred, with the exception of Georgia, which only requires quickening.

These wrongful death cases uphold the legal existence of the unborn child, for the action has been treated procedurally as a derivative one which is transmitted by the fetus to its beneficiaries at its untimely death. But a declaration of legal personality does not automatically make good law. These statutes, patterned after Lord Campbell's Act (1846), were intended to compensate the survivors, not the deceased victim. Logic does not demand that we apply the wrongful death statute to stillborn children. Whether or not the fetus has a legal personality is a false issue. The real question is whether or not there should be compensation to others for its wrongful death. There may well be, but it is a legal question not solved by biological facts.

No such juridical problem arises over compensating a plaintiff for prenatal injuries. If the injured fetus does not die, almost every state will allow recovery. Some jurisdictions require viability when the child is injured, but some allow recovery as early as the first month.[20] Since the child is especially vulnerable in the first trimester to many things, such as radiation, rubella, and thalidomide, the requirement of viability is unrealistic. It took a long time for the courts to allow recovery at all, however. In 1946, a District of Columbia court was the first to do so, in the case of *Bonbrest* v. *Kotz*. Referring to the Dietrich case and the notion that the child was part of the mother, the court said, "The law is presumed to keep pace with the sciences and medical science has made progress since 1884." [21] The court drew from the 1900 dissent of Judge Boggs in *Allaire* v. *St. Luke's Hospital* and from an influential 1933 Canadian case, *Montreal Tramways* v. *Leveille,* which held that no one should be forced to go through life bearing the seal of another's fault: "Therefore

when it was subsequently born alive and viable it was clothed
with all the rights of action which it would have had if actually
in existence at the date of the accident." [22]

Related to these actions for wrongful injury and wrongful
death is the action for wrongful birth. In the past, actions to impose liability for wrongfully causing one to be born have been
rare in tort litigation. In the future, however, such suits may
increase as the number of jurisdictions allowing liberal abortion
increases. A recognition of this possibility is suggested by the
"conscience clause" in recent liberal legislation which purports to
protect from liability doctors and others who refuse to perform
or permit an abortion which is against their moral principles.

Only a few cases have dealt squarely with the right not to be
born. No appellate court has allowed recovery against parents
or against nonparents. Most of the cases have concerned illegitimacy which, however, sets up a situation analogous to that
occasioned by a failure to abort.[23] In the suits by illegitimates,
there were two underlying difficulties: (1) The act that caused
the alleged harm took place before the conception of the plaintiff—five or six hours before he even existed; and (2) to permit
recovery, the court would have had to determine that nonexistence is preferable to existence as an illegitimate. The courts
had many other problems as well: the lack of precedents, the
tort rationale for the case, the measure of damages, and the
public policy against suits between members of the family, against
a proliferation of suits, and against encouraging abortion.[24]

Fortunately, it is possible for us to study the question of wrongful birth in a case concerning abortion, *Gleitman* v. *Cosgrove*,
which was decided by the Supreme Court of New Jersey in
March 1967.[25] It was a malpractice suit alleging the failure of
the doctors to inform the mother that it was possible for her
child to be born with birth defects. Her lack of information, she
claimed, deprived her of the chance to have an abortion. The
mother alleged that when she was two months pregnant, she
told her doctor that she had contracted German measles a month

before, but that he assured her that the disease would have no effect on her unborn child. At five months, she spoke to another doctor, also a defendant, who, she alleged, gave her the same reassurance. The child, however, turned out to be severely handicapped by sight, hearing, and speech defects, and perhaps to be mentally retarded.

The court made four basic assumptions for the purposes of its decision: (1) that the testimony of the plaintiffs was true—a procedural concession due to the fact that the trial was decided on the defendants' motion for judgment of dismissal, although, incidentally, there was evidence that the doctors told her that there was a 20 percent chance of child defects, but that they would not perform an abortion; (2) that the woman could have gotten an abortion for rubella somewhere that would not have subjected her to criminal sanctions but did not do so because of the defendants' statements; (3) that nothing the doctors could do would have changed the medical situation of the child; and (4) that the abortion was not necessary to preserve the life or health of the mother.

The New Jersey law made it a crime to perform an abortion "without lawful justification." The majority opinion stated: "The only justification so far held lawful by our courts is preservation of the mother's life." [26] Although the court expressed a clear bias against allowing eugenic considerations to control, it did so somewhat ambiguously.[27] "A good faith determination in accordance with accepted medical standards that an abortion is medically indicated" would apparently protect the physician from criminal liability.[28] Justice Francis, in a concurring opinion, took a stronger stand: "In my judgment the 'without lawful justification' exception applies only when the death of the mother can be reasonably anticipated to result from natural causes unless the child is destroyed." [29] In his dissent, Chief Justice Weintraub considered a eugenic abortion to be lawful but recognized the influence of the majority and concurring opinions: "When the highest court of the State even intimates the practice may be criminal, I would doubt that a reputable doctor or reputable institution would take the risk." [30] The holding in the case did not, however, turn on the illegality of the eugenic abortion.

Justice Proctor, in the majority opinion, took a less technical and more broadly human approach. He wrote: "The infant plaintiff is therefore required to say not that he should have been born without defects but that he should not have been born at all . . . that his very life is 'wrongful.' " [31] As for the measure of damages, the Justice wrote: "The infant plaintiff would have us measure the difference between his life with defects against the utter void of nonexistence, but it is impossible to make such a determination." [32] Although Chief Justice Weintraub dissented from the refusal to allow recovery by the child's parents, he concurred in the denial of recovery by the child: "Ultimately, the infant's complaint is that he would be better off not to have been born. Man who knows nothing of death or nothingness, cannot possibly know whether that is so. . . . To recognize a right not to be born is to enter an arena in which no one could find his way." [33]

The decision of the court was five to two against allowing the child to recover, because the conduct complained of did not give rise to damages cognizable by law. The decision was four to three against allowing the parents to recover, because they suffered no damage cognizable by law, and, even if they did, strong public policy prevented any recovery.

To summarize, the past trends and present state of American law concerning the rights of the unborn, especially manifest in tort law, is to equate the legal and natural personality. From a tort- or property-law point of view, this identity need not be so, but the fact that it is, highlights dramatically the great need to recognize the natural and legal personality of the unborn child before the criminal law, where its very life demands protection.

The Political Consensus on Human Equality

To understand the impact that our political commitment should make on the abortion controversy, we must consider two aspects of the consensus on human equality: its positive formulation in the United States, and its negative embodiment in Nazi Germany. But first we need some preliminary observations on the role of a consensus, because of the confusion that exists betwen the notion of public opinion or majority preference and that of consensus, and because of the general unawareness of the indispensable function of a political consensus in our society.

The word "consensus" has lost precision as it has gained in popularity. Adolf Berle, Jr., political theorist and presidential advisor, takes care to distinguish "public consensus" from "public opinion":

> "Public opinion" is sometimes misleadingly used as a syno-
> nym. Actually, public opinion is a shorthand phrase expressing
> the fact that a large body of the community has reached or may
> reach specific conclusions in some particular situation. These
> conclusions are spontaneously, perhaps emotionally reached,
> usually from some unstated but very real premises. The "public
> consensus" is the body of these general unstated premises which
> has come to be accepted. It furnished the basis for public opin-
> ion. Public opinion is the specific application of tenets embodied
> in the public consensus to some situation which has come into
> general consciousness.[34]

Berle speaks of limitation by public consensus, for every political and even economic organization must have a sense of self-
restraint or it will perish. This "public consensus" is "the
existence of a set of ideas, widely held by the community and
often by the organization itself and the men who direct it, that
certain uses of power are 'wrong' that is, contrary to the established interest and the value system of the community." [35] The
"real tribunal" which applies the public consensus, translating it

into public opinion and to which the American system is finally accountable, is made up of the "Lords Spiritual, the keepers and the developers of the public consensus." [36] These are the wise and the honest, the careful university professors, the well-trained specialists, responsible journalists, leaders of the business world, and respected politicians. Their concern is that core of conceptions and ideas that every organization essentially forms. As Berle said some years earlier, "A political force is a centrally attractive idea or conception, surrounded, or organized by, an apparatus." [37] Men must continue to select from among the political forces available, but "if they make a wrong selection, the chosen political force, soon or late, breaks up and disappears. In politics, as in nature, there is freedom to choose. In politics as in nature, bad selection weakens the ability to survive." [38]

Walter Lippmann focuses on this problem, which is at the root of our abortion controversy, in a somewhat different and perhaps more traditional way. The "public consensus," he calls "the public philosophy of civility" which good citizens accept and apply.[39] Consequently, all proposed legislation, such as a liberal abortion law, must be tested by this "public philosophy." Lippmann does not speak of the metaphysical abstractions of the professional philosopher but rather of the way of life of the body politic whose beliefs and values have inspired the great documents of the liberal democracies of the West from the Magna Carta to the Constitution of the United States.[40]

This public philosophy or public consensus is a dynamic principle informing and vitalizing our community life. It is a changing and evolving thing, a flexible instrument for perfectible man. The most serious problem that the abortion controversy poses is not on the level of the particular statute, be it restrictive or relaxed, but on the level of the public consensus. In making an abortion decision, we have the responsibility of looking long and penetratingly at the changes that easy abortion may ultimately bring to the public consensus. We must gaze upon this projected image of our society until we see it for what

it is in terms of the human dignity of all men. The abortion decision is not a snap judgment, an *ad hoc* resolution of a personal
crisis. It is a far-reaching policy determination about how to
evaluate men. We are rethinking our principles of life and death,
of freedom and despotism, as guidelines for the future of man.

A. The Positive Platform

After this brief excursus on the meaning and importance of
the public consensus, we are better able to estimate the ideological effect of liberal abortion laws on the political structure
of the United States. Walter Lippmann insists that if free institutions are to be preserved those who enjoy them must also
maintain them. Our citizenship is both a privilege and a responsibility.[41] We must be aware of the major values of our free
institutions if we are to be efficacious in protecting them against
the entropic effects of human negligence, selfishness, and domi-
nation.

The two elements of the American consensus that loom largest
and brightest on the political horizon and that characterize our
constitutional democracy are liberty and equality. Human dignity is an empty and mocking term unless it includes these two
properties. Despite the proliferation of wars and rebellions,
this age more than any other seems conscious of the demands
of human dignity. This century of technological marvels is also
the century of liberty. The *Declaration of Human Rights* of the
United Nations, the *Declaration of Religious Liberty* of Vatican
II, the steady progress in American civil and criminal courts in
protecting and fostering a multidimensional equal freedom before
the law evidence the evolving moral conscience of man and his
ever-deepening awareness of the implications of human dignity.

We have seen the new element that liberal abortion has introduced into the law. We have seen how property law, criminal law,
and tort law bear enduring witness to society's recognition of the
rights of the unborn. The question is: Can we deprive this voice-

less minority of its vested rights? Should not these traditional rights continue to be protected in this age of liberty and equality? Does not the Constitution itself prevent this abridgment?

The Constitution of the United States helps us center on the basic issues. This constitution has, as have most modern constitutions, two functions: the creation and maintenance of authority, and the declaration and maintenance of community ideals. These two functions establish both the process of authoritative and controlling decision as well as the fundamental ideology or policy judgments upon which decision is based. Change is still possible. Political structures and ideals are creatures of the community. But in a constitutional democracy radical change, a reversal in fundamentals, is purposely made difficult. A built-in stability tends to preserve this society precisely as this society. The Constitution of the United States articulates, develops, and preserves the community decision on human dignity spelled out so clearly in the Declaration of Independence: "We hold these truths to be self-evident, that all men are created equal, that they are endowed by their Creator with certain inalienable Rights, that among these are Life, Liberty and the pursuit of Happiness."

The Preamble to the Constitution speaks of the resolve to "secure the blessings of liberty to ourselves and our posterity." The Seven Articles do not explicitly deal with the two concepts of liberty and equality, but the Fifth and the Fourteenth Amendments do. The wording of both is substantially the same. The Fifth limts the power of the federal government; the Fourteenth limits the power of the states and adds a guarantee of equality. The Fifth reads: ". . . nor shall any person . . . be deprived of life, liberty, or property without due process of law. . . ." The Fourteenth reads: ". . . nor shall any State deprive any person of life, liberty, or property without due process of law, nor deny to any person within its jurisdiction the equal protection of the laws." The universal scope of these historic words is obvious, referring to "all men," to "ourselves and our posterity," and to "any person."

The growing sensitivity of Americans to the rights of minorities characterizes U.S. constitutional history. Most conspicuous is the struggle over civil rights for Negroes. There has been, despite innumerable delays and setbacks, tremendous progress since Lincoln emancipated three million slaves on January 1, 1865 toward ever-increasing recognition of equality. A valid analogy exists between the struggle over Negro rights and the struggle over fetal rights, but since it is only an analogy there is an important difference. A primary reason why the unborn should have these constitutional protections is rooted in the legal character of the civil rights which have been possessed by the unborn from the earliest days of the common law up to the present. The controversy over liberal abortion is essentially a power struggle, specifically a struggle over vested rights. It differs radically from the slavery question of the last century. The abolition of slavery gave legal rights to those who never possessed them; the liberalization of abortion abolishes the legal rights of those who have possessed them for centuries. The child and its father are being deprived of rights almost exclusively in favor of the will of the mother. For example, abortion on demand would mean that a woman could deprive her child of the fortune that he would have inherited from his willing father and even deprive him of his life for no other reason than that she does not want to bear the child. The traditional protections of property law and criminal law are torn from the child. Liberal abortion proposals, above all abortion on demand, are a qualified kind of outlawry—an ancient British proceeding which put a man beyond the protection of the law and permitted him to be killed by anyone at any time. But outlawry was for criminals, and as Mr. Justice Fortas said in a dissent in *Powell* v. *Texas,* a case on alcoholism, "Criminal penalties may not be inflicted upon a person for being in a condition he is powerless to change." [42] Admittedly, the mother's role in the mystery of generation is special;

the traditional justification for abortion took cognizance of this difference; but motherhood can never justify despotic dominion over fetal life and death. An innocent life should never be sacrificed on the altar of expediency.

Societies and individuals within them often possess blind spots in matters of right and justice that shock the dispassionate observer. H. L. A. Hart, the Oxford jurist, illustrates this point from the writings of Mark Twain: "Huckleberry Finn, when asked if the explosion of a steamboat boiler had hurt anyone, replied, 'No'm; killed a nigger.' Aunt Sally's comment, 'Well it's lucky because sometimes people do get hurt,' sums up a whole morality which has often prevailed among men." [43] The frequent reference to abortion as a "crime without victims" shows that this moral blindness is still possible. In sharp contrast are the words of John F. Kennedy, uttered in a time of interracial crisis: "This nation . . . was founded on the principle that all men are created equal, and that the rights of every man are diminished when the rights of one man are threatened." [44] The liberalization of abortion initiates an ideological revolution. Our political union for civil liberties is in principle rent asunder by this partisan selectivity.

The U. S. Supreme Court may not decide the constitutionality of liberal abortion laws, at least for some time. But the Fourteenth Amendment is not, for that reason, ineffectual in the abortion controversy. As a social ideal, it forces us unceasingly to rethink our practices and to refine our community conscience.

B. The Negative Embodiment

Liberal abortion rests on principles, not of equality and freedom, but rather of discrimination and utility. The principles that all do not have equal rights but that some can be sacrificed for the benefit of others has been used in the past far beyond the area of abortion to justify the killing of infants, of mental and physical defectives, of the sick and the aged, of supposed genetic or racial inferiors, and of unproductive consumers. It is too easy to decry as odious and unfair comparisons between liberal abortion proposals and, for example, the practices of the Third Reich. Yet we are now more than halfway between 1945 and 1984; and as Santayana wrote, "Those who do not remember the past are condemned to relive it."

Putting mutual recriminations aside, we ought calmly to be able to examine liberal abortion to see whether or not it would give a legal precedent and procedure for other kinds of socioeconomic or eugenic killings. Since many proponents of liberal abortion are extremely upset at any reference, however qualified, to Nazi practices, certain preliminary statements are necessary so that the climate of. mutual concern will not be replaced by one of fruitless antagonism. First, liberal abortion, even abortion on demand, does not necessarily lead to any other kind of eugenic or socioeconomic killing. Lawmaking is a process of drawing guidelines in which logic is a flexible servant, not a master. Second, the proponents of liberal abortion do not necessarily want any other kind of eugenic or socioeconomic killing. The humanitarian motives of most such proponents are beyond criticism. They are not "Big Brothers," or sadists, or crypto-Nazis, but rather dedicated persons intellectually and emotionally involved in alleviating obvious suffering. Third, and this factor is the crucial one, the principles used to justify liberal abortion can just as readily justify the other kinds of eugenic and socioeconomic killings.

The operative idea in liberal abortion is to eliminate the problem by eliminating the problem child. The oldest expedient of all, destruction, is the "final solution" to the perennial problem of the unwanted, those persons who are judged to be harmful or useless to society. The contagious power of this lethal idea prompts us to turn to recent history to show how easy it is for man to betray his own dignity. It is a psychological oversimplification to attribute the scourge of cruel and undeserved deaths at the hands of the Nazis to a spontaneous deviation of the

Germanic mind. Long before the mass exterminations were perpetrated the ideological motivation, the legal structure, and the institutional framework were ready and waiting. The idea was not new. In 1920, when Hitler was thirty-one and when his memorandum on "mercy killings" was two decades in the future, a jurist and a psychiatrist, Karl Binding and Alfred Hoche, published a book in Leipzig which was so popular that two years later there was a second edition. The title, *The Release of the Destruction of Life Devoid of Value,* awkwardly but accurately summed up the argument: The law should not penalize the killing of those whose lives are worthless. The work, widely discussed and scientifically defended, was symptomatic of the moral and political climate during the years of Hitler's early manhood. There is no conclusive evidence that Hitler actually read the book; nevertheless, its thesis somehow became a major policy of the Third Reich. The development was by stages, according to a technique already envisaged in *Mein Kampf*—the use of intermediate or tactical goals whereby procedures unacceptable in completed form are enacted piecemeal. Each stage of legislation, ostensibly the last, is eventually qualified to conform to the original over-all plan. Looking back, it is easy to see long-range premeditation, for the mass murders were the logical, although not inevitable, development of earlier legislation.

The sterilization law of July 14, 1933 was a crucial step in this creeping legislation which led to the death camps.[45] The title, "Law for the Prevention of Offspring with Hereditary Diseases," gave little hint of the lethal techniques of "prevention" that would eventually be devised and the broad interpretation that would be given to the words, "hereditary diseases." The pattern, however, had been set. The grounds for sterilization were broad and flexible: mental deficiency from birth, schizophrenia, circular (manic-depressive) lunacy, hereditary epilepsy, hereditary St. Vitus's Dance, hereditary blindness or deafness, serious hereditary physical malformation, and severe alcoholism. The diseased person himself, or more significantly, a civil service doctor or the head of a sanitorium or nursing home for its inmates, could make the application for sterilization. A Eugenics Court and a Eugenics High Court were to hold hearings and consider appeals. The strength of the law was in Paragraph 12: "Once the court has finally decided on sterilization, it must be carried out even against the will of the person to be sterilized." This law was signed by Adolf Hitler and by Wilhelm Frick, the Minister of the Interior, who was to be primarily responsible for the "mercy killings."

The eugenic program quickly moved from those unfit to produce life to those unfit to enjoy life. The monstrous step to euthanasia followed the pattern established by the sterilization law: a eugenic purpose—the sociomedical betterment of the nation; a broad classification of the unfit; institutional facilities already established for sterilization; and psychiatrists willing to determine the value of human lives. In the very beginning, Jews were not allowed to enjoy the "benefits" of this euthanasia program, but shortly the machinery of mercy killing was put to work on the "final solution to the Jewish problem." Once a judgment of worthlessness could justify eugenic killings, the move from medical to sociomedical and socioeconomic indications demanded only a minor rationalization. Racial extermination was as logical as sterilization, and certainly on an ethical par with the killing of "useless eaters."

The millions of Jews murdered overshadows the significant number of German victims. In both situations, the public interest —the purifying and protecting of the race—was the justification for this grossly discriminatory sacrifice of human lives. The well-being of the Third Reich allegedly necessitated the extermination of the unfit. The Czechoslovak War Crimes Commission made a detailed statement on the killing of ill and aged people in Germany: "There were—after careful calculation—at least two hundred thousand mainly mentally deficient, imbeciles, besides neurological cases and medically unfit people—these were not only the incurable cases—and at least seventy-five thousand aged people." [46]

The commission attributed these deaths to a secret law issued in the summer of 1940. Whether this was ever a binding command is disputed. There is extant, however, a signed memorandum by Hitler, dated September 1, 1939: "Reichsleiter Bouhler and Dr. Brandt M.D., are charged with the responsibility of enlarging the authority of certain physicians to be designated by name in such manner that persons who, according to human judgment, are incurable can, upon a most careful diagnosis of their condition of sickness, be accorded a mercy death." [47]

Whether given full authorization or not, the extermination of the unfit was a public secret, known to the German people, to their rulers, and to many outside Germany. In 1940, the Holy Office of the Catholic Church in Rome was asked "whether it is licit, upon order from the public authority, to kill directly persons who, although they have committed no crime which merits death, are nevertheless, owing to psychic or physical defects, unable to be of any use to the nation, and are judged rather to be a burden to it and to be an obstacle to its vigor and strength." The reply, approved and confirmed by Pope Pius XII on December 2, 1940 and ordered to be published; was: "In the NEGATIVE, since this is against the natural law and the divine positive law." [48]

On August 13, 1941, Bishop Hilfrick of Limburg wrote a letter to the German Minister of Justice. Copies were also sent to the Minister of Church Affairs and the Minister of the Interior. The latter, Wilhelm Frick, was the creator and head of the German police as well as the highest controlling authority over concentration camps. Through his medical division, he controlled the Nazi asylums and medical institutions in which the mass sterilizations and "mercy killings" occurred. The letter of Bishop Hilfrick, later used as evidence in the Nuremberg trials, did not lessen the killings, but it did testify to the operation of one such factory of death. He wrote in part:

About 8 kilometers from Limburg, in the little town of Hada-mar, on a hill overlooking the town, there is an institution which had formerly served various purposes and of late had been used as a nursing home; this institution was renovated and furnished as a place in which, by consensus of opinion, the above-men-tioned Euthanasia had been systematically practiced for months —approximately since February 1941. . . .

Several times a week buses arrive in Hadamar with a con-siderable number of such victims. Schoolchildren of the vicinity know this vehicle and say: "There comes the murder-box again." After the arrival of the vehicle, the citizens of Hadamar watch the smoke rise out of the chimney and are tortured with the ever-present thought of the miserable victims, especially when repulsive odors annoy them, depending on the direction of the wind.

The effect of the principles at work here are: Children call each other names and say, "You're crazy; you'll be sent to a baking oven at Hadamar." Those who do not want to marry, or find no opportunity, say, "Marry, never. Bring children into the world so that they can be put inside the bottling machine." You hear old folks say, "Don't send me to a state hospital! After the feeble-minded have been finished off, the next useless eaters whose turn will come are the old people." [49]

In the evolution of this methodical destruction, psychiatrists played a predominant role. They were discussing ways and means long before the killings were ever permitted. They were the enthusiastic supporters and innovators once the permission was granted. Frederic Wertham sums up their unbelievable con-tribution:

They were the legislators who laid down the rules for deciding who was to die, they were the administrators who worked out the procedures, provided the patients and places, and decided on the methods of killings; they pronounced a sentence of life or death in every individual case; they were the executioners who carried the sentences out, or—without being coerced to do so—surrendered their patients to be killed in other institutions; they supervised and often watched slow deaths.[50]

Paradoxically, under the Nazis the sanctions for abortion were increased. The Penal Code of 1871 recognized no justification for abortion at all. In 1926, these sanctions were lowered by Parliament. On May 9, 1943, the Nazis raised the sanctions against abortion. The reasons for the change in the law were consistent with the legalization of euthanasia. Even this move against the liberalization of abortion was based on principles of expediency rather than respect for life and for human dignity. It was a question of underpopulation, a wartime manpower shortage. Significantly, Jews were exempted from the abortion prohibitions.

In recalling the horrors of Nazi inequality, we sometimes experience a sense of ambivalence; we want to believe that it could never happen here, yet we are sensitive to indications that it might happen here. Two examples will illustrate the response that certain suggestions have elicited. In California in 1967, Governor Ronald Reagan refused to sign an abortion bill passed by the state legislature until it removed a provision permitting abortion when there was a grave danger of fetal defects because, he said, it was "only a step away from what Hitler tried to do." Secondly, some Negro militants have stated that the motivation of some of the proponents of liberal abortion is genocidal. It certainly is possible to put strong pressure on poor people who happen to form racial groups to force them to adopt family planning procedures, even those involving abortion. Recent Maryland legislation has taken cognizance of the possibility of economic coercion being used to force the poor into undergoing abortions. It has a provision stating explicitly that the refusal of a person to submit to abortion may not be used as a basis for denying any public benefits to such person.

If we look at the actualities instead of the labels, if we look at the principles instead of the motivations, we find that liberal abortion reveals a fearsome kinship with Nazi practices, whereby human life and human dignity become a mere function of political and socioeconomic expediency. That similarity does not imply, however, that liberal abortion is genocidal, as has been suggested. Although article II of the Genocide Convention speaks of the measures imposed to prevent births and includes sterilization, castration, contraception, and abortion, a necessary element in genocide is the intention to destroy in whole or in part a national, ethnic, racial, or religious group. The allegation that liberal abortion is genocide is more rhetorical than realistic. The real point of similarity, if we have to compare the two, is that both of them rest on principles of discrimination and utility. Both are techniques of expediency whereby the weaker are sacrificed for the sake of the stronger.

III

In conclusion, a final question must be answered: Have we in emphasizing the crucial role of the power struggle, of the political dimension of liberal abortion, managed to bypass that jurisprudential trouble spot which is the relation of law and morals? I do not think so. Actually, law and morals are harmonized through the public policy of society. Liberty is still in possession and morality is enforceable only if the common good of society requires it. Our constitutional democracy is structured on an essentially moral component of the common good—the equal dignity of all men before the law. Fundamental to our political ideology is the proposition that in a society of equals no man is expendable. Our society cannot assimilate the Nazi notion of "useless mouths." Nor can it play the diabolical game of marking undesirables for extinction. The thrust of liberal abortion is to the heart of the democratic community. "If we are to keep our democracy," Judge Learned Hand insisted, "there must be one commandment: Thou shalt not ration justice."

An abortion decision must be made. In fulfilling this awesome responsibility, let us be aware not only of the pathetic vulnerability of the unborn but also of the precariousness of our own political achievement. For ultimately, liberty that is not shared is lost.

Chapter Six

THE LEGAL IMPLEMENTATION

Law has a dual function: It points a finger and it makes a fist. The primary or normative prescription requires the secondary or sanctioning prescription. Although most obvious in the area of crime, this duality is characteristic of all law, Torts, breaches of contracts, ultra vires corporate acts, imperfectly drawn deeds to land—each item of disorder has its sanction to the extent that it involves an interest protected by the state. Society for survival and for progress needs more than good advice: It must have machinery to enforce sound patterns of conduct.

The formal structure of the crime of abortion is clear. The prohibition, the exceptions, the persons protected, the persons to be punished, and the penalty, usually appear on the face of the statute. As do all laws, abortion laws implement a social policy giving preference and priority to one set of values rather than to another competing set of values. Legislation, however, is not usually a simply once-and-for-all verbalization of community goals. Law-making is a continuing process, a constant working out of the competing claims of human interaction for the maximization of the common good.

How difficult a task this harmonization of interests is, can be seen from the great variety of legal solutions to the same identical problem. Occasionally someone remarks that the diversity of abortion laws proves either the impossibility of legislating in this area at all or the defectiveness of most present laws. It proves neither. The United States has more than fifty different jurisdictions, so when we speak of American law, for example, regarding divorce, liquor, or automobile insurance, we do so only on a comparative basis. This diversity is inevitable as long as communities are free to make the laws by which they are ruled. The states which have already liberalized their abortion laws have followed the American Law Institute's Model Penal Code but each in its own way, with changes in many details and in some major provisions.

Our task is to work out legal guidelines for a sound abortion decision. Preliminary insights and evaluations, the contribution of history, science, philosophy, morality, and politics are wasted unless we make a policy judgment. Academicians leisurely argue the pros and cons, but lawmakers must arrive at a decision. Even to do nothing is to make a choice. As participators in the decision-making process, we must determine our legislative stand on abortion. Our responsibility is to implement with justice a policy arrived at through wisdom and love.

In earlier chapters, we considered many legal aspects of the abortion decision: the history of the abortion laws, their social and political implications, and their practical results. Here, we consider more specifically the legal implementation of community policy. In doing so, we ask four questions: First, what is the effect of traditional laws, although they are not fully enforced? Second, what is the effect of the two types of liberal proposals, the extreme and the moderate? Third, what are the merits of a substantive compromise on a moderate proposal to avoid an extreme enactment? And finally, what procedural amendments must be appended to a liberal law so that it does not overstep its substantive boundaries?

I

When the discussion over the liberalization of abortion reaches an impasse on the level of science, morality, or politics, a simple pragmatic resolution is sometimes suggested. The argument runs: Since traditional abortion laws are unenforced and unenforceable, they should be repealed as useless dead letters which bring true laws into disrepute. Here are a series of observations to explain the wisdom of upholding the present laws, although, admittedly, they have not solved our sociomedical crisis.

1. No abortion law, traditional or liberal, will solve all the problems that cluster about an unwanted pregnancy. Laws are not magical incantations that make wickedness and suffering disappear. Laws are but one part of a larger synthesis, one of the many means of persuading citizens to be law-abiding. Education, religion, health, economic security, work, recreation, and affection, are some of the other factors that keep people from breaking the law. They are more important than the criminal code in doing so.

2. The sanction, even in an abortion law, is the last step in a process which, at least in the individual case, has failed. Every time that the law imposes a sanction, it deprives a person of good things because of his guilt in doing bad things. It restricts freedom because of an abuse of freedom. But to concentrate on punishment is to concentrate on the wrong end of the criminal process. If the success of a criminal code were measured by the number of punishments it imposed, seventeenth-century England with its rash of hangings would be the golden age of English criminal law. The true test of the efficacy of an abortion law is not how many people it punishes but how many abortions it prevents.

3. Abortion statistics do not tell us how well or how poorly the present laws function in preventing illegal abortions or how well moderate abortion laws would succeed in doing so. The available statistics on illegal abortions run from two hundred

thousand to one million two hundred thousand. Clearly, we are ignorant of the function of the traditional abortion laws.

4. Abortion is a particularly difficult area to control by legal means. The abortionist and the woman conceal their complicity. The victim dies and disappears before its existence is publicly known. With no complainant and no witness, the prosecutor has not even a *prima facie* case. When an offense is reported, if it does not involve an abortion mill or a maternal injury or death, the prosecutor will frequently use his discretion for leniency, as he does in other areas of the criminal law.

5. Abortion is not unique in its unenforceability. Some comparisons will help us keep abortion laws in perspective. For example, perjury is rarely prosecuted, though it daily vitiates civil, criminal, and family court proceedings. Obscene and abusive phone calls total in the millions with relatively few prosecutions, despite laws against such calls in all fifty states. Each year there are over three million complaints of larceny. At least that many more, and perhaps double or triple that number, go unreported. The number is growing: Grand larceny has increased 107 percent in the years 1960–66. Significantly, only about 10 percent of the reported crimes are cleared by a conviction.[1] Is larceny a dead-letter law that should be abolished because it is unenforceable?

6. Traditional laws do keep down the number of fetal deaths. With liberalization, there is a great increase in the number of legal abortions. In California, for example, there were about six hundred abortions a year before liberalization. Under the new statute, there were about five thousand the first year. In Colorado, the increase in legal abortions was twentyfold. On the other hand, the number of illegal abortions does not seem to diminish appreciably, especially under the moderate A.L.I. type statute which, it is generally conceded, would justify, if honestly applied, only about 15 percent of the illegal abortions now performed. Finally, even in the foreign jurisdictions which have adopted abortion on demand, the total number of fetal deaths has in-

creased. Traditional laws, then, do limit the number of abortions performed.[2]

7. Though neither fully enforced or enforceable, traditional laws do impede the move toward liberalization, above all toward the ultimate liberal goal—abortion on demand. Since traditional laws are in possession, it takes much legislative effort to dislodge them. When, however, the process of liberalization begins, drastic reversals of policy can be introduced gradually by the technique of "creeping legislation" or what Wilbur Cohen, the former head of the Department of Health, Education, and Welfare, calls "slicing salami." Within a year after liberalization in California and Maryland, energetic and well-organized movements for abortion on demand have appeared. Former proponents of the moderate law are now its harshest critics. The lines of battle have formed once more but much nearer to full permissiveness. A strong stand against moderate liberalization postpones the confrontation over extreme liberalization.

8. The symbolic power of a criminal law is of immense help in the abortion controversy. A criminal law establishes a public policy. It indicates the community judgment that certain actions are socially harmful, that certain interests merit political protection. Traditional laws commit society to a high valuation of unborn life. To call abortion a crime and to list it under culpable homicide is to communicate a public censure of abortion. Likewise, to remove abortion from the criminal code and to make it a private medical matter communicates a neutral and even favorable attitude toward abortion. Jurists are familiar with the function of the legal label; for instance, vehicular homicide statutes were enacted because jurors were reluctant to convict a negligent motorist of an offense that sounded as wicked as manslaughter. In the Model Penal Code, proponents of liberal abortion transferred abortion from the section on criminal homicide, not to the section on offenses involving danger to the person, but to the section on offenses against the family, such as bigamy, polygamy, incest, endangering the welfare of children, and persistent non-

support, all nonlethal with the exception of abortion.[3] This move was covert recognition of the strength of a law simply because it is a law. It is stronger than a moral precept because it is a community commitment.

In brief, then, the value in upholding traditional laws against abortion is twofold: They limit the number and the spread of abortions, and they declare the community evaluation of fetal life. In this delimitative and declarative role, the traditional laws are a strong political force, a dynamic safeguard of human dignity and equality. Dr. Allan Guttmacher, president of the Planned Parenthood Federation, made an observation about a reform law, which, however, also suggests the function of traditional law: "The law doesn't determine the number of abortions as much as it does the attitude of the hospital and the doctor." [4] It is the attitude of the community about human dignity and equality that determines the kind of world we will live in.

II

Since we have seen the arguments for keeping the traditional laws on the books, we look next at the proposed changes in the law. Reform, however, can take many directions. Few seriously agitate for a complete legal prohibition of all abortions, even when performed to save the life of the mother. Similarly, few want abortion laws so permissive that anyone at all can operate on a pregnant woman. The absolutist position, whether prohibitive or permissive, is generally rejected. The confrontation, therefore, is between those who uphold the present strict laws and those who want broader grounds of justification.

Proponents of liberal abortion are divided into two camps. The extreme position, most notably that of the American Civil Liberties Union, is that of abortion on demand, qualified only by accepted medical standards. The moderate position, most notably that of the American Law Institute, is that of specific legislatively determined grounds. Although the moderate view has had the most adherents and has been enacted, at least in part, in six states, more and more proponents of liberal abortion are admitting a preference for abortion on demand. In practice, the differences between the two positions tend to disappear, but since they are conceptually distinct, we shall consider them separately.

The Extreme Position

The most radical of the proposals for relaxing the abortion laws is abortion on demand: "No woman should bear a child she does not want." Here is the final "emancipation of the female," giving her complete autonomy over her body. Contraception and abortion free her from the burden of child-bearing that has kept her in traditional dependence. Now she will be truly equal to the male. But even extreme permissiveness draws the line at illegal abortions—those resulting from the unauthorized practice of medicine. The model statute drawn by the American Civil Liberties Union (June 1967) illustrates this radically minimal prohibition:

A. It is a civil right of a woman to seek to terminate a pregnancy, and of a physician to perform or refuse to perform an abortion, without the threat of criminal sanctions.

B. Abortions should be performed only by doctors, governed by the same considerations as other medical practices.

The A.C.L.U. justifies its position positively be asserting the interests to be protected, and negatively by attacking the constitutionality of the traditional abortion laws.[5] First of all, the interests are those of the parents, primarily the woman. In a policy statement, the A.C.L.U. said that its efforts to abolish all laws imposing criminal penalties for abortions performed by licensed physicians for any reason "rest solely on our desire to protect and advance civil liberties—in particular the rights of privacy and equality and the freedom of each individual to decide for what purposes her body should be used." [6] The liberty and equality of the fetus is considered irrelevant. Second, the constitutional attack is nothing if not broadly based. Traditional laws are allegedly unconstitutional for the following reasons: they are too vague; they deny equal protection to lower socioeconomic groups; they are unreasonable and arbitrary toward the parents and to the doctors who cannot practice medicine according to their best professional judgment; they violate the interest of marital privacy protected by the *Griswold* v. *Connecticut;* they are violative of the First Amendment and the guarantee of separation of church and state because there is no valid reason for the existence of the abortion laws. In California, the A.C.L.U. affiliate summed up the case against the traditional statutes with numerical efficiency: the laws are unconstitutional because they violate the right to privacy guarantees of the First, Third, Fourth, Fifth, Ninth, and Fourteenth Amendments to the Constitution of the United States.

This right to privacy is the nub of the A.C.L.U. case against abortion laws. Here is a reactionary return to the *patria potestas* of the Roman Empire, but there is a modern twist. It is the *materfamilias* who makes the final decision over fetal life or death. In fact, there is a depaternalization of the American male in these proposals, for he is denied his equal rights as a parent about whether his offspring will live or die.

Since *Griswold* v. *Connecticut* and its frequently misunderstood right to marital privacy has a central role in the cerebrations of the A.C.L.U., it will be helpful in assessing the strength of the argument it uses to consider the basis for them in the case itself.[7] This analysis is especially necessary since there is a superficial similarity betwen the Connecticut birth control statute and typical abortion statutes.

The defendants in *Griswold* were arrested as accessories before the fact. They had given information, instruction, and medical advice to married persons as to the means of preventing conception. The substantive crime was formulated in Section 53-32 of the General Statutes of Connecticut (1939): "Any person who uses any drug, medicinal article or instrument for the purpose of preventing conception shall be fined not less than fifty dollars or imprisoned not less than sixty days nor more than one year or to be both fined and imprisoned." The Supreme Court, in 1965, reversed the conviction of the defendants on the grounds that the statute unconstitutionally intrudes on the right of marital privacy. The majority was unable to decide on the exact constitutional rationale for its reversal, yet all agreed that there was a right to marital privacy and that this statute had violated it. Mr. Justice Douglas found this protection in the penumbra of privacy emanating from the Bill of Rights and applying to Connecticut through the Due Process Clause of the Fourteenth Amendment. Mr. Justice Goldberg, Mr. Chief Justice Warren, and Mr. Justice Brennan argued that this "right of privacy in the marital relationship is fundamental and basic"—a personal right "retained by the people" within the meaning of the Ninth Amendment and protected by the Fourteenth Amendment from infringement by the states. Mr. Justice Harlan considered the statute to infringe on the Fourteenth Amendment because "the enactment violates basic values 'implicit in the concept of ordered liberty.' " Mr. Justice White argued that the statute violated the Fourteenth Amendment in that it is a deprivation of liberty without adequate justification. The dissenters, Mr. Justice Black and Mr. Justice Stewart, disapproved of the law but could not find that it violated any constitutional provision.

The precise limitations of *Griswold* preclude its application to the abortion laws. It establishes three major principles: First, the protected right of privacy is marital; second, unlawful sexual acts are not protected; third, this right of privacy is not absolute. Let us look at these three points in more detail and then see how the argument of the case relates to abortion.

First, what was asserted in *Griswold* was the right of marital privacy, the right "to be free of the regulation of the intimacies of the marital relationship." [8] The Court's concern was "an intimate relation of husband and wife and their physician's role in one aspect of that relation." [9] The focal point was sexual intercourse—lawful between husband and wife—and the attempt to regulate this lawful activity by forbidding the use of contraceptives.

Second, lawful activity was clearly assumed. Mr Justice Goldberg, joined by Mr. Chief Justice Warren and Mr. Justice Brennan, pointed out that the Court's holding does not interfere with the right of the state to regulate sexual promiscuity or misconduct.[10] Adultery, fornication, homosexuality, and the like are legitimately forbidden by the law. Mr. Justice White, too, acknowledged the validity of "the state's ban on illicit sexual relationships." [11] The case certainly does not stand for the proposition that all sexual activity between consenting adults done in private is permitted. Probably the holding can be extended to include within the zone of protected privacy so-called deviate acts between consenting husband and wife. Nevertheless, some regulation of marital intimacies still remains: for example, the right of the state to grant a divorce to a nonconsenting injured spouse on the basis of the refusal to have sexual intercourse, or of an insistence on unreasonably excessive intercourse or deviate sexual practices.

Third, this new right of privacy is not an absolute. It affirms that "there is a 'realm of family life which the state cannot enter' without substantial justification," [12] and that "where there is significant encroachment upon personal liberty, the State may prevail only upon showing a subordinating interest which is compelling," [13] Therefore, even in the realm of lawful marital intimacies, there can be a breaching of the zone of privacy for "legitimate state interests."

The inapplicability of the *Griswold* case to abortion laws rests on the essential difference between contraception and abortion. Although the goals of the two actions may be the same, for example, health or financial well-being, the means used are radically different. Contraception looks to the act of generation, abortion to the product of that act. The contraceptive relationship is between a man and a woman. In fact, as the *Griswold* opinions make clear, the protected relationship is that between husband and wife. Illicit unions are not immune from regulation and prohibition. The abortion relationship, on one other hand, is between parents and child. This additional party changes the whole structure of the situation. The freedom of the parents is limited by the rights of the child. We do not throw a cloak of privacy over everything that goes on, however lethal, between husband and wife, nor between parents and child. The zone of privacy cannot make the home a no-man's-land, an arena of lawless despotism for the unborn child.

The right of the state, in the matter of abortion, to interfere with parental privacy and desires is certainly based upon a "subordinating interest which is compelling." Here indeed is a "legitimate state interest." Fundamentally, it is this public interest in the due process and equal protection clauses of the Constitution that establishes firm boundaries to the expansion of *Griswold*. And yet even without relying on the Fourteenth Amendment, the inner logic of the decision would preclude its application to the abortion laws.

Recently, the U. S. Supreme Court in *Katz* v. *U. S.* has limited or at least pointed out the limits of protected privacy. In the majority opinion of Mr. Justice Stewart, who refers to the *Griswold* case, we read: ". . . the Fourth Amendment cannot be translated into a general constitutional 'right to privacy.' . . . But the protection of a person's *general* right to privacy—his right to be let alone by other people—is, like the protection of his property and of his very life, left largely to the law of the individual States." [14] Mr. Justice Black, in his dissent here, recalled his position in the *Griswold* case: "No general right is created by the [Fourth] Amendment so as to give this court the unlimited power to hold unconstitutional everything that affects privacy." [15]

Consequently, although *Griswold* is an important case in the history of man's deepening sensitivity to human dignity, its holding should not be turned against the very liberty and equality that it upholds. The zone of privacy was conceived of as a protection of liberty, not its betrayal.

The Moderate Liberal Position

The American Law Institute, through its Model Penal Code, has had a major influence on the present controversy. Its provision on abortion has become a focal point for proponents of change. It has unified their goals and given them a viable statute with the major details worked out in advance. The Model Penal Code has not been adopted anywhere, although it has been influential in the revision of the Illinois and the New York Penal Codes. The insanity test and the abortion provision have been its most discussed and most widely adopted measures.

Section 230.3 on abortion provides far more radical abortion reform than is usually suspected.[16] If, therefore, we analyze both the substantive and procedural parts of the provision, we may conclude that the moderate position of today will become the radical position of tomorrow—without having to change the letter of the law. One would reasonably assume that the first two subsections on unjustifiable and justifiable abortions would pre-empt the field. The grounds for justifiable abortion are well known: the physical or mental health of the mother, grave physical or mental defects in the child, and a pregnancy resulting from rape, incest, or other felonious intercourse. If these grounds are absent, if the pregnancy has lasted beyond the twenty-sixth week, or if there is a pretended abortion, the act is classified as an unjustifiable abortion.

A third A.L.I. category of abortion, one not generally recognized, could be called excusable abortion, for it is neither "justifiable" or "unjustifiable." The significance of this *tertium quid* is tremendous when seen in the context of recent biochemical advances. First of all, the Code, in Subsection 4, excuses self-abortion, whether accomplished by the use of instruments, drugs, or violence. Although one who induces or knowingly aids a woman in this act is guilty of a third-degree felony, the woman herself is not punished. There is no penalty against the possession of "anything specially designed to terminate a pregnancy," although the sale of abortifacients, other than to physicians, druggists, or their intermediaries, is made a misdemeanor. Since there is much less risk involved for the seller of abortifacient drugs than for the seller of marijuana, and no legal risk at all for the woman, these drugs should, when finally perfected, be readily and inexpensively available on the black market. The second area of excusable abortion is found in Subsection 7, which misleadingly states that the abortion statute does not apply to the prevention of pregnancy. Contraception, however, is not the primary object of this subsection. Pregnancy is redefined. The subsection reads: "Nothing in this Section shall be deemed applicable to the prescription, administration, or distribution of drugs or other substances for avoiding pregnancy, whether by preventing implantation of a fertilized ovum or by any other method that operates before, at or immediately after fertilization." Since implantation does not occur until five to eight days after intercourse, and since the woman's testimony is usually essential in determining the time of intercourse, there is an appreciable and flexible time period for use of many abortifacient techniques, such as intrauterine devices and anti-zygotic drugs.

The A.L.I. recommended procedure in abortion cases is clear and easy to follow, but totally inadequate in protecting the interest of the child. What are the requirements? The standard is an undefined substantial risk. The determining factor is the belief of two physicians who certify in writing the circumstances that they believe justify the abortion. Notice is to be submitted before the operation to the hospital and, if the abortion is justified by felonious intercourse, to the prosecuting attorney or the police. The operation, except in an emergency, must take place in a licensed hospital.

Since a human life is at stake, strict safeguards are imperative. Yet here the rules are almost a mere formality. One of the purposes of this kind of procedure is to free the doctor from any fear of criminal prosecution for his mistakes, but this goal is achieved by giving him awesome and unaccountable power over the life and death of another. By such a statute, he preserves his own legal immunity by unduly jeopardizing the lives of others. When the only problem was the safeguarding the life of the mother, the key was the obstetrical competence of the physician acting within the area of his own expertise. But now the crucial problem may well be found in areas of skill unrelated to his own—not only psychiatric and socioeconomic but even criminological. The honest belief of the physician in these areas is a ridiculous and irrelevant standard. Consider the complexities presented the physician by the rape-incest provision of most moderate proposals.

A rallying cry of the proponents of moderate liberalization has been pregnancies induced by rape or incest. In fact, one of the most influential cases for abortion reform, in England and in the United States, was the prosecution and subsequent acquittal of Dr. Bourne, who admittedly aborted a young victim of multiple rape. Mississippi, the first state to liberalize its laws, did so simply by adding a rape provision. Every state that has subsequently revised its laws has included a rape provision. All, except Georgia and Maryland, have also included an incest provision. England, on the other hand, has rejected the rape-incest ground. The sponsors of the bill felt its legal technicalities would make it impossible for physicians to apply. However, since these purely legal criteria with their popular persuasiveness are part of the A.L.I. model statute, we must consider these two grounds at some length.

First, what is *rape?* Rape is a felony, widely feared and harshly punished, sometimes forced but sometimes freely consented to. Rape is an area of substantive criminal law in need of radical reform. Rape is, in the word of the seventeenth-century English jurist, Sir Matthew Hale, "an accusation easily to be made and hard to be proved and harder to be defended by the party to be accused though never so innocent." [17]

The term "rape," naked and unexplained, has been a powerful lever for abortion reform. Rape is a concrete, deceptively clear concept—until one examines it. Its emotional impact belies its technical complexity. Here are some of its legal aspects.

What conduct should be called rape? Legally, rape is defined as illicit sexual intercourse with a woman without her consent. "Illicit" means that the woman is not the man's wife. "Sexual intercourse" means the slightest labial penetration by the male. Emission is irrelevant. "Without her consent" means either (1) without her *actual* consent, and includes but does not always imply that the act was done through force or threat, or against her will, or (2) without her *legal* consent because, though she had given her actual consent, she was under age, "below the age of consent." Consequently, two kinds of rape must always be distinguished: forcible rape and statutory rape. The common term covers two radically different situations, two radically different kinds of harm. To permit abortion in either case would demand a separate and distinct justification, as a more detailed analysis will show.

Forcible rape, accomplished by violence and cruelty, fits the usual image of rape, but it sets up a deceptive monolith. Force is not necessary for forcible rape. The only "force" required, if we can still use the term, is that necessary for the act of sexual intercourse. Force is not an element in the crime. It is but one kind of evidence of the woman's lack of consent, in fact, the most convincing kind for a jury.

A woman is generally required to resist to the full extent of her physical powers, or she will be held to have consented. Of course, there are exceptions to this rule. For example, the law recognizes that the fear of death or great bodily harm may justifiably limit her resistance. But exceptions are scrutinized carefully. For example, in Washington, D.C., where rape is a capital crime, there is an operative rule that unless the woman actually sees the gun or knife she is threatened with, her resistance must be maximal. Nevertheless, the essence of the crime is illicit intercourse without consent, whether the man uses violence or threats of violence, or deceit, or drugs, or whether he finds the woman drugged, drunk, unconscious, or asleep. (Incidentally, each of these situations has a complex body of case law analyzing and particularizing it.) If the woman consents, no amount of sadistic cruelty can turn the act into rape. If the woman is married to the man, neither lack of consent nor the use of violence can make the act rape.

When forcible rape is alleged, the basic illicitness of the act of intercourse is easy to prove: It is simply a question of whether or not the woman was married to the accused. The actual occurrence of intercourse, the participation by this defendant, and the lack of consent by the woman, however, are progressively more and more troublesome for the prosecution to prove.

Consent has a will-'o-the-wisp elusiveness. *Ex post facto* rapes are sometimes perpetrated weeks after a mutually agreeable union when, for instance, the girl discovers that her lover has another girl friend or that she is pregnant and he will not marry her. Dr. Alfred Kinsey used to say that the difference between a "good time" and a "rape" often hinged on whether the girl's parents were awake when she returned home.[18]

Statutory rape simplifies the problem immensely by making consent irrelevant. Only two questions are decisive: the age of the girl and the act of intercourse by the defendant. Every under-age and unwed mother is positive proof of statutory rape by someone, somewhere, sometime. Neither honest ignorance of the girl's age nor her own shockingly immoral past will usually excuse the man. This absolute liability made sense under the common law's ten-year age limit. It is reasonable, too, applied to the popular image of statutory rape: the seduction of a barely pubescent Lolita by a depraved, middle-aged man. But the facts are usually different. The overwhelming majority of statutory rapes take place between teen-aged contemporaries, though the girl may be a year or two younger than the man—a normal age discrepancy. Fortunately, grand juries are reluctant to indict a high school boy for a felony whose only crime has been to act in accordance with current mores. This is especially so since the age of consent is so high. For example, it is sixteen in Washington, D.C., eighteen in New York, and twenty-one in Tennessee. Allowing abortion where there is statutory rape is to allow every unwed mother under the specified age to abort her unborn child. Despite the crucial fact that the mother consented to the act of intercourse—otherwise it would be forcible rape—she is freed from any responsibility for the life of her child.

So far, we have seen, in broad outline, something of the legal aspects of rape. Statutory rape, as a justification for abortion, is equivalent to voluntary abortion for a large segment of the fertile female population, but its determination, at least at the pregnancy stage, is not difficult, whatever the moral and social problems may be. Forcible rape, on the other hand, in addition to similar moral and social problems, has serious fact-finding ones: the law is complicated; the evidence is elusive and contradictory; and the effects of a bad decision are devastating.

Next, what is incest? *Incest,* though coupled with rape in the A.L.I. provisions and in other liberal statutes for abortion reform, has radically different implications. Incest is defined as marriage, cohabitation, or sexual intercourse between persons within the prohibited degrees of consanguinity (blood relationship) or affinity (marital relationship). Incest was not a crime at common law because it was within the exclusive competency of the ecclesiastical courts. Consequently, in the United States, incest is always a statutory offense, but a serious one, a felony.

The full legal significance of incest does not appear from its definition, so we will consider the elements of incest in more detail. First, incest may be committed by attempted marriage, by cohabitation—living together with the appearance of marriage—and by sexual intercourse. Second, the prohibited relationship varies greatly with the jurisdiction involved. For example, in the District of Columbia, intercourse is not incestuous between a man and his sister-in-law or his stepdaughter. But in Tennessee, begetting a child with one's sister-in-law is punished by a ten-year sentence;

and in Iowa and Georgia, intercourse with one's stepchildren is equivalent to intercourse with one's own offspring. In most states, there is no difference, for purposes of incest, between half-bloods and whole bloods, or between legitimates and illegitimates. In some states, sexual relation between aunt and nephew or uncle and niece are only misdemeanors. Third, in some states, the prohibited relationship must be known by the parties for their act to be a crime: in others, ignorance or mistake about the relationship is treated as ignorance and mistake about age in statutory rape: It is no excuse. Fourth, incest statutes usually have the words "with each other" or "together." The interpretation varies. The minority of jurisdictions require mutual consent for incest; otherwise the crime is rape. If it is rape, it cannot be incest. If it is incest, it cannot be rape. The majority of jurisdictions, however, do not require the consent to be mutual, so that it would not be a defense to the charge of incest that the other party was underage and that the correct charge should at least have been statutory rape. Fifth, both parties to the incestuous act are equally guilty of a felony, unless there is some circumstance changing the character of the crime. Mutual consent to the illicit act is assumed, as in fornication and adultery.

Incest, as a reasonable justification for abortion, is vitiated by the fact that it is fundamentally a consensual crime—both parties are guilty. Incest is a monstrous kind of justification for the taking of the life of another human being because the parents of the child were partners in the crime that resulted in his conception. The child's mother, herself a felon, pleads her own misdeed as a justification for killing the fruit of the very crime that is pleaded as a justification.

This brief survey of the laws governing rape and incest barely suggests the complexity, substantive, procedural, and evidentiary, that surrounds the proof that an offense actually occurred. But in Mississippi the physician is free to abort "where the pregnancy was caused by rape," if he has the prior advice in writing of two reputable physicians.[19] How the legal decision is made is his problem. In North Carolina, the law is almost as simple. The physician can perform the abortion, "if he can reasonably establish that: The pregnancy resulted from rape or incest and the said alleged rape was reported to a law-enforcement agency or court official within seven days after the alleged rape." [20] Other states such as California and Maryland have more elaborate statutes, but if the rape provision fails, the mental health ground will undoubtedly prevail. Perhaps the English statute is more sensible in putting all these rape-incest cases under the mental health provision. Yet it is odd that, in the United States, the provision which has been most persuasive for liberalizing the abortion laws is the one least used and the one least susceptible of being justly administered, though the legally untrained physician have the best of intentions.

Looking generally at the liberal proposals, we find little difference, except in ease of obtaining an abortion, between the moderate and the extreme statutes. The vague standards of the mental health and the rape-incest provisions, the freedom given physicians in determining justification, and the rise of sophisticated scientific abortifacients make the moderate A.L.I. statute the equivalent of the A.C.L.U. statute. The main difference is the lack of legalistic posturing and rationalization in the latter. But under neither statute will a determined woman be ultimately denied a legal abortion.

III

Having weighed the relative merits of the two types of liberal proposals, the extreme and the moderate, we must face our third question, one of great practical importance. Is it possible for someone, opposed on principle to abortion, to make a sound political compromise? Or, to phrase it differently, must one who is convinced on scientific, moral, and political grounds that abortion is harmful, steadfastly oppose all liberal abortion reform? The problem of abortion strategy is crucial in a pluralistic society where respect for the personal freedom of others is paramount. No society can totally eliminate the tensions that arise from conflicting views, and no citizen should abrogate his responsibility of bringing to bear on the decision-making process his own convictions about societal health.

The strongest argument for acquiescing in and even cooperating in the liberalization of the abortion laws despite one's personal convictions against abortion is found in utilitarian ethics or its legal counterpart, sociological jurisprudence. Roscoe Pound formulates this concept of law:

> I am content to think of law as a social institution to satisfy social wants—the claims and demands and expectations involved in the existence of civilized society—by giving effect to as much as we may with the least sacrifice, so far as such wants may be satisfied or such claims given effect by an ordering of human conduct through politically organized society.[21]

In order to satisfy as many claims as possible, a plausible move might be to remove all prohibitions against abortion. This solution fails, however, because it overlooks an important segment of the population. For every woman who demands an abortion, there is a fetus who naturally and instinctively demands self-preservation. To resolve the impasse between the mother who wants the child to die and the child who wants to live, we must go beyond the statistical game of counting demands, not a fair game anyway since the unborn have no voice in the matter.

If all men agreed on the moral and political rights of the fetus, the abortion decision would be to keep the traditional laws on the books, perhaps with some modernization, and to enforce them to the letter. All the members of this pluralistic society, however, do not agree on the personal character of the fetus, the immorality of its destruction, or the political necessity of protecting its life. Consequently, our political decision goes in one of two directions. Either we allow each person involved to make his own choice without concerning ourselves with the affect of free

abortion on the welfare of the community, or we use all legitimate political power to ensure that what we consider best for our
society be legally implemented.

As we have seen in our consideration of the public interest,
not every act believed to be immoral need be forbidden by the
criminal law. There is legislative latitude in decision-making.
The test is the social necessity for that abridgment of freedom
which is law. Many agree that some restriction on abortion is a
social necessity. They oppose abortion on demand as socially
harmful. Yet this opposition is itself divided, for some oppose
any liberalization and some oppose only complete liberalization.
In view of the numerical character of political power, the expedient of compromise would seem desirable and even necessary: let all opposed to free abortion agree on a moderate bill
with a strong conscience clause guaranteeing that no one either
in the medical profession or in the population at large will be
forced to be involved in an abortion if it is against his principles
or even preferences. Plausible though this conditioned compromise with its built-in safeguard may seem, it has serious
flaws.

A. The superficial differences between the extreme A.C.L.U.
position and the moderate A.L.I. position disappear when it is a
question of modern abortifacients, the mechanical intrauterine
devices, and the sophisticated chemical compounds that prevent
implantation. Self-abortion in the early stages of pregnancy will
be the scientifically safe and sure method of the future, the most
private and the most widely used and, without new legislation,
perfectly consistent with Section 230.3 of the Model Penal Code.

B. The moderate position of the A.L.I., which has been
adopted generally by the liberalizing states, admittedly only
justifies abortion in some 15 percent of all the cases of illegal
abortion that occur annually. The passage of a moderate abortion bill does not eliminate the demand that something be done
about these illegal abortions. In fact, many support moderate
abortion only as one stage in the creeping legislation that is to

lead to abortion on demand and the "final solution" to the problem of illegal abortion. It would be naïve for anyone to think that the compromise passage of a moderate abortion bill will do more than temporarily delay the fight for free abortion. The agitation will intensify, but this time from a base closer to its ultimate goal.

C. Strategic maneuvers of accommodation undermine the genuineness of the political participation of those convinced that liberalization is not a good thing for society. Even a coalition vote for moderate abortion laws destroys the integrity of one's witness to the equal dignity of human life. It is impossible to vote for limited destruction of the unborn without justifying in principle the expendability of human life, all human life. The proponents of liberalization very deliberately overemphasize rape-induced pregnancies. Comparatively, the incidence of such cases is very small. The full-scale and heavily funded pro-abortion organizations do not envisage themselves as a rescue league for rape victims. They do realize, however, that to justify abortion after rape is to depart from the absolutist position on the direct inviolability of fetal life. Dialectically, the problem then becomes simply one of balancing interests, involving an essentially expendable fetus, in an effort to find what circumstances justify killing it and what circumstances do not. For those convinced that liberal abortion is wrong, a political alliance would be a betrayal not only of their principles but of their fellow citizens— and not merely the unborn. Vatican II, in suggesting the extent of the harm from abortion, gives us the measure of our responsibilities as citizens acting with justice and love:

> Whatever is opposed to life itself, such as any type of murder, genocide, abortion, euthanasia, or willful self-destruction . . . all these things and others of their like are infamies indeed. *They poison human society, but they do more harm to those who practice them than those who suffer from the injury.* Moreover, they are a supreme dishonor to the Creator.[22]

IV

Without compromising one's opposition to the liberalization of the abortion laws, one can structure proposed legislation so that the law in its final form will not be equivalent to abortion on demand, so that it will be as fair and as reasonable as possible within the limits established by the adopted grounds, and so that the abortions performed will be within these limits. This goal can be achieved by a careful formulation of the procedural aspects of the new law. In the controversy over the substantive grounds, one often loses sight of the importance of the procedural rules. The battle over liberalization may be won or lost on the substantive level, but the value of the implementing procedures is significant. Procedure is the methodology of the legal process. It sets up the ways and means of best fulfilling the law. Whether one is for or against liberalization, sound procedures are indispensable. Pro-abortionists want their law to work effectively. Anti-abortionists want the new law to function with the minimum of injustice. Both have an interest in avoiding abuses.

All who vote for a moderate abortion bill, therefore, presumably intend that it be implemented by appropriate procedural measures. An insistence on standards and clearly worked-out formalities is a normal and indispensable part of good law-making. The abortion decision, regardless of its degree of permissiveness, should be procedurally sound. A brief survey of the operative procedural elements in a liberal statute will give us a sense of what a well-functioning law ought to have:

1. The physician or surgeon should be duly licensed.

2. The hospital should be accredited or licensed. Abortions should be permitted only in such hospitals, not in doctors' offices where supervision and control are more difficult.

3. A residency requirement should be included to keep a liberal state from becoming an abortion mecca.

4. A time limit should be established beyond which no abor-

tion should be allowed unless necessary to save the life of the mother.

5. The standards for justification under the various grounds should be as reasonable and clear as the subject matter allows. Specifically, the rape-incest provision should have procedures guaranteeing that legal matters be determined by legal experts.

6. The written consent of the woman should be required as well as the consent of her husband, at least if they are living together. If the woman is a minor or an incompetent, written permission should be obtained from her husband, if she is married, or from her parents, guardian, or one *in loco parentis*, if she is not married.

7. A legal guardian should be appointed to safeguard the interests of the fetus except in an emergency to save the life of the mother.

8. There should be prior written approval of the abortion by a special hospital board, officially appointed and subject to review. The board should always have on it an expert in the medical field on which the petition for abortion is based. If the board is small, unanimity should be required.

9. There should be the right of appeal from the decision of the hospital board to a designated court of law.

10. Complete official reports should be kept of the number of petitions, abortions, grounds, doctors, etc. These should be submitted annually to state medical departments.

11. A conscience clause should be included to protect hospitals, hospital employees, doctors, and even the pregnant women, her husband, parents, or guardian, in their right to refuse to permit, to perform, or to undergo an abortion.

12. Appropriate and strict penalties should be established for the violation of law, since one of the goals of liberalization is to cut down on the number of illegal abortions.

The 1968 Maryland abortion statute is an outstanding example of the effective use of procedural safeguards.[23] Despite the enactment of a moderately liberal law the Executive Director of the Maryland Catholic Conference, Joseph G. Finnerty, Jr., could say, "In evaluating the impact of this bill, it must be viewed in light of the existing legal conditions in this state prior to its enactment. When one considers the uncertain state of the present law, it is rather difficult to determine the extent of the relaxation, if any, that the new law will cause." [24]

The former law permitted "the production of abortion by a regular practitioner of medicine when, after consulting with one or more respectable physicians he shall be satisfied that the fetus is dead, or that no other method will secure the safety of the mother." [25] Maryland was one of the very few states before 1967 that permitted an abortion to preserve the health of the mother. The new law spelled out the implications of the vague word "safety," thereby justifying the prior standard practice. It allowed an abortion if "continuation of the pregnancy is likely to result in the death of the mother," or if "there is a substantial risk that continuation of the pregnancy would gravely impair the physical or mental health of the mother." Thus, the only really new justifying grounds concerned the defective child and forcible rape. Statutory rape and incest were not included.

Here are some of the new procedural requirements in Maryland which tightened up the previously vague and informal area of legal abortion. All abortions must now take place in an accredited and licensed hospital or the abortion is criminal. No abortion can take place after twenty-six weeks of gestation except to save the mother's life. Prior authorization must be granted by a hospital review board which is appointed by the hospital. Previously all that was required was prior consultation with one or more respectable physicians. The hospital review authority must keep written records of all requests and the action taken on them. The director of the hospital must report to the Joint Commission on Accreditation and the State Board of Health, the number of requests, authorizations, performances, the grounds, and the medical procedures used. This report will be made public. The penalties for violations of this bill have been increased. A con-

science clause, which may well become a model for other jurisdictions, was included. It reads:

(A) No person shall be required to perform or participate in
medical procedures which result in the termination of pregnancy; and the refusal of any person to perform or participate
in these medical procedures shall not be a basis for civil liability
to any person nor a basis for any disciplinary or any other recriminatory action against him.

(B) No hospital, hospital director or governing board shall
be required to permit the termination of human pregnancies
within its institution and the refusal to permit such procedures
shall not be grounds for any civil disability to any person nor a
basis for any disciplinary or other recriminatory action against
it by the state or any person.

(C) The refusal of any person to submit to an abortion or to
give consent therefore shall not be grounds for loss of any
privileges or immunities to which such person would otherwise
be entitled nor shall submission to an abortion or the granting
of consent therefor be a condition precedent to the receipt of
any public benefits.[26]

Conclusion

The function of law is to implement a policy decision arrived
at by the community. It is derivative rather than original, but it
does have the creative role of taking the community decision and
incorporating it into the established system of rights and duties
that structure our civilized life.

The legal implementation of the abortion decision is crucial.
It is the last step in a long investigative and evaluative process.
In our reappraisal of the abortion laws, we have come to four
conclusions: (1) that to leave the traditional laws on the books
although they are largely unenforced is, nevertheless, to limit the
number of abortions and to declare the community stand on the
equal dignity of all; (2) that to liberalize the laws, whether by
a moderate or extreme provision, moves the community in the

direction of abortion on demand; (3) that to make a strategic compromise—the acceptance of a moderate proposal to avoid the enactment of an extreme proposal—while opposed to abortion on moral and political grounds is to destroy the basis of this opposition by supplanting the principle of human dignity and equality with the principle of expediency; and (4) that to work for legislative amendments, however, when the enactment of a liberal statute is inevitable, is to contain the substantive harm through sensibly chosen procedural safeguards.

When an abortion law is enacted, the community has, wisely or unwisely, made a commitment. The law is declarative of the value preference of the community. But even a good law does not solve all abortion problems, nor does a bad law destroy all hope of their solution. Abortion laws contract or expand the area of permissible action. But the abortion laws, traditional or liberal, must be supplemented by the efforts of the community, if the law is to fulfill its function even in the area where it is sovereign. Societal health depends on all the members of the community, each working within the area of his competence. The true solution of the abortion problem is not found in an abortion law, however enlightened, but in the dedicated efforts of the community to find remedies for the evils that occasion the demand for abortion. The law does its part, but that part is comparatively small.

Chapter Seven

THE VIABLE ALTERNATIVE

Criticism need not be negative. In criticizing liberal abortion, we have appealed to the positive values of human dignity and equality. This is not to suggest that proponents of reform are entirely negative, though they resort to that ultimate in deprivation—the killing of a living being. On the contrary, they are deeply concerned with human values, with the age-old problem of evil. We share their motivations but disagree with their recommendations. Merely to attack the proposals of those trying to solve a critical human problem without in turn offering other acceptable and workable solutions is to be irresponsibly obstructionist. Currently, the abortion decision is whether or not the grounds for abortion should be enlarged. Those who reject liberal abortion as legitimate must submit a viable alternative.

No single solution, however, can resolve the sociomedical crisis which gives rise to the demand for abortion. Even complete permissiveness would merely cure symptoms and would not eliminate the social evils of rape and incest, of poverty and ill-health, and whatever makes the pregnancy unwanted. There is no one remedy, no twentieth-century panacea—as abortion itself is sometimes pictured—but there is a complexus of remedies that together form the viable alternative to liberal abortion. There can be a realistic approach to human distress that preserves the life of the child while at the same time works to eliminate the conditions that occasion the demand for its destruction.

The Dual Role of Communication

Communication forms an essential component of the true alternative to liberal abortion. If sex, marriage, and the family are to function with optimal efficiency, the task of teaching and lawmaking looms large. Domestic relations can be the source of too much unhappiness for society to grow complacent. In this era of the "communications explosion," we can reach more people more effectively than ever before. We can "tell it like it is" concerning principles of behavior and we can correct perceptions through feedback, thereby improving the probabilities that future conduct will be informed by an evaluation of past performance. The communication process has two functions: to inform and to control. Each is a kind of message-sending, yet the one focuses on education, the other on legislation.

People must have sufficient information if they are to live effectively. If they are to make a sound abortion decision, it must be made in the context of a rational ethical and political structure. Sex education may solve part of the problem, for it helps dispel the ignorance and error which confuse the issue. The educational coverage and the implementing techniques vary with the medium and the audience. Lectures, counseling, books, magazines, newspapers, radio, television, and movies all are efficacious. They have been used recently in the United States and in England in promoting the liberalization of abortion. India is preparing to use public television sets in small villages to teach its people about birth control. Many cities in various countries have run effective campaigns through the mass media against venereal disease.

Studies of anatomy, physiology, and psychology form the obvious prerequisites for sex education, but without an embryological and familial orientation, they lack an essential dimension. Sex involves a tripartite relationship: man, woman, and child. Sex can be enjoyed apart from the family, even apart from another person, but it can never be fully understood or evaluated apart from the family. To communicate the full meaning of sex demands the total view. The clinical side of sex education is only part of the picture, because man is something more than an animal to be trained for breeding purposes. Ordinarily, in our times and in our culture, the mature man maximizes these values and achieves his destiny in the married state. Yet even the family, important as it is, is not an end in itself, an isolated achievement unrelated to the rest of life. The family is a dependent part of the larger society, the political community. The health of the family is a good gauge of the health of the body politic. Widespread abortion is a sign of its social sickness.

Laws, too, are means of communication. They are the messages by which people are controlled, their freedom limited, for the sake of the common good. Legislation must buttress education in its ensuring the health of the community. Education must instill sound family ideals and practical guidelines. It must develop a sense of reasonableness and responsibility rooted in a respect for human dignity and equality. But there must also be sound marriage laws which establish approved patterns of behavior enforced by a system of effective sanctions.

To the extent that the members of a democracy understand the value and function of the family, they will make the kinds of laws that reflect their understanding and foster their goals. In fact, a profound grasp of what family life should be prompts those who share in the decision-making process to legislate in many related areas so that human values will be increased. Specifically, education and legislation for family living will gradually remove the conditions of life which lead to the demand for abortion. This demand is based in a value judgment that after weighing the contingencies, good and bad, the lethal option should be taken. Laws that remove or lessen the unfavorable conditions make abortion less desirable even on purely pragmatic grounds.

What alternatives are available to enable us to avoid or to compensate for the unwanted effects which liberal abortion proposals seek to eliminate? Each of the four fundamental goals sought by such legislation—maternal life and health, avoidance of defective children, relief from the unfortunate consequences of criminal and other unlawful acts, and the maintenance of a sound socioeconomic basis of a good life for the living—is attainable basically by means other than abortion.

Maternal Life and Health

The best remedy to help avoid abortions to preserve the life or physical health of the mother is greater medical expertise. Today, abortion is rarely medically necessary to save the life of the mother and only occasionally medically necessary to avoid serious injury to her health. Most abortions on health grounds are done to preserve the mother's mental health. Whether or not abortion is ever indicated in such cases, or whether it can ever be determined that an abortion would help, is a question still hotly controversial. What is necessary in this area is a sounder diagnostic approach to the relationship of abortion to mental health. Much research must be done by the medical profession to establish need as opposed to preference. If abortion on mental health grounds is simply a strategic way-station on the road to abortion on demand, it is a medical subterfuge unworthy of the profession. If it is not, then sound research should justify this drastic remedy—a physical killing for the sake of another's mental health. Relevant too are the sequelae to a "psychiatric" abortion. Is it but a worsening of an already sick person?

Since we are concerned in this current abortion decision primarily with an extension of the traditional grounds for abortion rather than with a total abrogation of all grounds, abortion to save the life of the mother is a political irrelevancy. The same can also be said of abortion to preserve the health of the mother from serious harm—in the few states which make such an exception. Thus, the real issue in this area is whether nonserious harm to a mother's mental or physical health should be enough to justify destroying the child. The medical profession has not made its case. In fact, the very formulation of the issue is declarative of its imbalance.

Child Defects

The rubella and thalidomide tragedies of the early 1960s prompted the inclusion of the defective child provision in proposed legislation. The 1959 draft of the Model Penal Code did not list child defects as a justifying ground, though the final draft of the abortion section reflected the public response to these widespread misfortunes in Europe and this country.

Of all the states to pass liberal abortion laws in 1967, California alone refused to include as a grounds for abortion the risk that the child might be born with serious mental or physical defects. Governor Reagan, as we have seen, insisted that he would veto the bill if it included this provision because it was "only a step away from what Hitler tried to do." One must, nevertheless, recognize the great burden that the birth of a defective child may be, especially to a poor family. But instead of legislating these unfortunate children out of existence, we should implement the great number of constructive things that can be done to lessen the pressure for abortion in this situation.

First, we should increase our support of medical and scientific research which is already so successfully minimizing the incidence of defective children. Viral diseases are gradually being eliminated by immunizing drugs. Vaccines against rubella have been developed and may be available by the end of 1969.[1] Great advances have been made in isolating the teratogenic ingredient in thalidomide.[2] The Food and Drug Administration is working with scientists and doctors in the fight against lethal and disabling birth defects and in the search for tests and experiments to make sure that no harmful drugs are available to the public.

Second, we should intensify and expand our facilities and techniques for the total rehabilitation and education of defective children. In recent years, the Kennedy Foundation has contributed much in the fields of education and research. National campaigns to "hire the handicapped" have been broadened. Goodwill Industries has established a nationwide business run entirely by handicapped adults. But much more needs to be done and can be done to rehabilitate the unfortunate victims of birth defects.

Third, the parents of defective children have, in addition to their acute emotional burden, unusually heavy financial expenses. The "baby-sitting" fees alone for a permanently retarded child severely limit the normal social activities of many families. A variety of means is available for alleviating the special costs of providing for such children. The state, through its welfare program, or the private sector by means of an insurance program, could help the family compensate for their hardship. Public and private institutions do exist, but if a family wants to keep a defective child at home to ensure that it gets the love and attention no institution can give, state aid to the parents seems equitable, especially since totally adequate funding would be less than the cost of institutionalizing the child.

A fourth and closely related problem concerns parents or potential parents with transmittable defects. Sometimes the problem appears only if both parents have recessive genes for a disease such as phenylketonuria, galactosemia, or fibrocystic disease of the pancreas. The Greek government, in 1968, set up standards which would prevent marriage between persons with much more common diseases, including heart disease and tuberculosis. Voluntary birth control or voluntary sterilization are less coercive methods. Involuntary sterilization is perhaps preferable to enforced celibacy, but does recall the early sterilization laws of the

Third Reich. This avenue of thought leads us into the fearful manipulations of eugenics with its potential for gross abuse but hardly less so than liberal abortion.

Crime and Illegitimacy

Pregnancies caused by certain crimes are currently proposed as grounds justifying abortion. These crimes include incest, forcible and statutory rape, and, sometimes, even fornication or adultery. The most obvious alternative to abortion in such cases is the prevention and deterrence of unlawful behavior—a perennial task of every government.

Since all pregnancies resulting from such acts involve forbidden sexual behavior, adequate preventive measures require early sex education, including realistic information about birth control.

Long before the particular criminal or other act that results in illegitimate pregnancy, one or another of the parties involved may exhibit behavior patterns that suggest the need for counseling and psychiatric help. Although sex crimes and illicit sexual relations will never be totally eradicated, unwanted pregnancies among the properly counseled and educated, should not result as frequently.

Generally, both for adults as well as for juveniles, a sense of reverence for sex and the human person is the best way to reduce the numbers of these so-called criminal pregnancies. If they do occur, and if the woman has truly been victimized, the current trends toward compensating victims of crimes could be made to apply to her and to her child.

Every child conceived as the result of crime is an illegitimate child if the parents do not subsequently marry one another. In most of these "criminal pregnancies," the parents of the child cannot or will not marry one another. Consequently, the problem as far as the child's status is concerned is primarily one of illegitimacy.

Whatever the circumstances giving rise to the illegitimate pregnancy, the situation of a pregnant woman who is not married to the father of her child is almost inevitably one of deep personal and social concern. If pregnancy results from forcible rape, trauma and revulsion may seriously impair her "mental health." If she is merely below the legal age of consent, her "statutory rape," causing social embarrassment and economic problems in the care and unbringing of the child, is invoked as a crime to justify terminating the life of the unwanted child. If the pregnancy is incestuous or adulterous, shame and psychic tensions affecting the mother and other members of the family are caught up in the loose net of "danger to her mental health" to justify taking the life of the child. Granting the conditions of anguish that attend the hateful character of some of these acts, and the remorse and shame that accompany pregnancies of the unwed, two questions must be asked: What, short of abortion, can be done to eliminate such pregnancies? What can be done to relieve the hardships of the mother and child when they do occur?

Two general areas are important, the legal and the extra-legal. By reforming the discriminatory laws against illegitimates, hundreds of thousands of children born every year will not be second-class citizens. We are speaking here, in the words of H. D. Krause, "about the disadvantages that are imposed by law on the illegitimate, but that are not imposed on the legitimate child of divorced parents." [3] He lists five trouble spots. (1) Support. The father must support his illegitimate child but usually on a lower economic level and for a shorter time than he would support his legitimate ones. In Texas and Idaho, there is no support requirement at all. (2) Inheritance. At common law, the bastard was a *filius nullius* who could inherit from neither parent. Most states allow him to inherit from his mother, although not from her family at all, and not from his father except by will or after legal acknowledgment. (3) Name. The illegitimate cannot use his father's name despite its social or economic value to him.

(4) Custody. The rights of the father to supervise the child's life and the child's right to the father's company are limited even when the father supports the child. The best interests of the child and the rights of the father should be harmonized in the areas of parental authority, custody, visitation, and adoption. (5) State and Federal Welfare Laws. A trend has begun to treat the legitimate and the illegitimate child equally: for example, regarding the Social Security Act. Nevertheless, there is still no consistency in state laws, and the federal laws are usually interpreted according to state policy. The problem has been placed dramatically before the United States Supreme Court by two Louisiana cases: One, *Levy* v. *Louisiana,* involved a suit by five illegitimate children for damages for the wrongful death of their mother.[4] They sued the hospital, the attending physician, and the A.B.C. Insurance Companies, alleging negligence. The Louisiana court rejected their suit because, as illegitimates, they had no right to sue even for the wrongful death of their mother. In the other case, the Louisiana court barred parents from recovering for the wrongful death of their illegitimate son (*Glona* v. *American Guarantee & Liability, Inc.*)[5]. Both of these cases were reversed, though with dissenting opinions, by the Supreme Court of the United States.

The Canon Law of the Roman Catholic Church has over a half a dozen canons which deal with the problem of legitimacy and legitimization.[6] Unfortunately, they evidence the medieval mentality shared by the Anglo-American law. The rules are complicated, unrealistic, and often ridiculous. Since they deal with ecclesiastical status rather than the necessary temporalities of life, they are not usually as important or as harmful as the civil discriminations—but they are an anomaly in a post-Vatican II Christian community. Canon law currently bars illegitimates from the office of cardinal, bishop, abbot, and prelate nullius. An illegitimate cannot be a priest unless he joins a religious order with solemn vows. The purely legal character of this ecclesiastical bar sinister is seen in the power of the Holy See to declare any child legitimate whether his parents ever married or not, and to declare illegitimate a child conceived and born at a time when the marital rights of its parents were suspended because one of them became a priest or one entered an order with solemn religious vows. The harshness of the rules is minimized by various other techniques for legitimizing children, including a *sanatio in radice,* a "radical curing," of an invalid marriage which is so perfectly retroactive that the children are not merely legitimized but are legitimate for all canonical effects. Whatever the original effectiveness and purpose of these rules, they no longer have a place in ecclesiastical law. The revised Code of Canon Law is sure to eliminate these anachronistic and discriminatory practices. Until that is done, however, the stigma of illegitimacy which has some ecclesiastical justification contributes to the total atmosphere of community disapproval and discrimination that moves an unwed mother toward abortion as the only dignified way out.

Equally as important as legal reform are the extra-legal remedies. Here, where society's attitudes impinge most personally on the unwed mother, much work is necessary. Inexpensive maternity homes of various kinds should be made available, so that, for example, high school students can continue their studies and older women will not feel out of place. Counseling and psychiatric services should be expanded to facilitate emotional adjustment before and after the birth of the illegitimate child. Welfare assistance for medical and living costs should be provided for those who do not go to maternity homes and for those who choose to keep the child rather than place him for adoption. Adoption should be encouraged among couples and individuals who are capable of providing suitable environments for rearing children, and greater efforts should be made to create a system of foster homes so loving and secure that unwed mothers will not fear to release their children to the care of others. Rehabilitation programs for the women who need and want to start anew should be freely available at costs well within their ability to pay. Finally, a massive change in societal attitudes is called for—a shift from punishment to comfort, from distaste to sympathy, understanding, and love. It is strange that in the United States, where the entertainment level and popular ideals are so compatible with a sophisticated sex life, the girl who happens to become pregnant is treated so unkindly. A more civilized view, a more charitable attitude can do much to relieve the unwed mother of the desperation that comes from finding herself alone in a hostile and punitive world with so little care for her or her innocent child.

The Socioeconomic Challenge

The socioeconomic aspects of the abortion crisis cut through three basic and correlated problems: overpopulation, hunger, and poverty. In this country, overpopulation is not a present evil, but it may constitute a future threat. The fear that people will soon outrun available resources underlies much of the agitation for liberalized abortion, especially since the crisis stage has already been reached elsewhere. The justifications for abortion reform are usually phrased in therapeutic, juridical, eugenic, or socio-economic terms, but concern about overpopulation gives a psychological urgency to reform that is buttressed by that ultimate rationalization—its apparent inevitability.

In the United States, fears about the rate of population growth have both qualitative and quantitative aspects. Even while famine stalks less privileged lands, massive starvation is not yet perceived as a real threat to the present and future millions fortunate enough to be born here. Americans are concerned instead with the massive growth of urban centers and with the solution of problems, some of them racial, that this growth is generating. Their attention is focused on the social and economic costs of improving the quality of life for individuals living in an affluent society. The right to life for the living has been transformed in our day to a demand for the right to the good life. And spokesmen for and against liberal abortion share the emerging ethic of love that is an essential part of this ideal.

No one disputes the altruistic motives of those who grieve for the defective child and its heartbroken parents, for the victim of forcible rape, and for the mother dead from a pathological pregnancy. Loving concern for the quality of life also underlies the demands that illegitimates not be stigmatized, greater opportunities be given for the enjoyment of education and productive employment, and for a massive reduction of the psychic tensions brought about by the economic stress of having to provide for too many on resources that are all too few.

What is not consistent with an ethic of love is the insistence by some on "spaceship Earth" that it is necessary to kill unwanted intruders, the unborn, who threaten the optimum balance between those who live and the environment of potential scarcity. The alternatives to killing demand a greater expression of love and even more rationality than that of the most liberal proponents of abortion reform. These loving and rational alternatives paradoxically parallel the American Medical Association's blueprints for curbing infant mortality.[7] Among other things, they call for

- Supporting all constructive community efforts for the improvement of living conditions among the needy.

- Initiating and supporting programs of health education, including good maternal and child health practices, family life and sex education, and the appropriate use of health care resources.

- Offering help and advice to implement programs to elevate medical and other services to acceptable standards [for the economically deprived].

- Giving impetus to broad and inclusive programs for the care of unwed mothers.

- Promoting family planning programs and re-emphasizing policy on family planning whereby "the prescription of child-spacing measures should be available to all patients who require them, consistent with their creed and mores. . . ."

- Emphasizing the association between the mother's nutritional status and her performance during pregnancy and encouraging further investigations into nutritional influences which affect infant mortality and morbidity.

- Evaluating, by state and component societies, of existing maternal and child care resources and taking the leadership in the expansion and development of programs for delivering services in locations to be found deficient.

- Aiming current and expanded programs at relieving shortages in health manpower.

More concretely, these alternatives demand responsive action from all sectors of society—government, business, the family, education, religious and civic groups, as well as the mass media. They also require the most intimate self-assessment of individual character in the philosophic framework of an ethic of love.

A most obvious and direct means of avoiding a socioeconomic abortion crisis is the control of the number of conceptions. Here the alternatives are continence or contraception. Absolute continence is generally impossible for married couples. Nevertheless, the Indian Family Planning Minister Sripati Chandrasekhar proposed on Oct. 20, 1968 that every married couple in India should deny themselves sexual intercourse for a year. How successful this "no baby" year will be remains to be seen. Periodic continence or the rhythm theory of birth control, though morally acceptable to most people, is frequently an unsuccessful means of avoiding pregnancy. The American bishops in their annual meeting in November 1968, prompted no doubt by the controversy over the encyclical *Humanae Vitae*, made a million dollar grant to study and perfect the rhythm method. Contraception, however, is the most frequently used method of family planning in the United States. Since the 1965 *Griswold* case, the use of contraception is legal [8] and has, in fact, been widely subsidized by private and public funds.

Tremendous advances over the last few years in developing chemical or hormonal means of inhibiting the ovulatory function have already radically transformed the life of the woman in American society. A continuance of the same rate of scientific and medical research make imminent the breakthrough discovery of the "perfect contraceptive." A safe, foolproof, long-lasting, and inexpensive contraceptive, channeled through a well-funded counseling and medical service, could largely eliminate the fear of overpopulation and most unwanted pregnancies without recourse to abortion, but it would not eliminate all of the abortion problems.

The process of generation will continue. Wanted babies and unwanted babies will be conceived. Changing circumstances may turn wanted babies into unwanted babies for reasons now found in the traditional and liberal justifications for abortion. There will not, however, be the same sense of public urgency, since the terror of overpopulation will have been exorcised. Even if all considered themselves morally free to practice contraception, some problems would remain. For contraception, whatever its moral quality, does not eliminate the problem of the pregnant woman too ill to bear her child to term, or of the rape-induced pregnancy, or of the defective child, or of the impoverished home. Contraception may be considered as a legitimate help or a lesser evil, but it is not a complete solution to the problems that occasion the demand for abortion.

Family planning, with or without abortion, is not the only remedy to the problem of overpopulation. Essentially, it is a negative solution—a limitation on the number of humans to inhabit this planet. It is argued that family planning is the indispensable means of keeping life worth living. But for us to cease the relentless search for other and better ways would be to succumb to societal defeatism. Without more, without supplemental programs for progress, society stagnates in an entropic equilibrium. Without venturing too far afield in the realm of demography, we can suggest certain avenues of hope.

A convenient but frequently misread image, "spaceship Earth," can help us formulate some of these suggestions. On the one hand, we are asked to consider this planet as a closed system with limited resources which have to last a long, long time. There is no *deus ex machina* to help us keep things shipshape. Isolated in the unsearchable vastness of space, we must keep our environment unpolluted, our resources—especially air, food and water—adequate, our wastes reconvertible, and our population constant. We are asked to count our blessings which, like the hairs of our head, are numbered. As people grow old they sense the need for marshaling their assets, for conserving their strength, for making care and efficiency compensate for the loss of youthful vigor and enthusiasm. In the twentieth century, we, on Earth, have suddenly become conscious of aging.

We must learn how to conserve our energies and our resources. We must use our ingenuity and discipline to learn better and better ways of solving the old problems, which are ever-present problems: famine, overcrowding, poverty, ignorance, disease, and the preservation of human dignity and equality. Boulding speaks of "dismal theories" that overpopulation, atomic war, or entropy will get us if we don't watch out. The bomb presages a dramatic destruction of mankind; famine and entropy bring man to a whimpering end, without a bang. Human beings are fighting an uphill battle in a downhill universe. This gloomy projection is not the only alternative, however.

"Spaceship Earth" does not necessarily portend the dreary end of a closed system. The future does not consist solely of survival gymnastics whose value, other than distraction, lies simply in the postponement of the inevitable doomsday. A spaceship is also the symbol of an age of exploration and adventure, of the days of the pioneers of space. The new frontier of the twentieth century has opened the door to an underpopulated universe when an overpopulated earth has begun to be a threat to human life. Without indulging in the dreams of science fiction, we can see the "spaceship Earth" as a means of breaking out of this closed system into a vast, undeveloped potential which will be peopled and perfected by those we have begotten.

To advocate societal procrastination in the hope that some now uninhabited planet will become available would be suicidal and presumptuous. We must give ourselves to the means within our immediate grasp. Yet we must not yield to the defeatist expedient of solving tomorrow's problems with the techniques of yesterday. Our cybernetic age has not yet begun to envisage what it eventually will accomplish. We should not narrow our vision to the crudities of abortion. Certainly, it is the most grim assumption of all to hold that men can solve their future problems only by killing one another, that legalized and wholesale killing is an essential element in man's brave new world.

Two practical considerations will help us in determining our legislative policy about abortion *vis-à-vis* overpopulation. First, population control is not the most accurate formulation of the problem. The optimal number of people is a function of the amount of food available to feed them. Housing, health, and education facilities are essential but are secondary to that of food production. To most, overpopulation spells famine. If the people are well-fed, the other problems can in principle, be worked out. The world is big enough, intelligent enough, and wealthy enough to take care of all its inhabitants if it can feed them. But the problem of feeding a nation is complex. Social logistics demands organization and expertise, but it is rooted in adequate methods of food production and distribution. Sometimes we overlook the fact that agriculture was invented by man. Carbon 14 dating techniques place the beginning of agriculture in both Mexico and the Middle East by about 7000 B.C.[9] Perhaps this revolutionary environmental shaping was primitive man's answer to his own population explosion or hunger crisis. The domestication of plants was paralleled by the domestication of animals. These were the responses of the intelligence of man to the challenge of scarcity—the economic formulation of the problem of evil. Our task is not to make man more scarce by killing the unborn, but to make food less scarce by exploring the unknown riches of the world.

The relationship between population and production is crucial. For the United States, November 1967 marked an unprecedented achievement in harmonizing the two: the population rose to two hundred million people and the gross national product rose to eight hundred billion dollars. In the ten years from 1958 through 1967, the population of the United States increased 15.5 percent and its gross national product increased 82.8 percent. On a comparative basis, the feat is even more impressive: "A nation that, with 6 percent of the world's population, can outproduce all the Communist countries combined and account for more than 42 percent of the entire output of the non-Communist world, is bound to be envied, feared and often hated. But it is also bound to be emulated, particularly when its performance is compared with that of the world's other superpower. With 30 million more people than there are in the U.S., the Soviet Union has a G.N.P. that is less than half as large as America's." [10]

In striking contrast to the affluence of America is the stark fact of poverty. The report, *Hunger U.S.A.*,[11] shocked many into an awareness of the dimensions of poverty. It found, for example, that ten million Americans are chronically under-nourished, that some 280 of the nation's thirty-one hundred counties have serious hunger problems. These people are not starving, but they are suffering from a drastic shortage of the right amounts of the right kinds of foods. The United States has sufficient good food and has used it in helping nations like India. The causes of U.S. hunger are different from that of India, and to some extent is attributable to local customs and ignorance, as the House Agricultural Committee phrased it in challenging the findings of *Hunger U.S.A.*[12] The blight of poverty usually hinders people even in the wise use of available foods. In this nation, a program of food planning is more needed than one of family planning. No food shortage exists in the United States. But malnutrition stalks the land. Despite marvels of productivity, there are bottlenecks in distribution. But the hunger problem is a part of the larger problem of poverty and will only be solved when poverty too is solved. The United States may be emulated by other countries. It may teach the world many things. But it has much to learn also.

To suggest ways of solving the world poverty crisis, or our own, is neither necessary nor possible here. Yet poverty does have a close relationship to abortion. Although most legal abortions are performed on the well-to-do, the poor, who would seem to have the best socioeconomic grounds for abortion, frequently cannot afford even an illegal abortion. For too many Americans poverty is the climate of distress that makes abortion appear as an attractive escape from snowballing responsibilities. The specific remedies are many and controversial. Universal minimum wages, guaranteed annual income, tax relief, subsidies for poor mothers, family benefits, universal Medicare, marriage and psychiatric counseling, better housing, and the Job Corps are but a few of the possible avenues of restoration. We can never solve the problem of poverty-induced abortion without solving the problems of poverty.

Poverty is treated briefly here only because of the overwhelming immensity of the challenge. But those who are seriously opposed to liberal abortion, those who hold human life sacred and human dignity both a reality and an ideal, must also make an abiding commitment toward that "other America," our thirty million poor.

The second practical consideration is that laws are determined by the conditions of the community. We do not adopt liberal abortion laws because others have a population and poverty crisis. In making an abortion decision, an individual state—and that is the decision-making unit in the United States—should not be panicked by irrelevancies or unduly influenced by false precedents. The vote on liberalizing abortion is not a decision on a worldwide policy, but on a statewide policy. A good law answers the needs of the political community in enabling it to maximize its uniquely circumstanced potential.

What is the population picture in the United States. The Census Bureau reported that the birth rate for 1967 was 17.9 per thousand, the lowest in the nation's history.[13] The Population Reference Bureau, Inc. said that there was every indication that the birth rate would continue to drop.[14] The Metropolitan Life Insurance Company stated that during the last ten years the birth rate declined 28 percent.[15] *U.S. News & World Report* estimated that the 1968 birth statistics would be 3,335,000, the fewest births since 1945.[16] *Time,* in November 1967, predicted a U.S. population of 308 million by the year 2000.[17] *U.S. News & World Report* asked Dr. Ronald J. Bogue, past president of the Population Assn. of America, when the figure of 300 million would be reached. His answer in March 1968 was, "Probably not within the next hundred years." [18] The word "explosion" is certainly not applicable to the population growth of the United States.

Nor is the United States experiencing an isolated phenomenon. General De Gaulle, in October 1967, initiated a campaign for increasing the population—a minimum of three children for every French family.[19] The average is now 2.2 children. The birth rate in France has been dropping for three years and is one of the lowest in Europe. Although the forty-seven-year-old law prohibiting the sale of contraceptives was repealed three months earlier, De Gaulle is said to have personally barred Social Security reimbursements for purchases of contraceptives. The Chase Manhattan Bank's world business survey predicted that Europe's "superboom," with its 4.8 percent annual growth in its "gross national product" between 1950 and 1965, will taper off between now and 1975. "The primary reason: a slowdown in expansion of Europe's labor force, caused by low birth rates during and after World War II. The working-age population of Germany and Austria, for example, will actually decline over the next eight years." [20] Greece, due to illegal abortions, is having a population problem.[21] Its birth rate, which was 31.34 per thousand in 1930, dropped to 17.48 in the early 1960s. The problem is aggravated by the high rate of emigration of the labor force. Dr. Nicholas Louros, Professor of Obstetrics at the University of Athens and head of a government commission to examine the problem, said that before emigration, the population total of 8,600,000 rose 1 percent a year, but that there were one hundred thousand abortions. "In proportion, this is three times more than in any other country." He stated, also, that 35 percent of all married women have had at least one abortion. In the three years 1961–64, the population of Greece rose only 1.4 percent. Both the Greek Orthodox Church and the Greek government are concerned over what they consider a national calamity.

The example of Japan is instructive. Japan has about 100 million people who live on the islands Honshu, Hokkaido, Kyushu, and Shikoku, which together cover 142,688 square miles—an area somewhat smaller than Montana, with its 145,736 square miles. The United States has a population of 200 million, about twice that of Japan, but it has a territory of 3,628,150 square miles. The birth rate of the two nations is approximately the same. Japan is already showing some anxiety about underpopulation. In November 1968, the Japan Federation of Employers Association in Tokyo described the labor shortage as "acute," and as seriously limiting the country's economic growth. The government predicted that this shortage would increase in coming years, that the age group ranging from 15 to 19 years old would decline from 10.98 million in 1965 to 9.09 million in 1970 and 7.78 million in 1975.[22] In the face of these facts and figures, the declining birth rate in the United States marks any anxiety about this country's overpopulation as an uninformed or neurotic response totally irrelevant in the making of a reasonable abortion decision.

Undeniably, there are population problems in parts of the world. India and Latin America face crises bordering on disaster.

But the citizens of individual states in this country should not let the fate of their own unborn children be determined by the faulty economies of technologically backward countries.

Conclusion

Mankind, by and large, has managed to solve its problems by means other than destruction. We do not automatically kill the insane, the diseased, the defective, or even the criminal. Killings have occurred, often on a grand scale and usually to the shame of man. But human nature's great triumphs are not in breaking but in making, not in eliminating but in ameliorating. Every age has its problems. This era of technological greatness has conquered so many enemies of man that the population of the world has multiplied beyond measure. Now man threatens to be his own last enemy, conspicuous by the killing of his own defenseless offspring. The perennial challenge of life has been met with a defeatism out of place in an age of scientific wonders.

Abortion is not new, but the remedies for the problems that occasion the demand for abortion are. More than ever before, man's growing love of others and his sensitivity to human dignity and equality should motivate an unparalleled scientific creativity for the alleviation of problems that pressure otherwise good-hearted citizens into abortion. There is not just one response to this multidimensional challenge. But the combination of remedies forms a responsible and humanly sufficient alternative, the viable alternative, to abortion. Not all the problems are solved. Not all the heartache and suffering are removed. But man, as far as his power and intelligence enable him, can make an honorable decision consonant with human dignity. He moves from the specious appeal of the lethal shortcut which is abortion to the consistent choice of life over death, of birth over abortion, and entrusts the problems that births bring with them to the creative spirit of man and the loving mercy of God.

NOTES

CHAPTER ONE

1. W. J. Hamilton, J. D. Boyd, and H. W. Mossman, *Human Embryology* (Baltimore: Williams & Wilkins, 1945), p. 3.

2. L. B. Arey, *Developmental Anatomy*, 7th ed. (Philadelphia: W. B. Saunders Company, 1965), p. 86. Throughout this section on the phenotype, I rely largely on L. B. Arey, *op. cit.;* B. M. Patten, *Human Embryology*, 2d ed. (New York: McGraw-Hill Book Company, 1953); and W. J. Hamilton, *et al., op. cit.,* an older book but one rich in insights.

3. R. M. Wynn, "Intrauterine Devices: Effects on Ultrastructure of Human Endometrium," *Science*, June 16, 1967, pp. 1508–10; but see exchange of letters clarifying nomenclature, *Science*, September 22, 1967, p. 1465. Two other theories are that the IUDs function contraceptively by preventing fertilization in the Fallopian tubes or by causing the egg to descend too fast to be ready for fertilization. The most widely accepted view is that IUDs make the uterus an unfavorable environment for nidation. IUDs are popular because they are easy to insert and remove, inexpensive, safe, reliable, and suitable to most women, especially those who have had two or more children. Although apparently abortifacient, they work so soon after fertilization that they are equated, in the minds of users, with contraceptives.

4. Arey, *op. cit.,* p. 100.

5. Patten, *op. cit.,* Chap. 7, *passim.*

6. Arey, *op. cit.,* p. 18.

7. See also E. W. Dempsey, Ch. 2, "Histophysical Considerations," *The Placenta and Fetal Membranes,* C. A. Villee, ed. (New York: Wilkins & Wilkins Company, 1960).

8. *Dietrich v. Northampton,* 138 Mass. 14, 52 Am. Rep. 242 (1884).

9. Arey, *op. cit.,* 17.

10. Patten, *op. cit.,* 189.

11. Arey, *op. cit.,* 17.

12. See L. Lessing, "The Biological Revolution: Part II, "At the Controls of the Living Cell," *Fortune,* May 1966; C. P. Swanson, *The Cell,* 2d ed. (Englewood Cliffs, N.J.: Prentice-Hall, 1964); and E. H. Mercer, *Cells* (Garden City, N.Y.: Doubleday & Company, 1964).

13. For a personal history of the discovery of DNA see J. D. Watson, *The Double Helix* (New York: Athenaeum Publishers, 1968).

14. Niels Bohr, *Atomic Physics and Human Knowledge* (New York: Science Editions, Inc., 1961), p. 92.

15. *History of Animals,* 7.3.583[h].

16. Aristotle, *Generation of Animals,* I, 22, 730.

17. *Summa Theologiae,* I, 76, 1 c.

18. 8 *Libros Politicorum* 7:11.

19. L. Van Bertalanffy, *Modern Theories of Development,* T. H. Woodger, tranl. (New York: Harper & Bros., 1962), p. 173.

20. *Ibid.,* p. 174.

21. *Ibid.,* p. 41.

22. New York *Times,* October 7, 1968, p. 1, and October 13, 1968, p. E9.

23. *Ibid.,* May 30, 1968, p. C12.

24. *Ibid.,* October 13, 1967, p. 1; see also B. R. Migeon and C. S. Miller, "Human-Mouse Somatic Cell Hybrids," *Science,* November 29, 1968, pp. 1005–6.

25. New York *Times,* February 22, 1967, p. C31.

26. H. Selye, *The Stress of Life* (New York: McGraw-Hill Book Company, 1956), pp. 3 and 274.

27. *Ibid.,* p. 274.

Chapter Two

1. T. J. Meek, transl., "The Middle Assyrian Laws," in *Ancient Near Eastern Texts* 2d ed., J. B. Pritchard, ed. (Princeton, New Jersey: Princeton University Press, 1955), pp. 181, 184–85. "Seignior" is Meek's term to indicate a noble or gentleman.

2. A. Goetze, transl., "The Hittite Laws," in J. B. Pritchard, ed., *op. cit.,* p. 190.

3. Sec. 1.2, text in Meisner, *Babylonian und assyrien,* 2 vols. (Heidelberg: Carl Winters Universitätsbuchandlung, 1920–25), I, 149–50.

4. See Kaufmann, *Gedenkschrift* 186 (1900), referred to by Rabbi Dr. Immanuel Jakobovitz, "Jewish Views on Abortion," 17 *Western Reserve Law Rev.* 480, at 484.

5. Philo, *De Spec. Legibus* 3:108–10. He makes the same reference in 117–18, and in *De Virtute,* 138. But as Jakobovitz, *op. cit.,* 497 note 57, points out, in the latter two statements he says that only he who kills a child already born is "indubitably a murderer."

6. *Talmud,* Tohorotn II, Oboloth 7:6.

7. See Jakobovitz, *Jewish Medical Ethics,* 184–91 (1962) on the basis for this in a Discussion of the Mishnah, *Talmud,* Sanhedrin.

8. *Republic* 5, 461c.

9. *Politics,* VII, Chap. 16, 1335b, 20–26.

10. *History of Animals,* 7. 3. 583^h.

11. Ludwig Edelstein, *The Hippocratic Oath*: Text, Translation, and Interpretation (Baltimore: Johns Hopkins Press, 1943), 3. See also 15 and 16.

12. Soranos, *Gynecology,* J. Ilberg, ed., in *Corpus Medicorum Graecorum* (London and Berlin, 1927), 1. 19. 60.

13. For the significance of this familial structure, see R. Sohm, *The Institutes of Roman Law,* J. C. Ledlie, transl. (Oxford: Clarendon Press, 1907), Bk. III, Chap. I, § 91, "The Family," p. 449, and § 101, "The Effect of the Patria Potestas," p. 482.

14. Seneca, *De Ira,* I, xv, at 145, Lock, ed. (1928).

15. For *Digest* references to the following, see R. J. Huser, *The Crime of Abortion in Canon Law* (Washington, D.C.: Catholic University Press, 1942), 10–11.

16. The most complete source for the ecclesiastical history of abortion is *The Crime of Abortion in Canon Law,* by Roger John Huser (Washington D.C.: Catholic University Press, 1942). Although it deals briefly with ancient laws, its main contribution is in tracing the development of the Church's abortion legislation up to the 1917 *Code of Canon Law.* John T. Noonan's article, "Abortion and the Catholic Church," 12 *Natural Law Forum* 85–131 (1967) is an excellent recent presentation which supplements Huser's book by its greater emphasis on the history of the teaching of theologians. The article profits from the fact that the author has covered most of the sources in his book on a related subject, *Contraception* (Cambridge: Harvard University Press, 1965). The work of both authors has been helpful in preparing this section on the Christian experience.

17. *Luke,* Chap. I.

18. See Noonan, *op. cit.*, p. 90.

19. C II, n.2.

20. C XIX, n.5.

21. *Legatio pro Christianis*, c.35.

22. *Paedagogus*, Bk. III, c 10, N.96, n.1.

23. *Octavius*, c 30, nn. 2–3.

24. *Epistola*, LVI, 2.

25. *Apologeticum ad Nationes*, 1.15.

26. *Refutatio Omnium Haeresium*, Bk. IX, c 12, n.25.

27. *Epistle* 52.

28. *Apostolic Constitution*, Lib. VII, cap. 2.

29. *Letters*, LCL, III, 20–23.

30. *Letters*, LCL, III, 34.

31. XXIV, 4.

32. *Epistola* XXII, c 13.

33. *Enchiridion on Faith, Hope and Charity* (421) 86.

34. *Ibid.*

35. *Ibid.*, 85

36. *Questions on the Heptateuch* (419), 80.

37. *On Marriage and Concupiscence* (419–20), 1.15.17.

38. Council of Elvira, Canon 63, J. D. Mansi, *Sacrorum Conciliorum Nova et Amplissima Collectio* (Paris: 1901–27), II, 16. Hereafter cited as Mansi.

39. Council of Ancyra, Canon 21, Mansi, II, 5.19.

40. Council of Lerida, Mansi, VIII, 612.

41. Canon 77, Mansi, IX, 858.

42. Mansi, XI, 981.

43. The abortion canons were contained in the part called the *Syntagma Canonum*, tit, XIII, c 10.

44. II, c 89.

45. *Ibid.*, II, Canons 66, 67.

46. *Decretum* X, c 181–83; *Collectio Tripartita*, III, XX, cc 9, 15–18. None of these were found in the collections of Regino and Burchard.

47. *Panormia*, VIII, cc. 12–14.

48. *Decretum*, Ad c. 8, C. XXXII, q.2.

49. Ad *Aliquando* of c. 7, C. XXXII, q.2.

50. V, 10, 2.

51. C. 20, X, *de homicidio voluntario vel causali*, V. 12.

52. *Codicis Iuris Canonici Fontes,* 9 vols. (Rome, 1923–39), n.165. Hereafter cited as *Fontes.*

53. *Fontes,* n.173.

54. *Fontes,* n.552.

55. See Huser, *op. cit.,* Part II, canonical commentary, 79–121.

56. *Casti Connubii,* 22 *Acta Apostolicae Sedis,* 562 (1930).

57. Pius XII, *Allocution to Midwives* (October 29, 1951), 43 *A.A.S.* 835.

58. Pius XII, *Allocution to the Association of Large Families* (November 26, 1951), 43 *A.A.S.* 855.

59. John XXIII, *Mater et Magistra* (May 15, 1961), 53 *A.A.S.* 401.

60. Paul VI, *Allocution to Members of the New England Obstetrical and Gynecological Society* (October 3, 1964).

61. Paul VI, *Humanae Vitae* (August 1, 1968), 60 *A.A.S.* 481, n.14.

62. *The Documents of Vatican II,* W. M. Abbott, gen. ed., J. Gallagher, transl. ed. (New York: Guild Press, 1966), 203.

63. *Ibid.,* 206.

64. *Ibid.,* 203.

65. *Ibid.,* 204.

66. *Ibid.,* 226.

67. *Ibid.,* 256.

68. *Ibid.,* 226.

69. *Ibid.,* 256.

70. Twiss, ed. *II Legibus et Consuetudinibus Angliae,* 278 (1879).

71. Coke, *III Institutes of the Laws of England,* 50, 3rd ed. (1660).

72. I Blackstone *Commentaries,* 1, 129–30.

73. Miscarriage of Women Act, 43 Geo. 3, c 58 (1803).

74. Offenses against the Person Act, 9 Geo. 4, c 31 (1828).

75. 7 Will. 4 and 1 Vict., c 85 (1837).

76. 24 and 25 Vict., c 100 (1861).

77. 24 Q.B.D. 420 (1890).

78. The Infant Life (Preservation) Act (19 and 20 Geo. V, c. 34), Sect. 1, Subsect. I.

79. 3 All. E.R. 615 (1938). Glanville Williams points out that "the variations between this report and that in the *Law Reports* [1 K.B. 687 (1939)] are so great that the judge must have almost rewritten his directions for the *Law Reports.*" 4 *Br. J. of Criminology* 558, n.7.

80. *Ibid.*

81. *Rex* v. *Bergamann and Ferguson is unreported,* but see 5 *Current Legal Problem* 134; [1948] 1 B.M.J. 1008.

82. *Regina* v. *Newton and Stunge,* London *Times,* May 20, 1958. [1958] 1 B.M.J. 1242.

83. The Abortion Act, 1967.

84. K. Davis, "Population Policy," *Science,* Nov. 10, 1967, p. 733.

85. Conn. Stat. Tit. 22 §§14, at 152 (1821).

86. 43 Geo. 3, c. 58.

87. Conn. Pub. Acts, Chap. LXXI §1, at 65 (1860).

88. Florida, Hawaii, Kansas, New Hampshire, New York, North Dakota, Oklahoma, Pennsylvania, South Carolina, and Wisconsin.

89. *Comm.* v. *Brunelle,* 341 Mass. 675, 171 N.E. 2d 850 (1961).

90. Connecticut, Minnesota, Missouri, Nevada, New York, South Carolina, and Washington.

91. American Law Institute, *Model Penal Code,* Proposed Official Draft, Section 230.3 (Philadelphia: American Law Institute, 1962), pp. 189–90.

CHAPTER THREE

1. See F. J. Taussig, *Abortion Spontaneous and Induced* (St. Louis: The C. V. Mosby Co., 1936).

2. R. E. Hall, *Am. J. Obst. & Gynec.* 91: 518 (1964), and C. Tietze, *Am. J. Obst. & Gynec.* 101: 784 (1968).

3. New York *Times,* June 9, 1968, p. 33. In California, according to Dr. E. W. Jackson of the State Health Department, legal abortions in 1968 will total about five thousand, an eightfold increase over previous yearly average. *NC News Service,* Oct. 12, 1968, p. 4.

4. M. S. Calderone, M.D., ed., *Abortion in the United States* (New York: Paul B. Hoeber, Inc., 1958), Sec. 10, "Report of the Statistics Committee," p. 180.

5. C. Tietze, M.D., "Statistics of Induced Abortion," International Conference on Abortion sponsored by the Harvard Divinity School and The Joseph P. Kennedy, Jr., Foundation, September 1967, to be published by Harvard University Press.

6. Calderone, ed., *op. cit.,* p. 50.

7. P. H. Gebhard, W. B. Pomeroy, C. E. Martin, C. V. Christenson, *Pregnancy, Birth and Abortion,* Science Editions (New York: John Wiley & Sons, 1958).

8. See discussion in Calderone, ed., *op. cit.,* p. 55.

9. Gebhard, *et al., op. cit.,* pp. 15–17.

10. M. E. Kopp, *Birth Control in Practice* (New York: Robert M. McBride & Co., 1934), Part II, pp. 47–78.

11. R. Stix, "A Study of Pregnancy Wastage," 13 *The Millbank Memorial Fund Quarterly*, October 1935, No. 4, p. 364.

12. Taussig, *op. cit.*, p. 26.

13. In Calderone, ed., *op. cit.*, p. 50.

14. D. G. Wiehl and K. Berry, 15 *Millbank Memorial Fund Quarterly*, 229 (1937).

15. P. K. Whelpton and C. V. Kiser, *ibid.*, 26: 182 (1948).

16. Johannes Andenaes, from a paper on abortion in Scandinavia delivered at the University of Chicago Conference on Abortion, May 1968, p. 2. See generally, C. Tietze, M.D., "Statistics on Induced Abortion," delivered at the Harvard Divinity School and Joseph P. Kennedy, Jr., Foundation, International Conference on Abortion, September 1967, and "Abortion," 220 *Scientific American* 21 (Jan. 1968).

17. *Ibid.*, 4.

18. H. Hoffmeyer and M. Nørgaard, "Incidence of Conception and the Course of Pregnancy," 126 *Ugeskrift For Laeger*, pp. 355–71 (1964).
19. V. Skalts and M. Nørgaard, "Abortion Legislation in Denmark," 17 *Western Reserve Law Rev.* 498, at. 516.

20. *Ibid.*, p. 514.

21. *Ibid.*, p. 516.

22. Lars Huldt, M.D., *Lancet*, March 2, 1968.

23. *Ibid.*

24. See C. Tietze, "Statistics on Induced Abortion," *op. cit.*, *passim;* also K.-H. Mehlan, M.D., "The Socialist Countries," in Berelson, ed., *op. cit.*, pp. 207–26.

25. Andras Klinger, "Abortion Programs," in B. Berelson, ed., *Family Planning and Population Programs* (Chicago: University of Chicago Press, 1966), p. 476.

26. *Ibid.*, p. 474.

27. *Ibid.*, p. 475.

28. See New York *Times*, November 13, 1967, p. C16; see also A. Hellegers, 3 *Med. Opinion & Review* 89 (1967).

29. For data on abortion in Japan, see R. Hirano, paper delivered at University of Chicago Conference on Abortion, May 1968: "How Japan Solves Population Problems," in *U.S. News & World Report*, June 12, 1967, pp. 64–65; C. Tietze, Harvard-Kennedy Conference, *op. cit.;* Gebhard, *et al.*, *op. cit.;* M. Muramatsu, "Japan," in Berelson, ed., *op. cit.*, pp. 7–19.

30. Quoted in E. Quay, "Justifiable Abortion," 49 *Georgetown Law Journal* 184 (1964).

31. Allan Guttmacher, M.D., "The Shrinking non-psychiatric Indications for therapeutic Abortion," H. Rosen, ed., *Abortion in America* (Boston: Beacon Press, 1954), 13.

32. See Calderone, ed., *op. cit.,* pp. 102–3.

33. Robert Hall, M.D., "Therapeutic Abortion, Sterilization, and Contraception," 91 *Am. J. Obst. & Gynec.* 518 (1965).

34. K. Niswander, M.D., "Medical Abortion Practices in the United States," 17 *Western Reserve Law Rev.* 418–19 (1965).

35. R. Hall, M.D., "Commentary," *Abortion and the Law,* D. Smith, ed. (Cleveland: Western Reserve Press, 1967), 224. See also H. L. Packer and R. J. Gampell, "Therapeutic Abortion: A Problem in Law and Medicine," 11 *Stanford Law Review* 418 (1959).

36. *Rex* v. *Bourne,* Central Criminal Court, England 3 All Eng. R.615 (1938).

37. Guttmacher, *op. cit.,* p. 16.

38. Calderone, ed., *op. cit.,* p. 139.

39. *Ibid.,* Table 6-13, p. 93.

40. *Ibid.,* Table 6-10, p. 84.

41. E. Gold and associates, 55 *Am. J. Pub. Health* 964 (1965).

42. K. Niswander, R. Klein, and C. Randall, "Changing Attitudes to Therapeutic Abortion," 28 *Am. J. Obst. & Gynec.* 124 (1966).

43. Allan Guttmacher, M.D., "The Influence of Fertility Control Upon Psychiatric Illness," 115 *Am. J. Psychiat.* 683–91 (1959). See also Calderone, ed., *op. cit.,* p. 105.

44. H. Sim, M.D., "Abortion and The Psychiatrist," *Brit. Med. J.* 5350: 145–48 (1963).

45. H. Rosen, M.D., "Psychiatric Implications of Abortion," 17 *West. Res. Law Rev.* 445 (1965).

46. B. J. Lindberg, 45 *Svenska Läk-Tidn,* 1381 (1948).

47. B. Jansson, "Mental Disorder after Abortion," 41 *Acta psych. et neur.* Scandinavia, 87–110 (1965).

48. Alex Barno, M.D., "Criminal Abortion Deaths, Illegitimate Pregnancy Deaths, and Suicides in Pregnancy," 98 *Am. J. Obst. & Gynec.* 356–67 (1967).

49. *Ibid.,* p. 361.

50. Calderone, ed., *op. cit.,* p. 141.

51. G. Zillboorg, M.D., "The Clinical Issues of Postpartum Psychopathological Reactions," 73 *Am. J. Obst. & Gynec.* 305 (1957).

52. Calderone, ed., *op. cit.,* p. 125.

53. See Rosen, ed., *op. cit.,* p. 276.

54. Calderone, ed., *op. cit.,* p. 123.

55. E. Hakanson, M.D., "An Obstetrician's View," 50 *Minn. Medicine,* 26 (1967).

56. See *U.S. News & World Report,* June 24, 1968. The source is the U.S. Census Bureau, U.S. Department of Health, Education, and Welfare, with 1968 estimates by the *U.S. News & World Report* Economic Unit.

57. A Report by The Teamsters Joint Council No. 16, New York *Times,* July 1, 1968, p. C21.

58. New York *Times,* October 29, 1967, p. 36.

59. Federal Bureau of Investigation, *Uniform Crime Reports 1967* (Washington, D.C. 1968), 13.

60. "Probability of Pregnancy from Single Unprotected Coitus," *Fertility and Sterility,* Vol. II (October 1960), pp. 485–88.

61. *Uniform Crime Reports 1967, op. cit.*

62. This figure is two-thirds of the 27,100 crimes reported in the category, "Forcible Rape," Table 1-2, *Uniform Crime Reports 1967, op. cit.*

63. Allan Guttmacher, M.D., *et al.,* ed., *The Consumer's Union Report on Family Planning* (New York: Consumer's Union, 1962), p. 7. "For intercourse to result in conception, therefore, it must take place within a two and a half day period; from two days before the release of the egg to half a day after the event."

64. A. Hellegers, U.S.C.C. Abortion Conference, Washington, D.C., October 1967.

65. *Ibid.*

66. L. Z. Cooper, "German Measles," 215 *Scientific American* 35 (July 1966).

67. J. Rendle-Short, 2 *Lancet* 373 (1964) and S. J. Sallomi, 27 *Am. J. Obst. & Gynec.* 252. The findings of both are very close and average out to the above figures; see E. Y. Hakanson, 50 *Minn. Medicine,* 26 (1967).

68. D. Sheridan, 2 *British Med. J.* 536 (1964).

69. P. R. Ehrlich, *The Population Bomb* (New York: Ballantine Books, Inc., 1968), pp. 17–35.

70. Kingsley Davis, "Population Policy," *Science* (November 10, 1967), pp. 730–39.

Chapter Four

1. Thomas Aquinas, *Summa Theologiae,* I–II, 94, 2 c.

2. M. S. McDougal, "Perspectives for an International Law of Human Dignity," *Proceedings of Am. Soc. of Int. Law* (1959), p. 116.

3. See D. Granfield, "Force, Power and the Law," 12 *Cath. Univ. Law Rev.* 79 (1963).

4. Albert Camus, *The Myth of Sisyphus,* J. O'Brien, transl. (New York: Vintage Books, 1955), p. 16.

5. *Ibid.,* p. 49.

6. *Ibid.,* p. 3.

7. *Ibid.,* Preface, p. v.

8. Camus, *The Rebel,* A. Bower, transl. (New York: Vintage Books, 1956), p. 6.

9. *Ibid.*

10. *Ibid.,* pp. 7–8.

11. Viktor Frankl, M.D., *The Doctor and the Soul* (New York: Alfred A. Knopf, 1957), p. xii.

12. *Ibid.,* p. 129.

13. Frankl, *Psychotherapy and Existentialism* (New York: Washington Square Press, 1967), p. 129.

14. *Ibid.*

15. Thomas Aquinas, *Summa Theologiae,* II–II, 64, 7. For the history of this principle see J. T. Mangan, S.J., "An Historical Analysis of the Principle of the Double Effect," 10 *Theological Studies* 41 (1949).

16. Thomas Card. Cajetan, *Commentarium in Summa S. Thomae in Sancti Thomae Aquinatis Opera Omnia* (Romae, 1882 sq.), II–II, 64, 7.

17. Salmanticenses, *Cursus Theologicus* (Parisiis, Bruxellis, 1877), T.7, tr. 13, disp. 10, dub. 6, n. 221–47.

18. Joannes P. Gury, S.J., *Compendium Theologiae Moralis* (Lugduni, 1850; Ratisbonae, 1874) T.1, "De actibus humanis," c. 2, n. 6–10.

19. For more detailed moral analyses of these and related medical problems see Thomas J. O'Donnell, S.J., *Morals in Medicine* 2 ed. (Westminster, Md.: The Newman Press, 1960), Chap. 5, 153–235.

20. Pius XII, *Allocution to Midwives* (October 29, 1951), 43 *Acta Sancta Sedis* 835.

21. T. L. Bouscaren, S.J., *The Ethics of Ectopic Operations,* 2d ed. (Milwaukee: The Bruce Publishing Co., 1943), pp. 3–24.

22. Aquinas, *Summa Theologiae,* II–II, 64, 7 c.

23. *Ibid.*

24. *Ibid.*

25. Peter Knauer, S.J., "The Hermeneutic Function of the Principle of the Double Effect," 12 *Natural Law Forum* 149 (1967).

26. C. J. Van Der Poel, C.S.S., "The Principle of Double Effect," *Absolutes in Moral Theology?* C. Curran, ed. (Washington, D.C., Corpus Books, 1968), p. 209.

27. Charles Curran, *A New Look at Christian Morality* (Notre Dame, Ind.: Fides Publishers Inc., 1968), p. 243.

28. R. M. Perkins, *Criminal Law* (Brooklyn: The Foundation Press, 1957), p. 850.

29. Joseph Fletcher, *Situation Ethics* (Philadelphia: The Westminster Press, 1966), p. 39.

30. American Law Institute, *Model Penal Code,* Proposed Official Draft, Section 4.01 (Philadelphia: American Law Institute, 1962), p. 66.

31. *Ibid.,* Section 3.04, pp. 47–49.

CHAPTER FIVE

1. 85 *S. Ct.* 1678, 1717, 381 U.S. 479 (1965).

2. *Report on the Committee on Homosexual Offenses and Prostitution,* CMD 247 (1957), in *The Wolfenden Report* (New York: Stein and Day, 1963), Chap. II, Par. 13, p. 23.

3. *Summa Theologiae,* I–II, 96, 2, c.

4. *Ibid.*

5. *Ibid.,* 3, c.

6. See R. M. Perkins, *Criminal Law* (Brooklyn: The Foundation Press, 1957), p. 106. But abortion is an exception even to the general law of necessity: ". . . there is no rule of law which permits the intentional killing of an innocent person, even to save the life of a slayer or the lives of several." p. 850.

7. For a further analysis of these three approaches see David A. Gordon, "The Unborn Plaintiff," 63 *Michigan Law Review* 579 (1965).

8. See *Santa Clara County* v. *Pac. R.R. Co.,* 118 U.S. 394 (1886).

9. Michaelmas Term, 28 & 29 Eliz., 4 Coke 7 f. 7 (1586); Wilson, ed., 77 Eng. Rep. 421 (1777).

10. I Blackstone, 1 *Commentaries,* 129–130. 4th ed. (1771).

11. See Chap. II, on "The English Experience," 8.

12. 2 Hawkins, *Pleas of the Crown,* 2. 51. 9, Curwood, ed. (1824).

13. *Talmud,* Erakhin 1:14; *Talmud,* TOSOPHOTH, Erakhin 7a., referred to in Rabbi Jakobovitz, *Jewish Views on Abortion,* 17 *West. Res. Law Review,* 480. 497 (1965).

14. 138 Mass. 14, 52 Am. Rep. 242 (1884).

15. 184 Ill. 359, 56 N.E. 638 (1900).

16. 229 Minn. 365, 38 N.W. 2d 839 (1949).

17. *Keyes* v. *Construction Serv. Inc.*, 340 Mass. 633, 165 N.E. 2d 912 (1960).

18. *Torigian* v. *Watertown News Co.*, 352 Mass. 446, 225 N.E. 2d 926 (1967).

19. See Anno: "Action for Death of Unborn Child," 15 A.L.R. 3d 992 (1967); see also dissent in *Leal* v. *C. C. Pitts Sand and Gravel, Inc.*, 41 S.W. 825 (1967).

20. *Sinkler* v. *Kneale*, 401 Pa. 267, 164 A. 2d 93 (1960). See W. L. Prosser, *Torts*, 3d ed. (1964), Sec. 56, p. 356, citing nine jurisdictions allowing recovery for prenatal injuries in early stages of pregnancy.

21. 65 F. Supp. 138, 143 (D.D.C., 1946).

22. 4 D.L.R. 337, 344 (1933).

23. *Zepada* v. *Zepada*, 411 Ill. App. 2d 240. 190 N.E. 2d 849 (1963) and *Pinkney* v. *Pinkney* 198 So. 2d 52 (1967). Two adulterine bastards unsuccessfully sued their fathers. See also *Williams* v. *State* 18 N.Y. 2d 481, 276 N.Y.S. 2d 885, 223 N.E. 2d 343 (1966) in which an illegitimate unsuccessfully sued the State of New York for its negligence in allowing his mother to be sexually assaulted.

24. See, 22 A.L.R. 3d 1441 for an analysis of these elements as well as more general considerations.

25. 49 N.J. 22, 227 A2d 689 (1967).

26. *Ibid.*, 694.

27. *Ibid.*, 693.

28. *Ibid.*, 694.

29. *Ibid.*, 698.

30. *Ibid.*, 707.

31. *Ibid.*, 692.

32. *Ibid.*

33. *Ibid.*, 711

34. Adolf Berle, Jr., *Power Without Property* (New York: Harcourt, Brace & World, Inc. [A Harvest Book], 1959), p. 111.

35. *Ibid.*, p. 90.

36. *Ibid.*, p. 14.

37. Adolf Berle, Jr., *Natural Selection of Political Forces* (Revised edition; Lawrence/London: University of Kansas Press, 1968), p. 35. See also pp 43–44.

38. *Ibid.*, p. 31.

39. Walter Lippmann, *The Public Philosophy* (New York: The New American Library, 1950), p. 79.

40. *Ibid.*, pp. 77–78.

41. *Ibid.*, p. 101.

42. 88 S. Ct. 2145 (1968).

43. H. L. A. Hart, *The Concept of Law* (Oxford: The Clarendon Press, 1961), p. 196.

44. 1963 *Public Papers of The Presidents of the United States—John F. Kennedy* 468 (1964).

45. *Nazi Conspiracy and Aggression,* Office of U. S. Chief of Counsel for Prosecution of Axis Criminality (Washington, D.C.: U. S. Government Printing Office, 1946), Vol. V, pp. 880–83.

46. *Ibid.,* Vol. II, Chap. XVI, p. 673.

47. *Ibid.,* Chap. XV, p. 55.

48. T. L. Bouscaren, II *Canon Law Digest* (Milwaukee: The Bruce Publishing Co., 1946) 96–97.

49. *Nazi Conspiracy and Aggression, op. cit.,* Vol. II, Chap. XVI, pp. 671–72.

50. Frederic Wertham, *A Sign for Cain* (New York: The Macmillan Company, 1966), p. 165.

Chapter Six

1. For larceny statistics see, Federal Bureau of Investigation, *Uniform Crime Reports 1967* (Washington, D.C., 1968), pp. 22 ff. For the number of unreported crimes see, *Report by President's Commission on Law Enforcement and Administration of Justice* (Washington, D.C., 1967) pp. 20 ff.

2. For sources for these figures see Chapter II, n.3.

3. American Law Institute, *Model Penal Code,* Proposed Official Draft, Section 230 (Philadelphia: American Law Institute, 1962) pp. 187–93.

4. Washington *Post,* June 16, 1968, p. G2.

5. See N. Dorsen, "The Position of the Civil Liberties Union," Harvard University-Kennedy Foundation International Conference on Abortion, September 1967.

6. Washington *Post,* March 25, 1968, p. A3.

7. 85 S. Ct. 1678 (1965).

8. Mr. Justice White, *op. cit.,* p. 1691.

9. Mr. Justice Douglas, *op. cit.,* p. 1680.

10. Mr. Justice Goldberg, *op. cit.,* p. 1689.

11. Mr. Justice White, *op. cit.,* p. 1693.

12. Mr. Justice White, *op. cit.,* p. 1691.

13. Mr. Justice Goldberg, *op. cit.*, p. 1698, quoting from *Bates* v. *Little Rock*, 80 S. Ct. 412, 417.

14. *Katz v. U.S.*, 88 S. Ct. 510–511 (1967).

15. *Ibid.*, 523.

16. *Model Penal Code, op. cit.*,
Section 230.3   Abortion.

(1) *Unjustified Abortion.* A person who purposely and unjustifiably terminates the pregnancy of another otherwise than by a live birth commits a felony of the third degree or, where the pregnancy has continued beyond the twenty-sixth week, a felony of the second degree.

(2) *Justifiable Abortion.* A licensed physician is justified in terminating a pregnancy if he believes there is substantial risk that continuance of the pregnancy would gravely impair the physical or mental health of the mother or that the child would be born with grave physical or mental defect, or that the pregnancy resulted from rape, incest, or other felonious intercourse. All illicit intercourse with a girl below the age of 16 shall be deemed felonious for purposes of this subsection. Justifiable abortions shall be performed only in a licensed hospital except in case of emergency when hospital facilities are unavailable. [Additional exceptions from the requirement of hospitalization may be incorporated here to take account of situations in sparsely settled areas where hospitals are not generally accessible.]

(3) *Physicians' Certificates; Presumption from Non-Compliance.* No abortion shall be performed unless two physicians, one of whom may be the person performing the abortion, shall have certified in writing the circumstances which they believe to justify the abortion. Such certificate shall be submitted before the abortion to the hospital where it is to be performed and, in the case of abortion following felonious intercourse, to the prosecuting attorney or the police. Failure to comply with any of the requirements of this Subsection gives rise to a presumption that the abortion was unjustified.

(4) *Self-Abortion.* A woman whose pregnancy has continued beyond the twenty-sixth week commits a felony of the third degree if she purposely terminates her own pregnancy otherwise than by a live birth, or if she uses instruments, drugs or violence upon herself for that purpose. Except as justified under Subsection (2), a person who induces or knowingly aids a woman to use instruments, drugs or violence upon herself for the purpose of terminating her pregnancy otherwise than by a live birth commits a felony of the third degree whether or not the pregnancy has continued beyond the twenty-sixth week.

(5) *Pretended Abortion.* A person commits a felony of the third degree if, representing that it is his purpose to perform an abortion, he does an act adapted to cause abortion in a pregnant woman although the woman is in fact not pregnant, or the actor does not believe she is. A person charged with unjustified abortion under Subsection (1) or an

attempt to commit that offense may be convicted thereof upon proof of conduct prohibited by this Subsection.

(6) *Distribution of Abortifacients.* A person who sells, offers to sell, possesses with intent to sell, advertise, or displays for sale anything specially designed to terminate a pregnancy, or held out by the actor as useful for that purpose, commits a misdemeanor, unless:

(a) the sale, offer or display is to a physician or druggist or to an intermediary in a chain of distribution to physicians or druggists; or

(b) the sale is made upon prescription or order of a physician; or

(c) the possession is with intent to sell as authorized in paragraphs (a) and (b); or

(d) the advertising is addressed to persons named in paragraph (a) and confined to trade or professional channels not likely to reach the general public.

(7) *Section Inapplicable to Prevention of Pregnancy.* Nothing in this Section shall be deemed applicable to the prescription, administration or distribution of drugs or other substances for avoiding pregnancy, whether by preventing implantation of a fertilized ovum or by any other method that operates before, at or immediately after fertilization.

17. Matthew Hale, *The History of the Pleas to the Crown,* Vol. I (London, 1678), 635.

18. Quoted in P. H. Gebhard and Assistants, *Sex Offenders* (New York: Harper and Row, Publishers, Inc., Bantam edition, 1965), p. 178.

19. *Miss. Code Ann.* §2223,1(b) (1966).

20. *N.C. Gen. Stat.* §14–45.1 (1967).

21. Roscoe Pound, *The Philosophy of Law* (New Haven: Yale University Press, 1922, Rev. ed., 1955), p. 47.

22. *The Documents of Vatican II,* W. M. Abbott, gen. ed., J. Gallagher, transl. ed., *Pastoral Constitution on the Church in the Modern World,* n.9, p. 226 (italics supplied) (New York: The Guild Press, 1966).

23. *Md. Ann. Code,* Art. 43, §149, E, F, G (1968).

24. *National Catholic News Service* (April 3, 1968), p. 14.

25. *Md. Ann. Code,* Art. 27, §3 (1957).

26. *Md. Ann. Code,* Art. 43, §149 F (1968).

CHAPTER SEVEN

1. In 1962, the rubella virus was first isolated and grown in a laboratory. Four years later, Drs. Meyer and Parkman had developed a vaccine against it. See L. Z. Copper, "German Measles," 215 *Scientific Amer-*

ican 30–37, July 1966. On Oct. 16, 1968, the National Institute of Allergy and Infectious Diseases, Bethesda, Md., announced that successful results of field trials using rubella vaccines indicated that the vaccine may be licensed and on the market within a year. Washington *Star*, Oct. 17, 1968.

2. Dr. Heinz Wuest, M.D. has isolated the harmful agents in the thalidomide molecule, a combination of a form of glutamic acid and a form of phthalic acid. These findings are of more than retrospective interest, for as Dr. Wuest remarked, "it is quite possible that other compounds containing these acids will be investigated as new drugs." New York *Times*, September 13, 1968, p. C30.

3. H. D. Krause, "The Non-Marital Child." I *Family Law Quarterly*, 4.

4. 391 U.S. 68 (1968).

5. 391 U.S. 73 (1968).

6. *Code of Canon Law*, Canons 116; 232, §2, 1°; 320 §2; 331 §1, 1°; 984 §1; 1015; 1038; 1051; 1117.

7. Recommendations approved by the American Medical Association's House of Delegates at Annual Convention in San Francisco, June 1968. Reported in *A.M.A. News*, July 1, 1968, p. 6.

8. 85 Sup. Ct. 1678; 381 U.S. 479 (1965).

9. Walter Sullivan, "How Agriculture Began," New York *Times*, January 29, 1967, p. E6.

10. *Time*, November 10, 1967, p. 23.

11. *Hunger U.S.A.*, a report by the Citizens Crusade Against Poverty.

12. House Agricultural Committee Report. See New York *Times*, June 17, 1968, p. M66.

13. *Herald Tribune* International Edition, Aug. 3, 1968.

14. Washington *Post*, February 26, 1968, p. 8.

15. *Ibid.*, July 29, 1968.

16. *U.S. News & World Report*, June 24, 1968, p. 64.

17. *Time*, November 24, 1967, p. 70.

18. *U.S. News & World Report*, March 11, 1968, p. 60.

19. Washington *Post*, October 8, 1967, p. A23.

20. *Newsweek*, Business Trends, October. 2, 1967, p. 69.

21. New York *Times*, June 22, 1968, p. C7.

22. New York *Times*, November 10, 1968, p. 16. See also *U.S. News & World Report*, June 12, 1967, pp. 64–65.